RETURN OF THE FALLEN ONES

Nephilim Histories, the Antediluvian World, Anunnaki Chronology and the Coming Cataclysm

Jason M. Breshears

THE BOOK TREE

San Diego, California

ISBN 978-1-58509-153-9

Cover art
©

Zvereva Iana

Cover layout & design

Jason M. Breshears

Published by
The Book Tree
P O Box 16476
San Diego, CA 92176

www.thebooktree.com

We provide fascinating and educational products to help awaken the public to new ideas and
information that would not be available otherwise.

Call 1 (800) 700-8733 for our FREE BOOK TREE CATALOG.

Special Note

Annus Mundi [Year of the World]

   Over 2000 years ago in Egypt, the Greek antiquarians and scholars studied the oldest writings in the world and revived a nigh extinct system of recording the time periods between historic events, known as the Annus Mundi chronology.

   This system has been adopted for this work because of its simplicity and compatibility with the oldest time-keeping methods in the world. The history of its usage and reconstruction is more fully explained in this author's prior works.

   The Annus Mundi timeline merely provides us with a continuum as opposed to the scores of other calendars that maintain dynastic breaks or merge with other systems as to the BC to the AD.

About the Author

Jason M. Breshears is a researcher of occult antiquities. Four of his previously published works are nonfiction with extensive bibliographies concerning fascinating information on ancient civilizations, cataclysms and the modern establishment's attempts to suppress these discoveries from the public today. These works are published by Book Tree in San Diego.

The Lost Scriptures of Giza (2006)

When the Sun Darkens (2009)

Anunnaki Homeworld (2011)

Nostradamus and the Planets of Apocalypse (2013)

Other books by Jason M. Breshears

Secret to Changing Your Life (2017)

Giants on Ancient Earth (2001/2017)

fiction: *The Oraclon Chronicles*

Beyond Dagothar (2017)

The Cragly of Cindereach (2017)

Greric and the Witch of Dimwood (2017)

Breshears' research, articles and discoveries are found at
nephilimarchives.com

Contents

Archive I

Anunnaki Origin of World's Oldest Calendars

It is a remarkable fact that today's time-keeping system was inherited from the earliest recorded civilization: Sumer. This distant culture preserved the method of reckoning time by the calculation of periods of 60 seconds, minutes, hours and days from an even more remote society that once thrived before an immense cataclysm popularly known as the Flood brought an end to these advanced thinkers. The Sumerians were in fact a remnant extension of this forgotten people for it is noted by historians that the Sumerian stone records make no mention of any other lands of origin and the places called Sumer and Akkad were not even known to the earliest inhabitants. (1)

This 60-base, or *sexagesimal*, system was preserved by the occupants of Sumer after this catastrophe, adopted by the mysterious Akkadians and again copied by the Bablonians. The Sumerians recorded their chronologies meticulously, dividing their cultural history between regnal years of kings that ruled before the Flood and those that exercised kingship afterwards. It is one of the more enigmatic of the Sumerian King-Lists that is the focus of this study, a 4000 year old record of Eight Kings that are very cryptically referred throughout Euphratean texts as the *Seven* Kings whose reign ended disastrously with the Deluge:

"When kingship was lowered from heaven, kingship was at Eridu. Eridu, Alulim king and reigned 28,800 *shars*. Alalgar reigned 36,000 shars. Two kings reigned its 64,000 shars. I drop Eridu, its kingship to Badtibira was carried..."

The shar is a unit of time that has perplexed scholars. Because historians have not detected any obvious reasons for asserting that the shar is anything other than a standard year they have uniformly designated it thus, effectively rendering Sumerian annals to the stuff of mythology. The shar-year theory makes these kings to have lived lifespans of tens of thousands of years. Another very misunderstood aspect of these annals from Sumer accentuating the problem of falsely assigning these records a mythological status is that the Sumerians wrote that their kingship was *dropped* from heaven. As will be shown, this is a precise astronomical phenomenon experienced by the Sumerians that will prove astonishing throughout this study. The Eight Kings and their reigns are as follows:

King of Sumer	Reigns [shars]	City [PreFlood]
Alulim	28,000	Eridu
Alalgar	36,000	Eridu
Enmenluanna	43,200	Badtibira
Emmengalanna	28,000	Badtibira
Dumuzi	36,000	Badtibira
Ensipazianna	28,800	Larak
Enmenduranna	21,000	Sippar
Ubartutu	18,600	Shurrupak

"Five cities were they, Eight Kings reigned their 241,000 shars. Then the Flood swept over. After the Flood had swept thereover, when kingship was lowered from heaven, kingship was in Kish." (2)

The traditional conclusion of the shar-year theory will lead the casual observer to conclude that these kings ruled successively for a period of 241,200 years, and that one king alone, Enmenluanna, ruled 43,200 years by himself. This interpretation is simply untenable. Though there are hundreds of historic references in the annals of antiquity to the incredible longevity of the antediluvian [preFlood] people and the even longer lifespan of the giants, we cannot hold to the possibility of kings living to reign for periods of 43,000 years and more. Our very earliest confirmable stone tablet records extend back to 2200 BC and dates prior to this are subjected to such conservative analysis they are usually assigned to the realm of fable or are assumed anachronistic.

The answer to the shar mystery lies in none other than the Book of Genesis. Prior to its inclusion into the Hebraic scriptures Genesis 1 was already a very old cosmological record that Moses copied from another source, a curious creation account he used to prefix the other Genesis texts. In Genesis 1 the very first mode of time-keeping introduced was from "…evening to morning," being the first day. The antediluvians recorded time by the passage of *days*. This was simply because the world before the Flood was biospherically different from our world today. The present axis-tilt inclined toward the plane of the ecliptic [sun's equator] did not exist in those days. Earth experienced no variation in temperatures because of a denser mesosphere of moisture that trapped heat and effectively dispensed light and reflected away harmful radiation due to a perfect vertical axis of 90° that allowed earth to orbit the sun in 360 days as opposed to our slightly slower rate of 365.24 days. Without *seasons* there was no reason for the ancients to ascribe any importance to the passage of years [orbital periods]. Genesis 2 explains this biosphere perfectly in revealing in that in those days prior to the Flood there was no rain, only a mist watered the earth every morning and evening. This is what one would expect to find under such a pristine tropical climate beneath a thick marine canopy above. This is biblically referred to as the *firmament above.*

The traditional relic of factoring the evening as coming before the morning has survived in modern holiday traditions such as New Year's *Eve*, All Hallow's Eve [Halloween], Christmas Eve and Midsummer's Eve. It was the eve that marked the new beginning. (3) Hebrew reckoning marks the eve as the start of a day. The day as a unit of time is appreciated much in the regulation of festivals and feasts and in the Book of Jubilees we find the measurement to determine lifetimes was counted in *days*. (4)

The records of the Sumerians themselves dispel the shar-year theory and reveal the origins of our present time-keeping system used globally today. Thousands of cuneiform tablets have been excavated and translated that show precise tabulations of *sunsets* and *moonrises* (5), a system of measurement linking Genesis 1 to ancient Sumer. So meticulous were the Sumerian calculations that they divided the day into 86,400 seconds with 24 hours of 60 minutes each having 60 seconds. (6) The numbers 6, 60 and 600 were of extreme import to them and they were aware that their 60-base system was 1/6th of the circle of 360° that they had designed after the original orbital period of Earth around the sun before the Deluge. The sexagesimal system truly linked time with *space* and unified terrestrial periods of measurement with astronomical periods involving this planet's movement and relationship to other moving objects within this solar system.

Now with the shar being a single *day* [an evening and morning] the 241,200 shars of the Sumerian King-List becomes *670 years* on a 360-day annual orbit. Throughout this book this 360-day year will be referred to as the *Draconian Calendar*, an epithet affixed to this system because the antediluvian polestar was Alpha Draconis. We find now that the longest reign of a king was *120 years*, or 43,200 days [shars]. With this revelation does a mystery unfold. In calculating the first six reigns of the King-List we find that each one is divisible by 120 days while the latter two are not. (7). The average reign was 84 years while the shortest was only 51 years before it was *cut off* by the Flood. The length of 120 years seems to have become a standard theme in many Sumero-Babylonian epics and histories. Just as there is a year and a greater counterpart astronomers refer to as the Great Year, so too does it appear that there was a shar [day] and a Great Shar [120 years].

Incidentally 120 days is a *third* of the Draconian Year and a third of this is a biblical generation [40 years].

This King-List record lies at the heart of many mysteries that will be revealed in this work. It is a history involving unusual kings ruling from a Pentapolis of cities, Seven Kings who enjoyed full regnal terms before the Deluge cut off the reign of the Eighth King. This is a Sumerian version of the final 670 years of history until the Flood.

By the time of the height of the Greek dominance of the Old World the shar had already been forgotten as a calendrical unit of time measurement. But a fragmented memory of it remained. Plato wrote in his Timaeus and Critias that earth's earliest traditions span back 120 centuries. (8) Curiously, on the other side of the world in remote America the Tsalagi [Cherokee] believed that 120 years was the limit of human longevity, a number associated with those who were called Keepers of the Fire. (9) Let it be remembered that God in Genesis gave Noah 120 years warning before the Flood and Moses lived to exactly 120 years.

During the period of Greek expansionism and innovations in the arts and sciences lived a Babylonian historian-priest of Bel named Berossus. He was also referred to as a Chaldean astronomer [280-246 BC] who wrote an extensive history of Babylonia in Greek probably during the reign of Antiochus II of Syria. (10) His histories were made unique because he had exclusive access to the oldest Babylonian archives and he was able to read the ancient cuneiform. Unfortunately his works have not survived but fragments of his books have been recorded by Josephus, Tatian, Eusebius, Pliny, Vitrivius, Syncellus, Apollodorus, Abydenus and Polyhistor. (11) The cuneiform texts studied by Berossus were centuries old, some over a thousand years in age which were merely copies of even older Akkadian and Sumerian tablets. Berossus even boasted that he had access and had studied original inscriptions of the beings that preceded the appearance of mankind on earth. (12) These were they whom the Babylonians called the *Anunnaki* and they will shortly be the focus of this calendrical study.

Because of transliteration problems, language rifts, corruptions inadvertently introduced in to copies made from older copies of the histories preserved by Berossus some of his conclusions were slightly corrupted, but even the corruptions allude to the correct interpretations. For example, the Babylonian Zodiac is supposed to have dated back from the time of Berossus exactly 6700 years, which is actually an exaggerated *670 years* of the older Sumerian King-List. (13) Further, Eusebius, celebrated Church Father calculated Berossus' chronology of Babylonia to span back 2,150,000 years (14), but this sum merely exhibits his confusion between the shar being a year or a day. The actual records reveal that 216,000 shars [days] and not 2,150,000 of them was exactly 600 years [Draconian years of 360 days]. Eusebisus could have been attempting to isolate the even greater sum of 6000 years [2,160,000 shars is 6000 Draconian years].

Also of note is that other king-lists have been found, some being Babylonian versions of older Sumerian records. One such list of preflood kings numbers Seven Kings and is known as British Museum Tablet W-20030, with six of the Seven Kings equated with the Sumerian list. (15) This disparity may be due to the fact that only seven regents finished their reigns, the Eighth having his rule interrupted by the Flood. Another king-list preserved by Berossus and cited by Alexander Polyhistor mirrors the Genesis genealogy of ten patriarchs, having ten antediluvian kings who ruled collectively for *120 shars*. [43,200 days]. (16)

It was the memory of the Flood and these ten rulers (patriarchs not to be confused with the Eight Kings) that gave rise to the Atlantean mythos. Plato recorded the teachings of Solon of Athens who had visited Egypt and learned the histories from their venerable priesthood. The Egyptian scholars told Solon that the ancient world was sunk beneath the ocean in its *tenth* generation. (17) Atlantis is the collective embodiment of the preflood traditions. The Ten Kings of Atlantis were venerated in a temple said to be on the Atlantic continent that had ten statues of pure gold of the ten kings and their wives. The original Atlantic tradition was a historic story from Egypt that Solon rewrote into an epic verse, according to Plutarch. Interestingly, the Egyptians told Solon that the world was destroyed periodically at long intervals of time because the bodies moving around the earth deviate from their courses. (18) Aside from the Atlantean beliefs, the biblical ten-king dynasty before the Great Deluge seems to have been remembered universally. Iranian legends recall a ten king dynasty in antiquity, called the Men of Ancient Law. In India were remembered the Ten petris, or fathers. The old Germans and Arabs had ten patriarchal fathers in the beginning of their histories, all kings and the Chinese begin their ancestral annals with the Ten Emperors, men that lived before the dawn of historical times. The Chinese stories tell that just after the reign of the Ten Kings, after the Creation, mankind struggled against fierce and gigantic monsters back when people lived unusually long lives. (19)

Unlike the more peaceful memories of the ten kings or patriarchs the Eight Kings of Sumer are remembered as a dynasty of iniquity, the cause of the Flood itself and the catastrophic events that collapsed the earlier heavens [firmament], pushed earth out of its place and ruined the perfect Draconian calendrical system. These Eight Kings are also dissimilar to the ten patriarchs because they are not historically identifiable outside the King-List, being commemorated over and again only within the Sumerian, Akkadian and Babylonian fragments that mention the Seven [or Eight] Kings. The patriarchs have the entire biblical and extracanonical records stemming from them and their descendants but the Seven Kings as well as the Eighth do not return to the world's literary scenes until the apocalyptic text known as the Book of Revelation. In Revelation they are described as demonic and this corresponds with their Sumerian identities. The very first king was Alulim, an epithet denoting one who is possessed with an evil spirit [alu]. In Sumerian the designation for this demon is A-LA and it was noted for its ability to change its form at will. (20)

The records of the past concerning these Eight Kings are prolific in the surviving Mesopotamian annals, and all contain one startling fact. From the start there were only Seven Kings, the Eighth was one of the Seven who returned to rule again. In these texts these Kings are referred to as the *Anunnaki*. There are seven deities named in the most ancient texts but the lists contain eight kings, the last never named, but the ideograms indicate only seven regents. (21) The later Babylonians considered the Eighth to be the Dragon of Chaos named Tiamat, a Goddess of the Deep (22) and the Akkadians before them held that the Seven Gods were merely heads on the Great Dragon who is the Eighth. (23) In the Vedic texts the Rishis were Seven Sages immortalized in the stars according to the Vayu Purana who were numbered as Eight. (24) The Rishis visited earth when humanity was in its infancy, thus identifying these Sages as the Anunnaki. Incidentally, the Anunnaki are specifically called the Seven Sages who built the walls of Uruk in the Epic of Gilgamesh. Even an obscure fragment in the Bible concerns this arcane enigma. In Ecclesiastes we read "...give a portion to seven and also to eight, for thou knowest not what *evil shall be upon the earth.*"

A female was often associated to the Seven Kings. She was called Dingir-DAM-NUN-GAL-E-NE or Damkina. (25) These seven were also called the Sons of Isharra (26) that intriguingly maintains a root word pertinent to this study: I[shar]ra. Antiquarian Gerald Massey in the 1880s wrote in his *Ancient Egypt Light of the World* that the goddess may have been the originator of the Seven, a primordial Genitrix who is mysteriously also identified as a masculine deity. He also addressed this problem in his epic *The Natural Genesis*, writing that the Seven Kings were the sons of Anu, Babylonian god of heaven. (27) This confusion between a male and female originator may simply be due to preferential ideologies between patriarchal and matriarchal cultures over time, also by historians and redactors handling newer copies of older texts. The goddess link may be due to the fact that the Chaos known throughout antiquity was also personified as a female, even the word for *deep* in Genesis 1:2 is in feminine tense. Either way the belief in seven deities having their beginning with an Eighth is not exclusively Mesopotamian. The Egyptians, later Gnostics and others as will be shown recalled their kingship. (28)

The earth is very old. Of all the chronologies and calendrical systems of long ago that have survived and those used today very few, if any, claim to span all the way back to a creation event. Most of them stretch back in time to the supposed beginning of *mankind* or some major event in early history that depopulated our planet. One of the dating systems thought to go back the furthest and with the best accuracy is the Annus Mundi Chronology [Year of the World]. Alexandrian scholars in Egypt were familiar with Annus Mundi dating but even then there were varying versions and just as the Egyptian priestly classes altered their own sacral calendars to suit their socio-religious purposes so too did Alexandrian scribes and Christian writers modify AM [Annus Mundi designation used throughout this book] dates to correspond with assumed calendrical points in other dating systems. Over time this dating has resurfaced, been lost again, reverse-researched to again put it back together up until the present. The Greek astronomer in charge of the Library at Alexandria during the reign of Ptolemy III was Eratosthenes [276-196 BC]. He interpreted Egyptian dynasties as containing periods derived from Genesis dating and was familiar with the Annus Mundi dating. (29) Flavius Josephus who gave us his *Antiquities* was acquainted with AM system, even claiming that Solomon became king circa. 3100 AM. (30) The Egyptian Book of Sothis preserved by Syncellus [800 AD] recorded events in AM years and Geoffrey of Monmouth, celebrated author of *Historia Regum Brittanae* [History of the Kings of Britain] also used the Annus Mundi Chronology to ascertain that the city of Londonum was founded 1004 years before Christ's birth. Even texts from secret societies like Masons published in the past three and four hundred years date events by Annus Mundi reckoning, principally the Inigo Jones Document and Wood Manuscript.

Unlike the Julian/Gregorian system the Annus Mundi Calendar is without a break or merging with any other calendar. The greatest and most accurate reconstruction of the AM system was performed by Stephen Jones and published in his *Secrets of Time*. He began Year 1 with Adam's expulsion from Eden, which corresponds exactly with the start of the Hebraic Chronology. For some perspective let the reader understand that as of this writing in 2017 AD [Anno Domini] it is the Year 5911 Annus Mundi. Next year, 2018 AD, will be 5912 AM, or **88** years short of 6000.

That the Sumerian record of the Eight Kings extends back 670 years prior to the Flood unveils some startling revelations. Hebrew reckoning is divergent from Annus Mundi calculations in events *after* the Flood, but in dating the Deluge both agree with the testimony of many ancient writings with the Year 1656 [Hebraic/Annus Mundi], which translates into the Gregorian system as 2239 BC. Subtracting 670 years from 1656 AM is 986 AM [2908 BC]. Amazingly, this is the exact time that the antediluvian prophet-king Enoch ascended into heaven to exercise *kingship* over the remaining 66.6% of the Anunnaki that remained in heaven in obedience to the Creator after 33.3% of them were imprisoned, with a small minority of these angelic [Anunnaki] offenders free to roam the earth. As shown in this author's work entitled *Lost Scriptures of Giza* the Sumerians and many others remembered Enoch and his testimonies he gave against the Anunnaki. Enoch's ascension at Achuzan [later called Giza after Pyramids constructed] initiated a 70 year countdown to 1056 AM [2839 BC], a period marking the changing of *kingship* of earth from mankind to the Anunnaki. In 2839 BC the Anunnaki began 600 years of rulership over humanity until the Flood ended their reign of wickedness. The first regnal year of the Anunnaki Kings [1056 AM/2839 BC] was also the same year that the famous Noah was born, builder of the Ark. This is confirmed in Genesis where we learn that Noah was 600 years old when he entered the ark and the world was destroyed by flooding. It is absolutely beyond coincidence that these two entirely different methods of time-keeping merge to this incredible year 600 years prior to the cataclysm.

Though this is a stunning parallel, the Egypto-Coptic record of the building of Giza and the Great Pyramid is even more profound. The Giza Complex was finished at 2815 BC [1080 AM] after 90 years of construction that started in 990 AM [2905 BC]. Construction began 60 years after the death of Adam, the patriarch of mankind, who died in 2965 BC [930 AM], and while *Lost Scriptures of Giza* provides the full account of the building of the pyramid complex and Sphinx by the instructions of Enoch who had received them from heaven, the following account was not elaborated. This Egypto-Coptic history amazingly aligns with Sumerian chronology. This ancient Coptic manuscript was found in a tomb in the Monastery of Abou Harmeis. The text was translated into Arabic by a monk of the Monestary of Al Kalmun:

"In the first year of King Diocletian [3rd. cent. AD] an account was taken from a book, copied in the first year of King Philippus, from an *inscription of great antiquity* written upon a tablet of gold, which tablet was translated by two brothers—Ilwa and Yercha—at the request of King Philippus, who asked them how it happened that they could understand an inscription which was unintelligible to the learned men of his capital? They answered, because they were descended from one of the ancient inhabitants of Egypt, who was preserved with Noah in the Ark, and who, after the Flood had subsided, went into Egypt with the sons of Ham, and dying in that country left to his descendants (from who the brothers had received them), the books of the ancient Egyptians, which had been written one thousand seven hundred and eighty-five [1785] years before the time of Philippus, nine hundred and forty-six [946] years before the arrival of the sons of Ham in Egypt, and contained the history of the two thousand three hundred and seventy-two [2372] years; and that it was from these books that the tablet was formed. The contents of the books were:

> ...we have seen what the stars
> foretold; we saw the *calamity*
> *descending from the heavens*, and
> going out from the earth, with the
> inhabitants and plants...

The two brothers calculated what time had elapsed from the Flood to the day when the translation was made for King Philippus; and it appeared to be one thousand seven hundred and forty-one years [1741].'" (31)

This translation was made for King Philippus in 498 BC, or 1741 years after the Flood in 2239 BC [1656 AM]. The text goes on to explain how and why the Great Pyramid was constructed before this catastrophe, which is largely the focus of *Lost Scriptures*. Interestingly though, Ilwa and Yercha conclude their translation for this king with—

"...in this manner were the Pyramids built. Upon the walls were written the mysteries of science, astronomy, geometry, physics and much useful knowledge, which any person, who understands our writing, can read..." (32)

This passage further supports this author's contention that the Great Pyramid was indeed covered in myriads of writings that had over millennia faded to obscurity. According to the Appendix in the book *Origin and Significance of the Great Pyramid*, "This statement was translated from the Coptic into Arabic 225 AH [After Hijrah]." (33) This was 839 or 840 AD.

Annus Mundi reckoning and Hebraic records reveal that Egypt was settled 341 years after the diluvian catastrophe. This would be 1899 BC [1996 AM]. Remember, this is the *post*-flood occupation of Egypt. There was also a civilization centered there prior to the Flood that was Sethite, having little connection to the ancient Egypt we know about today. 1899 BC was during the reign of Anam of Sumer who occupied Egypt and is remembered by the earliest Egyptians as Mena [Menes] or Min according to Herodotus in Book II of his *Histories*. (34) This was during the life of Abraham and only a few years before the excavation of Giza from flood sedimentation that half buried the site. The Coptic record holds that the pyramids were built and inscribed with the knowledges from which their information derived 946 years before the arrival of the sons of Ham to Egypt. This would be 2843 BC [1052 AM], *only four years* difference from the Sumerian King-List regnal year of 2839 BC [1056 AM] when the Seven Kings began their reign the same year Noah was born. Due to the expanse of four thousand years in these calculations a variance of 4 years is virtually precise. But this may have been a deliberately contrived disparity. As shown in *Lost Scriptures of Giza* there were once 144,000 white polished limestone casing blocks upon the surfaces of the Great Pyramid, all with minute inscriptions from bottom to top, and there are four years between these two dates which under the preflood Draconian System would be exactly *1440 days* [360 x 4]. Reader recall, before the Flood the prime unit of measuring time was by *days*, which leads us to our next calendrical study.

The bewildering Mayan Long-Count Calendar is not so mysterious once compared with the Annus Mundi system. Scholars have determined that this olden American calendar has a start-date of August 12th, 3113 BC, a date that baffled Mayan scholars. The Mayan Calendar will end once 13 baktuns are completed, and incredibly, these baktuns are expansive units of time that are measured at exactly *144,000 days* each. Thus the entire Mayan system concludes at 1,872,000 days, which reads 13.0.0.0.0. The fact that days were the prime unit of calendrical reckoning to the Maya whose system began in remote antiquity on par with early Sumerian civilization, a culture also counting their periods in days instead of years is telling indeed. 3113 BC extends back to 782 AM [3113 BC] which is only *13 years* prior to the date Sumerian scholars ascribe to Etana, the Enoch of the Sumerian King-lists; *11 years* from the start of the Brahmanic Kali Yuga Age of India in 3102 BC [793 AM]; and *8 years* after the beginning of the Mayan Itza Temple of the Cross Calendar.

The Mayan system as well as the others noted here began during the reign of the prophet-King Enoch. Its start date in conjunction with the building of the pyramids and reign of its principle architect [Enoch] and allusion to a time in the Last Days hints that this system was intended to start at a very significant date in the beginning that commemorated another time period in the *end*. And as *Lost Scriptures* clearly demonstrated, this was the chief purpose of the Great Pyramid—an apocalypse recorder and prophetic time capsule. Though antiquarians associate the Egyptian ruler Khufu with the

Great Pyramid the actual title appears to be a Mayan Itza description meaning *sacred area* [K'UFU]. (35) Though this is not to be addressed until later in this thesis the author makes it very clear that he agrees with the start-date of the Mayan Long-Count in 3113 BC, for reasons to be disclosed, but he is adamantly opposed to the modern scholarly interpretation that this system of 13 baktuns ends in 2012 AD because chronologists today assume that earth's 365.24 day orbital period making the year has always remained constant, and this is far from the truth. Recalibrating the Long-Count to 13 baktuns of *Draconian* days [360-day years] gives us 5200 years [52 being sacred to the Maya] and provides us an incredible date important to our study later in this book. The Maya considered the 365.24 day-year to be *vague*, and they would never have adopted the vague year for their historic Long-Count. Even the greater sum of 144,000 days [baktun] exhibits the use of the lower denominator of 360 [360 x 4 = 1440].

But these facts and divisors do not only apply to the Mayan Long-Count. The truly remarkable Brahmanic system is even closer in synchronicity to the Sumerian system than the ancient American. The Kali Yuga age of India marks the beginning of mankind's degeneration into evil and has a start-date of 3102 BC [793 AM], exactly *11 years* after the beginning of the Long-Count. (36) The Kali Yuga age was predicated on the idea that the Age would come full circle to an end after 6000 years. Note that the Kali Yuga was the Fourth Age of India and did not start with the beginning of Brahmanic reckoning. The proximity of these start-dates is laden with implications. All four of these references, the Temple of the Cross, the Mayan Long-Count, Etana record and Brahmanic Calendar all fall within a *21 year* period that perfectly averages out at 800 Annus Mundi [3095 BC] if we conclude that the Mayan Temple of the Cross Calendar was designed to start contemporaneously with the Long-Count instead of seven years priorly. And this conclusion is not without further confirmation from the Maya themselves.

The Maya Itza Temple of the Cross Calendar has been assigned a start date of 3121 BC [774 AM] and the Mayan records claim this system began with the *ascension of a goddess* from the earth who is represented by a rather grotesque glyph. The inscriptions in the Temple read that Lady-Beast-With-Upturned-Snout was over *800 years old* at the time of her ascension. (37). Of course this was Enoch, however, an 800 year-old woman was not uncommon during those days prior to the Flood. The 800 reference could refer to 800 Annus Mundi or the 800 could be a numerical disguise for the Eight Kings because the Lady-Beast is no doubt equated with the Sumero-Babylonian Dragon Tiamat, the seven-headed dragon that supports the Eighth. In the biblical apocalyptic Book of Revelation she is called MYSTERY BABYLON and the Harlot. Are we to delegate this as mere coincidence? Are we to assume Mayan records in the Temple of the Cross any less accurate than the scientific calculations in the Mayan Dresden Codex that contains Venus almanacs so precise they ensure an accuracy of within *two hours in five hundred years* of Venus calculations? (38) We are reminded here of a most truthful statement made by Robert B. Stacey-Judd in 1939 AD who wrote that beneath the stories of world mythology there is truth, veiled in various disguises and "...by careful comparison with somewhat analogous accounts from widely scattered areas, fundamental charactorists frequently show remarkable parallels. If therefore, extraneous data disclose that a certain amount of fact underlies most myths and legends, let us, for the time being consider them as a medium of information, subject to the more definite acceptance of substantiation through other sources." (39)

Keeping this in mind we note that the Mayan and Brahmanic histories are fused together by the goddess motif, for the Kali Yuga was modeled after the Indian Goddess of Destruction Kali. She had *eight* arms (matriarchal memory of the Scorpion King) and was a frenzied, bloody woman with weapons of war in each hand. Other Native American cultures probably distantly related to the Maya maintained traditions concerning Spider Woman who was linked to the number 8 [arachnid having 8 legs] and the creative act of weaving web. (40) In early Mexico the spider was the surrogate of evil and cold, known as the Arch-Deceiver and enemy of mankind. The mother-goddess connection is prevalent everywhere in the early Americas, the genitrix of a malignant race of Stone Giants. These giants sought to exterminate mankind before they were hurled over the great abyss. The Aztecs tell of these giants during the reign of Tlaloc (Mexican Enoch), a man who lived for 364 years until an evil goddess began to rule and the world was destroyed in a Flood. This is a direct memory of Enoch, who lived 365 years being translated into heaven, the 364 recalled because it aligns the Mexican calendar into periods of 52 years (52 x 7 is 364). This goddess's name was Ixcuina and she is faulted for the flood, she further being remembered as being represented by a *constellation* that fell from the sky. This primordial woman that caused the Deluge is told of in old Cornwall, Wales and Brittany as well as across the globe in early Persia. The Hopi too remembered a wicked goddess who had access to a ladder that reached the world's axis. (41) These details are distinctly Euphratean in origin. Ishtar of the Babylonians and Innana of Sumer also were identified with ladders to reach heaven and were both connected to flood myths involving divine necklaces with beads that represented the Anunnaki. Another title for Innana was Aruru and she had a necklace of lapis lazuli beads similar to the divine necklace of jewels worn by the Japanese goddess Amaterusa. This Japanese story tells that after the passage of seven generations [which would be during *eighth* one] of gods appeared the Izanagi and Izanami. (42) These beings are no doubt a corruption of the Sumerian Anunnaki [A-NUN-NA-GE]: Iz[anagi]. Izanami is merely a Japanese female version of Izanagi. The goddess associated to the Seven in Egypt was called Sefket-Aabut, the Goddess of the Laying Down of the Foundation, of the repetitions of seven, the Guardian of the cycles of 30 and *120 years*. Over her head was a seven-rayed star and about her neck was a rainbow scholars identify as the same symbol of Ishtar's collar of jewels. (43) The 7-pointed star as seen in *Lost Scriptures of Giza* was important to the architectural mechanics of the Great Pyramid and 120 is the Sumerian Great Shar in use when the pyramid complex was constructed upon the firm foundation in Egypt. Even in late Greek antiquity this mythos was still circulating. It was said that a god of forging made a wonderful necklace and it was given to Harmonia, a goddess. Despite its divine origin the necklace was to bring about the end of a later generation. (44)

Though most theologians and scholars would scoff at the idea, there is enough evidence to assert that the world's oldest chronological systems all shared a common origin, a universal time-keeping system known throughout the old world that was fragmented with the rifts created in civilization over millennia. That they seem to align is merely half the mystery. The other half of this puzzle is why they all appear to have been designed to align at a *600-year countdown* to the Great Flood in 2239 BC [1656 AM]. And the reason for this will prove to be a shocking revelation, as we will find.

The Sumerian, Babylonian, Akkadian, Vedic, Hebrew, Mayan, Coptic and many other calendars all share the same characteristics because when these systems were first implemented the entire world was a single civilization with a phenomenal calendar that unified terrestrial and astronomical time. We have discovered herein the day-shar and the Great Shar, or 120-year period. But just as one day can be magnified into many, now we must peer into the mysteries of the year and its greater counterpart: the Great Year.

The Jewish historian Flavius Josephus wrote an extensive history of his people after the Romans virtually destroyed his nation. He wrote that the people before the Flood lived extremely long lives, a fact he cites from several other earlier historians such as Berossus of Babylon, Manetho of Egypt, Mochus, Hestiaeus, Hieronymous, Hesiod [Theogany] and others. In his famous *Antiquities* he wrote:

"Let no one comparing the lives of the Ancients with our lives, and with the few years which we now live, think that what we have said of them is false; or make the shortness of our lives at present an argument that neither did they attain to so long a duration of life; for those Ancients were beloved of God Himself, and because their food was then fitter for the prolongation of life, might well so live so great a number of years; and besides, God afforded them a longer life on account of their virtue and the good use they made of it in *astronomical and geometrical discoveries*, which would not have afforded the time of foretelling [the periods of the stars] unless they had lived *six hundred years*; for the *Great Year* is completed in that interval." (45)

The astronomers prior to the Deluge were aware that an important cycle concluded every 600 years. Oriental chronologists measured the Great Year as a day of 600 actual years and a night of the same length. (46) This identifies a cycle of 1200 years, which will prove vital to our thesis later in this archive. In Timaeus Plato inferred that history repeated itself when the heavenly bodies regained their original positions. This is called the Great Year. (47) Proclus was a student of Plato who determined that the length of the Great Year was to be found by a *conjunction of planets*. (48) The planetary cycles align every 216,000 days [600 years], a period the Italian astronomer Cassini referred to as the most perfect astronomical cycle known. (49) Those planets that synchronize are the five anciently known planets of Mercury, Venus, Mars, Jupiter and Saturn. This epoch was considered sacred, the solar years not being as important but rather the *days* necessary to complete the 216,000-day cycle. For example, the Greeks, Romans and Etruscans recalled such a cycle but instead of 600 solar years they used a 608 lunar calendar to produce virtually the same effect. (50)

Considering all of this we come to the conclusion that the Sumerian King-list first regnal year began with the first of 600 years to the Flood, the Sumerian record of five cities perhaps even alluding to the *five planets* that signified the start of the reign of the Seven Kings in 2839 BC [1056 AM]. Because this date was the 1056th year since the start of the Annus Mundi and Hebraic chronologies then the beginning of Sumerian Anunnaki kingship and birth of Noah happened to fall upon the same year that the Ancients according to Josephus discovered the *Great Year*. 600 years prior to this year was also a significant Anunnaki-related event that will be revealed in this archive but until *two* events occur there was no way to discern when a Great Year began or ended. 2839 BC was the second termination of a Great Year therefore distinguishing the epoch. 600 years prior could not have been preceded with a 600-year period because the calendars only span back 1056 years, not a full 1200.

The Flood was an apocalypse that had been predicted and the next apocalypse that had been predicted, as will be shown, will involve global *fire* instead of water; flood of flames. And just as the diluvian cataclysm was aligned astronomically so too has it been known from times of yore even before Hipparchus [recognized father of astronomy] that the Great Year was integral to determining the *ekpyrosis*, or end of the world by conflagration. (51)

It is the Sumerian records lately translated that link the Anunnaki to the Eight Kings of Sumer before the Deluge. The Sumerian King-Lists do not refer to them as Anunnaki, however, their reign of 600 years that began exactly 70 years after Enoch's ascension to power is our greatest clue to their identity because in these Sumerian texts the Anunnaki are called by the common ideogram NER, which means the SIX HUNDRED. (52). Berossus preserved this fact as the *neroi* and in Vedic literature of India it was written that each Avatar [deity descended from heaven] visited earth for 600 years. (53) Another reference to the NER is found in a Babylonian calendar code concerning the Anunnaki:

The gods of heaven, the gods of earth,
    The Great Gods, fifty are they.
The gods of fate, seven are they.
    The Anunnaki of heaven, three hundred;
The Anunnaki of Earth, SIX HUNDRED. (54)

Scholars have missed the amazing significance of this passage. The total number here is 957, a sum without significance calendrically, geometrically or otherwise. But if we exclude the apparent reduplication of the Anunnaki in line 5 we are left with 357 "gods of heaven," as opposed to the 600 Anunnaki of *earth* we excluded. The number 357 is incomplete as the number of "gods" [preflood annual days] without adding the Sumerian Triad of Enlil, Anu and Ea, thus equaling 360 gods of heaven, or degrees in a perfect circle used to measure *distance* and *time*. The gods of heaven are the stellar deities that mark time, but are governed by the seven "gods of fate," which are the five anciently recognized planets, the sun and moon.

This astronomical code exhibits that the 600 Anunnaki only align with *earth* when the Gods of Fate [planets] seem so on a 360-day annual calendar and that they only rule for 216,000 days [600 x 360]. Now, these periods are themselves governed by 50 Great Gods. As will be shown throughout this work 50 years is a number linked to *generations of earth time*, equal to a Hebrew calendrical Jubilee [7 x 7 years plus a rest year is 50] and similar to the human generation that is only 40 years. The Seven Anunnaki were not given an unbroken period of reign upon earth but appear to have been themselves ruled by the movement of stellar bodies. Akin to the Babylonians were the Assyrians, also descended from Sumer, and according to Jamblichus, they

"...have not only preserved the memories of the Seven and twenty myriads of years, as Hipparchus says they have, but likewise of the whole Apocatastes and periods of the Seven Rulers of the World." (55)

The NER is a mysterious unit of measurement but all of this information lends credit to the supposition that it was long ago quite popular. Another title for the Sumerian goddess preserves this memory, being NER-uda, the goddess linked with the Seven Anunnaki in several texts. The uda suffix is apparent in many Sumerian titles, such as in the Sumerian name of Nimrod [the Mighty Hunter]: A-MAR-*UDA*-AK, who happened to have ruled over Anunnaki after the Flood [or so he claimed]. Many ancient things are remembered in this way. The Greeks recall a survivor of the Flood named Deucalion, who was also called by the title of NEReus. Nereus was the Old Man of the Sea, an obscure deity associated to Noah, whom Hesiod wrote was "...a trusty god and gentle [something the sea is not], who thinks just and kindly thoughts and never lies." (65) Nereus had 50 daughters after the Flood that were the cause of much strife. This name means 'wet' and was the name of an early Christian known to Paul. (57) The infamous Roman Emperor Nero derives his name from him.

Though Sumerian records tell of the Anunnaki and Seven Kings as having lived and ruled prior to the Flood they also reveal that these beings antedate the antediluvian world and even humanity, their existence having been archaic long ere mankind was created. They were originally a part of the hosts of the heavens that served a Godhead but they rebelled in pre-Adamic times. The Seven were from ancient heaven (58) and were cast down from their positions in a devastating war that destroyed the solar system, scarred the moon and pushed earth away from the sun to freeze until it returned to orbit centuries later. They made war against Enlil, the Chief of Old Time and were condemned by Enlil to enjoy their kingship over humanity [prophesied back in early heaven] for a period not to exceed *50 shars*, or 6000 years [50 x 120]. Earth became the center of conflict between the Godhead and the rebellious Anunnaki before mankind was even created.

Sumerian, Akkadian and Babylonian stone tablets and stellar inscriptions describe the Anunnaki as having literally *fell down* from heaven. The tablet reads, "Those Seven, the evil gods, who swoop like the Deluge, swoop upon the *world* like a storm." (59) They are the seven serpents of death no doubt all connected to the Eighth, or Dragon. They are also constantly referred to as "Those who observe and see," or IGIGI, better known as the Watchers (60) and in the Secrets of Enoch text the Watchers are called the "many-eyed ones." (61) Indra in the Indian epics wore a robe "covered in eyes," [fulfilling the office of Watcher] and incidentally in the Rig Veda he is called the *7-Slayer.* (62) Watchers have long been connected to the serpent motif and those having read *Lost Scriptures* will know that the oldest root words in several archaic languages for serpent, snake and dragon were syllables all connected to *seeing, observing* and *discerning.* Enoch was commanded to testify against the Watchers, "…those that sinned with the daughters of men; for they had commenced to mix with the daughters of the earth, so that they were defiled; and Enoch testified against them all." (63)

The Babylonian historiographers and scribes were convinced that the Seven Kings came from the heavens and they designated these beings as the Children of Anu who rebelled (64), which is understandable because the older Sumerian writings tell that the Anunnaki were the Sons of Enlil [Lord Wind]. (65) To advance this position is the fact that the Hebraic texts of Jubilees, Genesis 6 and several extracanonical works convey that the Sons of God took [abducted forcibly] the daughters of men, fathering a race of giants. The Anunnaki, called Nephilim [Fallen Ones] in scripture descended upon the earth and created a counterfeit theology involving many "sons of God" rather than just One who was foretold in the Elder Prophecies to visit the earth to announce judgment. In the Old Testament books the Anunnaki offspring are a race of giants called the *Anakim.* The radical AK is found in both Anunn[AK]i and An[AK]im and is a syllable of great antiquity found in many languages and almost always meaning *mighty* or a variant thereof. (66) It is commonly found among the titles of rulers and kings like in the Sanskrit Ganaka [king], Akbar [great] and Cormac, the High King of Ireland. Balak was king of Moab, Shishak of Egypt and Gwrnach was a female giant in the Arthurian legends and the syllable serves as the root for the strongest of all trees: the oak. O[AK]. (67) Anak was also a Philistine title of rank thought by some scholars to have come from the Mycenaean region of Anak. (68) It was also Phoenician for *prince* (69) and it was a part of many Graeco-Aegean titles and names: Anaxagoras, Anaxamander, Anaxidrides.

Because the Anunnaki were called the Children of Anu the later Babylonians misinterpreted the original and very old records of the Sumerians concerning these A-NUN-NA-GE [Anunnaki], for there is no evidence that NUN meant "heaven." (70) This was merely traditional etymology leading the later Babylonian scribes to interpret the epithet as "Offspring of Heaven and Earth." But the Sumerians did not convey this meaning at all. The Sumerian word NUN is synonymous with *apsu*, the Underworld, a common title used in many names of old. Apsu literally means the *deep* as in the mythical NUN-KI-GA, or City of the Deep. The Sumerian underworld was thought to be filled with water; the fountains of the deep and the idea and etymology can be traced back to Sanskrit as well where we learn that ap is the word for water. (71) The very earliest records held that the Anunnaki came from the *Deep*. (72)

Curiously the Deep has a dual meaning. To the credit of the Babylonians the apsu was not only the terrestrial oceans but was also a metaphor for the vastness of space, especially the lowest regions below the horizon that were alien to the Sumerians. Both were considered an abyss [bottomless pit]. In some writings the Anunnaki were seven Masters of the Underworld and Gloomy pit (73) and one text reads: "In the Abyss of the Deep they are Seven..." (74) The dual reference to the heavens and underworld are also seen in Akkadian hymns that read, "They are Seven, they are Seven! In the depths of the Ocean they are Seven! In the heights of the Heaven they are Seven!" (75) This dichotomy is also apparent in the Egyptian Book of the Dead concerning the Sons of Revolt: "...whether the fiends descend from out of heaven, or whether they come forth from the earth, or whether they advance on the waters, or whether they come from among the *Star Gods...*" (76)

The fall of the Anunnaki from heaven is often linked to a curious description given to them as Seven Mountains. (77) This imagery connects the Anunnaki to the Watchers of the Enochian and Hebraic traditions. Enoch traveled through heaven and came across a dreadful place between heaven and earth called the Prison of the Stars where in the Abyss he witnessed "Seven stars like great *burning mountains*," described later in the Book of Enoch as ...mountains burning with fire." (78) The imagery invoked in the texts is of a *comet* that hurls through the vastness of space [abyss] from the direction of the Deep [regions far below ecliptic in southernmost area of our solar system]. The Anunnaki/mountain motif link reappears in the book of the Revelation of the Last Days:

"...and I saw a woman sit upon a scarlet colored beast, full of names of blasphemy, having *seven heads* and ten horns...the beast that thou sawest was, and is not; and shall ascend out of the *bottomless pit* [abyss] and go into perdition [ruin], and they that dwell on the earth shall wonder...and here is the mind which hath wisdom. The seven heads are *seven mountains*... And there are Seven Kings; five are fallen, and one is and the other is not yet come; and when he cometh, he must continue a short space. And the beast that was, and is not, even he is the *Eighth*, and is of the Seven..." (79)

The *Lost Scriptures of Giza* disclosed ample evidence exhibiting that motifs and symbols of the Revelation record were not known to the Greeks and this is the case also with the imagery of *mountains* identified as powerful supernatural beings. The Revelation text had already been recorded and seen by Enoch and later virtually lost into fragments preserved within the scattered books and traditions of cultures even thousands of miles apart. These Seven Mountains are the seven Anunnaki of Sumer and Babylonia, also called the Seven Kings, Sages and Igigi. In India they were the Seven Avatars, the Maruts and the Seven Rishis. The Egyptians remembered them as the Seven Sons of Revolt, the Masters and Builder Gods. The Hebraic traditions called them the Sons of God, the Watchers and Nephilim while the Graeco-Aegean cultures recalled these divinities as the Gygantes [giants], the Cyclopes and the Titans.

Lost Scriptures served to show that the Enochian records and the Revelation had come from the same source material, a vast corpus of information abbreviated for dissemination for both contain passages mirroring each other laden with iconography and language unknown to the Greeks and other civilizations extant at the time of the *second* composition of the Revelation by John 2000 years ago. However, these writings would have been perfectly understandable to the average literate Sumerian. The apocalyptic language of the Revelation and references to the Seven indicate that the history of the Anunnaki did not end with the Great Flood, but that these arcane beings have yet another role to play in the Last Days. This is inferred in the riddle provided in the Revelation just cited about the Seven Kings, and then the Eighth who is a part of the Seven. The evidence suggests that the Eighth is the same as the Anunnaki King who never finished his rule because he was "cut off," the Flood bringing his kingship to a premature end.

With the discovery of the NER [600] as an Anunnaki dating system separating the beginning of the Anunnaki kingship to the Flood, we find that the 600-year count holds true *backward* in time as well. In fact, to this author's astonishment, he calculated 600 years back to the *exact* year the Anunnaki *first appeared on earth* among men in the year 3439 BC [456 Annus Mundi] when one-third of humanity was killed in flooding and earthquakes exactly 1200 years before the Great Flood in 2239 BC [1656 AM]. This occurred according to Hebrew annals during the reign of King Cainan in the days of Enos in the 456th year of mankind's expulsion from Eden. This flooding and massive human fatalities is described in the Book of Jasher, the Jewish Haggadoth texts (80) and the Roman conqueror of Jerusalem named Titus is said in the Genesis Rabbah text to have remarked that he was aware that the God of the Jews had anciently punished them with water during the generation of Enosh before the Flood. (81)

The 3439 BC year of the first appearance of the Anunnaki appears to be the message of the Descendant Passage that leads into the Subterranean Chamber's abyssal pit, for Astronomer Royal for Scotland, Piazzi Smyth in 1880 AD published his research that he believed that the pit underneath the pyramid represented the Abyss in Revelation while also asserting that his calculations showed that the tunnel leading below the monument pointed directly at *Alpha Draconis* in about the year 3440 BC. This estimate is in fact *one year off.*

The first arrival of the Anunnaki on earth before the Flood is a very popular tradition in the Book of Jubilees, books of Enoch, the Dead Sea texts of Qumrum, Genesis 6, the Books of Adam and Eve and Testaments of the Patriarchs that were either composed or copied by Alexandrian scribes.

The works concern the arrival of the Watchers known to men as the Sons of God who descended and committed horrible sexual trespasses against the daughters of men and fathered a race of violent giants. Even the obscure Apocalypse of Baruch text reads, "...some of them descended, and mingled with women." (82) The Book of Enoch preserves a story that 200 Watchers descended to earth upon a place called Ardis atop Mount Armon. These Watchers had followed the Seven kings in primordial times and held a special council together over a very troubling proposition. They were awaiting judgment for their past rebellion but while waiting they were afforded an opportunity to descend to earth and take for themselves wives and father progeny in the world, hybrids between Adamic men and angelic beings capable of manifesting physical forms. The text reads, "Then they swore all together, and all bound themselves by mutual execrations [curses]. Their number was 200, who descended upon Ardis, which is at the top of Mount Armon." (83)

The anger of the Creator at the Anunnaki was not unjustified. They did not merely rebel against His authority but deliberately tampered with the natural order of His creation seeking to alter the divine image of God [man] into something unacceptable and corrupt, ultimately destined to suffer similar judgment. God commanded Adam and Eve, and by extension all humanity, "...be fruitful, multiply and replenish the earth." Thus, the act of coupling and procreation was by divine decree. The Anunnaki taught men hybridization techniques to "invent" newer animal variations. The Jasher texts read that man was taught "...the mixture of animals of one species with another." (84) This was first done by the Anunnaki themselves when they took the daughters of men in the days of Jared and fathered giants, called the Nephilim, a title that derives from a root meaning "an untimely falling from the womb."

The sciences of the Anunnaki were also designed to promote sexual intercourse in *violation* of the Edenic command to multiply. The Fallen Ones taught mankind the techniques of *abortion*, and in the Book of Enoch the knowledge of how "...to kill an embryo in the womb," was taught by the dark angel Kasyade and one of the many reasons God decided to eradicate the Nephilim species with the Flood. (85) The Jasher record states that sexual contraceptives were used to prevent unwanted pregnancies in women before the Flood, "...to render them barren, in order that they might retain their figures and whereby their beautiful appearance might not fade." (86)

Though accepted by modern society even 2000 years ago in the days of Jesus abortion and contraceptives were practices used widely. In the Epistle of Barnabas we find that "Thou shalt not destroy thy conceptions before they are brought forth; nor kill them after they are born." (87) These practices were first introduced by the Anunnaki and have been found among the sciences of the Egyptians 4000 years ago who were employing effective chemical contraceptives of acacia spikes, honey and dates which was used as a spermicide. Modern science had found that acacia spikes contain lactic acid, a natural spermicide. (88) Knowing that the redeemed of humanity would one day replace the fallen ranks of the Anunnaki, these corporeal beings taught hybridization, abortion, sexual contraceptives, more effective ways of warfare, and sought to popularize adultery and homosexuality because they sought desperately to slow down human reproduction so as to further lengthen their own delaying of divine punishment. Their end could not come until mankind has produced the necessary 33.3% that heaven lost in the Rebellion. This is why, according to the Babylonian *Atrahasis Epic*, the Anunnaki sought to kill mankind with a plague before the Flood because of the human population explosion in those days. (89)

That the Seven Kings were also guilty of sexual trespasses is seen in a Babylonian fragment: "In the midst of the earth they grew up and became strong; and...Seven Kings brethren were made to come as *begetters*..." (90) All of this evidence suggests that the opportunity to mingle with mankind was not an extended one. As we will see, long ago they were afforded the chance to pile up more sins upon their judgment every 600 years. Now the descent upon Mount Armon was exactly 600 years before the first regnal year of the Seven Kings which began 2839 BC [1056 AM], the descent of the Watchers having been in the year 3439 BC [456 AM] which was four years prior to the birth of Enoch's father Jared. The Jubilees text reads that Enoch's father was specifically named Jared in commemoration of the descent of the Watchers. (91) This four years between their descent and his birth was 1440 days [360 x 4] and intriguingly, Jared's name is built from a root meaning *descent* ['ared]. (92)

A most profound mystery unfolds within the names of Ardis, Armon and Jared. All of them are constructed from a very old root: [AR]dis, [AR]mon and '[AR]ed. This syllable is a phonetic relic from the antediluvian world seen also in the root for *dragon* [arad], which incidentally is a derivative of an even more primal root for *watcher* [ira]. (93) In Egypt the Brotherhood of the Seven Stars was called Kabiri, originally referred to as the Ari [eyes] of Kheb [Kab], the earliest name for Egypt. (94)) In the Old World *dragons* were comets and unknown, threatening celetial bodies. AR is the ancient Egyptian word for *hail,* or a *shower of stones. (*Worlds in Collision p. 67) The Seven sages known to the Greeks were also related to this arcane syllable and remarkably, one of the names of these Sages preserved also the Sumerian syllables earlier noted in this study. Anacharsis is this name, constructed from the roots AN [heaven], AK [great] and AR. Interestingly, kosmos in Greek has gematrical value of 600.

The phonetic root AR is also found in the olden and contemporary words for *circle*: gear, jaar, jaer, the Persian yare and the modern English year. (95) The ideological concept behind the year as a circle is understood by its orbital period around the sun. The inference behind this root is of circular time or cycles. This is reinforced by the fact that even the modern word for iron contains the primordial root [IR]on, which the ancients thought was a *heavenly metal* because it was found within meteoric rock. (96) Phonetically IR is merely a variant of AR and traced back far enough the two are probably the same.

This leads us to a perplexing conclusion. The Anunnaki *descended*, the Nephilim had *fallen*, meteorites fall from the sky like *burning mountains* and it is difficult to shake off the idea conveyed in the Sumerian King-Lists concerning the Seven Kings and how each kingship was *dropped down from heaven*. Further, meteorites were long ago called aeroliths, the conjunction here constructed from two words meaning sky and rocks, the former built from the syllable AR [aero]. These facts would naturally lead us to conclude that the underlying message unifying all of these ancient stories of the Anunnaki serve to convey a belief in the periodic descent of devastating asteroids or comets. We are not without more cogent evidences but first we must indulge in an entirely relevant and fascinating tangent. The knowledge of extraterrestrial metals according to Plato was known to Socrates who was criticized for claiming that the sun was made of stone. This was a good assumption on Socrates part since it had been known from very remote times that meteorites were made of rock and iron. Though ridiculed at trial before the Athenian Court he showed that his belief merely reflected what he had read in the books of Anaxagoras the Clozomenian. (97) Note the root word *anax*.

Socrates was one of the many antiquarians long ago who believed that sounds possessed archetypal meanings. If they are correct then this would be evidence that there was an original universal language later fragmented with its daughter dialects and languages merely preserving broken memories and scattered syllables identifiable by comparison to those same phonetic syllables preserved by other cultures. This is not an untenable theory. The syllable AR is traced back to Sumer and has survived in the Egyptian designation for *pyramid* [MER], meaning *place of ascension* [M-AR]. (98) The meaning affixed to this Egyptian term related to Achuzan, the area where Enoch ascended into heaven before the Flood where later was constructed the Great Pyramid.

This syllable is also found in Aram [one that deceives], in ard [he that descends] and in ardon [a judgment of malediction]. (99) Alexandrian Egyptians and Greeks called wandering deities identified with *planets* and *comets* [AR]chons that are diligently watched lest they deviate their celestial paths. An obvious observation to make now is that the ancients would not have worried about the movements of the planetary bodies nor of the more irregular comets had not some extraterrestrial object not already in man's distant memory wreak havoc upon civilization. Fear is born from experience and those things experienced by many are usually remembered in many ways. Another perplexing fact is that the antediluvian unit of timekeeping called the sh[AR] contained this root as well as the N[ER].

It is this incredibly complex syllable that actually *unites* the Sumerian shar and the Anunnaki NER, for in Sumerian the AR UB symbol [geometrical code for *comet*] is a perfect pentagram that had five equidistant points that contains a cryptic calendrical secret important to the ancients: five 120 year [shar] periods is 600, or a NER of the Anunnaki [120 x 5].

The pentagram is one of earth's oldest and most misunderstood symbols, its present meaning believed to be that of Satanic origin but this is very far from the truth. It is the geometrical sign for *judgment* and because divine judgment is due to the presence and longevity of evil, an evil interpretation has in more contemporary times been attached to the pentagram. The AR UB is formed of ten 108° angles which identifies the pentagram as the symbolic

Sumerian AR UB
[Plough Sign]

form of the number 1080. This number is of amazing significance to the Great Pyramid and calendrical mysteries for Giza was completed in 2815 BC which was the year *1080 Annus Mundi*. Additionally, from the start of the construction at Giza in 2905 BC [990 AM] to the exact time when Abraham had been in Egypt translating the Giza texts was 1080 years. Interestingly, the association to judgment is derived by the fact that the number 9 [number for judgment to Kabbalists, Hebraic mysticism] multiplied by the shar [120] is 1080.

Cited earlier in this archive was Josephus' passage concerning the pre-flood people's longevity afforded to them for the accurate discovery of astronomical and *geometrical* mysteries. We are left wondering if these truly advanced architects and mathematicians knew that by taking the five points of the AR UB and forming a *three*-dimensional geometrical image the result would appear as:

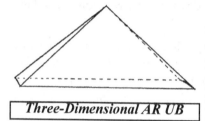

Three-Dimensional AR UB

The pentagram is a very informative symbol. As a symbol formed with one continuous line it was a representative image of linear time separated by *five* parts. It was also the Pythagorean symbol for knowledge (100) which the Great Pyramid ideologically conveyed in the earliest traditions and the Anunnaki freely gave us to our own detriment. This symbols leads us back to the beginning of our study of the Sumerian King-List which is actually an encoded AR UB is the disguise of a *pentapolis*. The *five* cities of the *Eight* Kings before the Flood were Eridu, Badtibira, Larak, Sippar and Shurrupak. These numbers in the Sumerian text cryptically provide us the angular dimensions of the Great Pyramid:

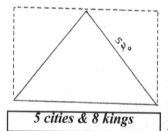

5 cities & 8 kings

Virtually nothing is known about any of these cities. Eridu is a variant of the Genesis Irad, the son of Cain and name of the first city. Badtibira was a Cainite city meaning "settlement of the metal worker." Larak seems to be a compound epithet containing three roots: 'l [god], AR and AK. Sippar was famous for having an antediluvian library that was rediscovered after the Deluge. A very old tablet discovered at the underground library of Ashurbanipal [666 BC] claimed to be a copy of a copy from Sippar concerning Enmenduranki, a man able to divine mysteries of heaven and earth. (101) Shurrupak according to the Epic of Gilgamesh was the pre-flood home of Noah [called Utnapishtim]. The particulars about these Sumerian cities are irrelevant. It's the fact that they form a *pentapolis* before they were totally destroyed in a massive cataclysm is what is important to remember.

The Sumerian idea attached to the AR UB is one of judgment. It literally means "...to cause earth to go up," which is why it was also called the Plough Sign. This archaic Sumerian sign is represented as the pentacle, the pentagram. The syllable AR has the further meaning of *to shackle, imprison*. The Creator is the Gardener and mankind His harvest. When His crops no longer bore

Him fruit [multiply and replenish the earth] for His labors [creative acts], He sent the Plough [AR UB] to break the ground [Earth] which resulted in a cataclysmic poleshift causing earth "to go up," as is described in the Revelation account when the "...heavens rolled like a scroll." The Plough was His instrument of destruction and because the olden root AR signified also a *mountain* (102) then it is a logical conclusion that all of these fragments when assembled paint a picture of a large mountain or asteroid that passed close to earth, a metaphorical *Passover* 1200 years prior to the Flood allowing Anunnaki to descend to earth in 3439 BC [456 AM] and then again 600 years later when the Seven Kings of Sumer [Anunnaki] began their kingship in 2839 BC [1056 AM], ruling for 600 years until the asteroid or a large fragment therefrom collided with earth destroying the planet just as a plough breaks up the symmetry of a garden furrow in 2239 BC [1656 AM] causing the Great Flood. While this theory is truly remarkable, another syllable from early history strongly supports it: UB, or AB which is phonetically comparable. The Sumerian word for the Four Regions of the World was UB, or sometimes AN.UB, according to Zechariah Sithin.

UB in AR UB is akin to the *fifth* Hebrew month: AB. This syllable appears throughout scripture to be associated with *death* and *fire*. [AB]ednego survived the fiery furnace in the book of Daniel; [AB]el was murdered by Cain; [AB] igail's husband died and she remarried King David; [AB]ihu displeased God and suffered a fiery death (103); [AB]imelech was a treacherous king who was killed by a *falling stone* (104). This is a very good analogy to a falling asteroid or for judgment descending from the sky as in [AR]megeddon. Also, [AB]ner was a commander in an army who was murdered by Jo[AB] after he slew Asahel with a spear "...under the *fifth* rib." (105) Abner is a compound epithet of AB and NER and curiously, the scriptures declare that Abner was the son of Ner. (106) This as a name is akin to the name of the father of Jeremiah's scribe: [NER]iah, meaning "light of Jah." His scribe's name was Baruch, a name derived from AR and AK. The earliest Chaldean and Semitic roots of NER mean "gleaming: lamp" [like a comet], the syllable derived from an older root meaning "fresh furrow, till the soil, break up [the ground]," these ultimately stemming from archaic roots meaning *fiery* and *fire*. (107)

Further, [AB]salom, son of David, conspired to murder his half brother before he was himself murdered by treachery (108). In Aramaic ar-ub means locust, which is a *destroyer of the harvest* and in Revelation locusts are released from the Deep and led by the Destroyer [of the Harvest] called [AB] addon once a *fiery burning mountain* impacts earth. Abaddon is the *Eighth King*, who was numbered as one of the Seven Kings but his reign according to the Sumerian king-Lists was "cut off" by the Deluge and he will return in the apocalypse to finalize his kingship over earth with his counterpart called the False Prophet a dark figure who enigmatically fulfills the role presaged by the office of the Apkallu who were religious leaders appointed to Sumerian kings. Abaddon's return is further confirmed in that this title is constructed from a root word [bad] that means "cut off from others." (109)

What empowers this thesis so profoundly is the irrefutable fact that this remote syllable even today in these modern times carries with it the exact connotations in English that is maintained in Sumer before the Flood. Examples abound. [AB]olish is "to put to an end," [AB]omination is "that which defiles," [AB]andon is "to desert," [AB]ash is "to destroy," [AB]ate is "to put to an end," [AB]breviate is "to shorten," [AB]dicate is "to give up," [AB]erration is "deviant from the norm," [AB]eyance is a "condition of suspended activity," [AB]hor is "to loath," [AB]ject is "low in hope," [AB]-jure is "to renounce solemnly," [AB]negate is "to renounce," [AB]ort is "to terminate prematurely," [AB]rogate is "to annul," and there are others to be found in any English dictionary but this final word is [AB]solutely amazing: [AB]racad[AB]bra, which is a magical incantation against *calamity*.

One would by now naturally assume that we are finished with this lengthy tangent but there is yet more to unveil critical to our thesis. The Sumerian AR UB is a geometrical representation of the number 5, linking 5 shars to the NER [120 x 5 = 600]. In the Revelation apocalypse the locust-demons are said to torment men under the kingship of Abaddon for *five* months with scorpion stings, and remarkably the *fifth* house of the Zodiac is Leo, in the Fire Domain of occult astrology, which was noted long ago as being the region of the skies where fire shall descend upon the earth in the last days as recorded by the Arabic scholar Makrizi. (110) In the older lunar zodiacs the *ninth* house was in Leo and was called [AR]chaam, Eye of the Lion, a mansion of the moon thought to bring discord to men and *hinder harvests*. The Zodiac is the Record of Heaven and is an unbelievable catalogue of latent messages concerning the Last Days easily decoded once one grasps the mathematics involved in the design of the Great Pyramid, a virtual apocalypse decoder of timeless stone. Reader Beware: The following archives may reveal to you more than you sought to know.

Returning back to the initial syllable in AR UB we find it recorded in the biblical texts as a geographical region bordering Israel that was originally inhabited by giants:

"I have given AR unto the children of Lot for a possession. The Emims dwelt there in times past, a people great, and many, and tall, as the *Anakim*; which also were accounted giants, as the Anakim; but the Moabites called them

Emims [terrors] …giants dwelt there [AR] in old time; and the Ammonites called them Zamzummims." (111)

This passage is of peculiar significance in two aspects. One is the cleverly concealed AB syllable in Mo[AB] in reference to the land of AR and the other is the fact that the biblical Anakim are in another passage in the Bible in the book of Joshua that cites these giants to have been descended from an ancestral figure known as ARBA. (112) The Anakim were the offspring of the Anunnaki and ARBA was a Babylonian designation for the Four Great Gods at the four corners of heaven. (113) ARBA and AR UB are interchangeable; ARBA further identifying the Four Watchers covered in eyes at the four corners of the throne of God [the heavens] seen by Enoch, Ezekiel and John as having the faces of a bull, lion, eagle and man. This was what the Sphinx at Giza was built to physically commemorate, a zodiacal mystery unveiled later. Suffice it to say that the Giza Sphinx was constructed as a testimony against the Watchers and their abominable earthly offspring.

The coming of the reign of the Anunnaki Kings and the horrid wickedness that would transpire with their emergence and kingship over the nations of the world prior to the Flood was not unknown to the antediluvians. Enoch read from an *ancient record from heaven* that foretold that after he would be taken from the earth "…great wickedness shall arise, and fraud [spiritual deception] shall spring forth," and afterward would come the Flood. (114) Note that the phraseology employed here is of wickedness springing forth as if emerging from *below*. This language and imagery precisely describes the power vacuum created by the disappearance of Enoch and how the Sumerian Seven Kings filled in the void of kingship until the Flood. The exponential increase in evil coinciding with the appearance of the Anunnaki Seven Kings 600 years before the Deluge is paralleled by their first appearance among humankind 600 years earlier when they descended upon Mount Armon in the days of Jared. The Jewish historian Josephus wrote this passage about the Sethites before the Flood in the days of Enoch's father: "Now this posterity of Seth continued to esteem God as the Lord of the Universe, and to have an entire regard for virtue, for *seven generations*; but in the process of time they were perverted, and forsook the practices of their forefathers…" (115) Josephus recorded that the Sethites became evil only *after* the angels descended and took the daughters of men. Jared was born in 3435 BC [460 AM], or 1440 days after the descent of the Watchers. Seven *human* generations of 40 years each is 280 years [40 x 7] and from 280 Annus Mundi [3615 BC] to Jared's birth was 180 years [60 + 60 + 60] and 3615 BC [280 AM] to the completion of the Great Pyramid by the Sethites at Achuzan [Giza] is exactly *800 years*, the monuments finished in 2815 BC [1080 AM]. This 800 years just might be the origin of the 800 year-old goddess of the Maya that began their Temple of the Cross calendar. These seven generations mentioned by Josephus are the same as the Japanese Way of the Gods mythos cited earlier concerning the appearance of the Izanagi and Izanami after the closure of seven generations. It was then that mankind began turning away from the Elder Faith of the Godhead as originally conveyed to mankind. By the time of Enoch's birth and kingship the giants were multiplying as the Anunnaki practiced exogamy against the Cainite families that were willing to trade their daughters in exchange for the knowledge they could provide. It was Enoch who prophesied that the "offspring of the Watchers," would tyrannize over humanity before being destroyed by the agency of water. (116) This history is the reason why we have two versions of Sumerian Kingship before the Flood. One king-list refers to ten kings that mirror the biblical ten patriarchs while the other more obscure text revealed in this book mentions Eight Kings known historically as the Seven. The Seven Kings began their kingship of the world after Enoch's departure and evidently part of antediluvian civilization still recognized the original patriarchal rulership while the majority were inclined to be ruled by the Anunnaki.

A curious coincidence seemingly latent among these traditions is that when the Anunnaki descended in Jared's day they numbered two hundred, which is only a third of an Anunnaki NER. This fact is made stranger once considering that at the arrival of these 200 Anunnaki [Watchers] one *third* of humanity died in devastating flooding. If we assume that the Anunnaki kingship could not have begun until their number was full, 200 more of them having descended to earth 600 years after they originally descended in Jared's time, then somewhere in the *past* we will discover this hidden Anunnaki descent to earth. 200 appeared before Enoch was born, 200 more at the first regnal year of Anunnaki kingship but we are missing 200 more in order to fulfill the NER [600].

So far we have identified three NER points on the olden calendar. The first NER we've discovered is the descent of the Watchers in 3439 BC [456 AM]. The second NER was 600 years later with the start of the reign of the Seven Kings immortalized upon the stone Sumerian King-List record that began in 2839 BC [1056 AM] when Noah was born. And the third NER was 600 years after this was the Great Flood in 2239 BC [1656 AM]. But these three NER points only identify a 1200-year period, from 3439 to 2239 BC [456-1656 AM]. This 1200 years is exactly ten Sumerian great shars [120 x 10] and just happens to be the key that links together earth's *oldest* dating systems, the 1200 years decodes many calendrical mysteries of our ancestors.

The emergence of the Anunnaki among men and their kingship during the pre-flood world was so important to archaic historians that they designed entire chronological systems beginning with the start of the first regnal year of the Seven Kings 600 years prior to the diluvian apocalypse. While this has indeed proven to be a fascinating study we have evidence of yet another calendrical begin-date of our earliest timekeepers. The confusions between divergent systems of calendrical reckoning appear to have been caused by the intentional recognition of two dates in antiquity that thematically identifies the same topic [descent of powerful beings to earth]. The two events were at first known to be separate but later redactors confused over the obvious similarities in the descension accounts wrongly attempted to merge what were specifically designed to be separate calendars. Aside from the Hebraic and Annus Mundi chronologies, which were actually the same system before the Hebrew system fell before corrupt scribes, no known calendrical history spans back to the beginning of mankind. All evidence exhibits that our most ancient calendars reach back to either the *first* descent of the Anunnaki in 3439 BC [456 AM] or the second *descent* in 2839 BC [1056 AM] when Sumerian King-ship began. This becomes axiomatic with the following facts.

Returning to Berossus, the Babylonian priest-historian who lived during the beginning of the Alexandrian era we find that he recorded that the ten kings prior to the Deluge ruled for a total of 432,000 years (117), an absolutely ridiculous number of years for ten men to live even successively. He misunderstood many of the olden tablets he had in his possession. Berossus also claimed that this period of the ten kings [biblical patriarchs] was equal to *120 shars*. Berossus' miscalculations were common with many cultures that attempted to understand their own ancestral records. The number 432,000 was not of years but of actual *days* on a Draconian 360-day count for this is the *exact number of days in 1200 years* [1200 x 360]. 432,000 days is the same as two NER [600 + 600]. Thus the Babylonian histories *begin* with the descent of the Watchers 1200 years before the Flood.

The last of the ten kings of Berossus' account was Xisuthrus, the Babylonian Noah. This patriarchal king lived in the city of Sippar in Sumer which we found earlier on the Sumerian King-List as one of the pentapolis of Anunnaki-controlled cities. The tradition reads that Xisuthrus was warned of the coming Deluge and commanded to "...commit to writing a history of the beginning, progress and final conclusion of all things down to the present term, and bury these accounts securely in the city of Sippara, City of the Sun." (118)

The Babylonians were not the only ones who preserved this confusion over the actual length of the 432,000 "years." The Brahmans of India reckoned their history in vast ages of the gods and like most historical cultures even among themselves there existed disparate interpretations concerning the actual length of these time periods. Some in India believed that from beginning to end of earth time would pass 432,000,000 years. (119) This belief may have stemmed from the fact that at the end of 432,000 "years" the Old World had met its end. Like the Babylonians, Greeks, biblical book of Daniel and other lesser known traditions, the Brahmans ascribed various metals to their Ages of the World: Gold, Silver, Brass and Iron:

Krita Yuga	1,728,000 'years'
Trita Yuga	1,296,000 'years'
Dvapara Yuga	864,000 'years'
Kali Yuga	432,000 'years'

Recall now that the scholarly interpreted begin-date for the Kali Yuga age cited earlier was only *11 years* from the start of the Mayan Long-Count calendar. 432 is simply 144 x 3, or the most abbreviated form of the Mayan Long-Count of 13 baktuns [144,000 days x 13]. So, 432,000 days is three Mayan baktuns, and three baktuns is exactly 1200 years under the pre-flood system. Further, *12* baktuns is the same as the entire Krita Yuga Age of 1,728,000 *days* [144,000 x 12]. The common origin of all these dating systems is evident.

Vedic scholars are at variance over the Kali Yuga dating but even their disparities conform to our thesis. Note that all four ages of the Brahmans are multiples of 432,000. The Dvapara Yuga is 432,000 x 2 and the others are x3 and x4. If added all together the Four Ages are 4,320,000 'years.' A Anunnaki NER is 216,000 days [600 years] and two NER is 432,000 days, or 1200 years. The logical abbreviation of 432,000 from years to days is confirmed in the Vedic text called the Laws of Manu, which cites that the Kali Yuga Age was only *1200 years*. (120) The lowest denominator between these old calendars from the East to the West of the Americas is the number 12, which squared produces 144. Zoroastrian beliefs also maintain the Four Age concept, holding that these ages were all 3000 years each. (121) 3000 x 4 is 12,000. Hesiod, the first of the Greek epic authors, wrote that the history of earth was divided between Four Ages, the first being 4800 years [1200 x 4] and the last being 1200 years. (122) This is merely a Grecian version of Brahmanic ages. The Scandinavian Norse remembered this number in their traditions of Valhalla concerning the Norse god Heimdall who was the Watcher of Asgard [heavenly city] and captain of the 432,000 Einheriar who were warriors that defended the Hall of the Dead. (123)

Arabic traditions concerning the Ad hold that their patriarch lived centuries before the Flood, namely *1200 years* before. In the Quranic passages the Ad were a race of giants who left behind mysterious stone monuments and ruins. During those days one named Ash-Shedad ordered the construction of a terrestrial paradise called Iram, after the name of his great grandfather, a place later known as Irem of the Columns, structures so majestic they have never been equaled (Great Pyramid complex). These stories are rooted in biblical history, for Irem is listed as a pre-flood patriarch. The Great Pyramid was anciently called a *pillar*, because it was so huge people later thought that it supported the weight of heaven. Additionally, Irem is the root in p[irem]id. The Arabic legends reveal that the pyramid complex monuments were built *after* the appearance of the giants, and this is historically accurate. The Anunnaki appeared in 3439 BC, the Giza Complex was not finished until 2815 BC, 624 years later. Zecharia Sitchin inadvertently confirms this interpretation of the 1200 years for he published that he discovered in the Sumerian records that the Anunnaki descended to earth 432,000 'years' before the Deluge, which of course were 432,000 days (shars), or 1200 years of 360 days each. 3439 BC descent to the 2239 BC Flood was 1200 years.

These calendrical discoveries were all predicated on the fact that the larger unit of *years* was in fact exaggerated and later substituted for the original unit of *days*. This method of calculation was designed so as to conceal information from those not initiated into the Mystery Schools and cults that sought to 'protect' these secrets from the unworthy public. A prime example of the discovery of this practice is found in Osirian texts from Egyptian papyri that contain calendrical codes interpreted by the late D. Davidson in 1924 AD. These texts claim that "…one day counts for a month," and Davidson figured that this applied as well with months-to-years. The Egyptian texts provided dating formulas for a period of 12,420 days, which he calculated accurately as 414 x 4 months, or 1656 'months' [years]. This was actually a priestly code for *1656 years* commemorated in the Ptolemaic festival, which was celebrated with papyrus *boats*. Because of this he concluded that the priest class secretly taught and knew that the Flood of Noah [papyrus boats modeled after the Ark] occurred in the 1656th year of the pre-flood calendar. (124) As noted earlier the Great Flood was in 1656 Annus Mundi [2239 BC].

Now that we have determined that these historic dating systems were originally designed to begin with Anunnaki descents upon earth we are not surprised to find that the Babylonian Deluge Tablets convey that it was the Anunnaki that caused the Flood. (125) Could it be that they were faulted for more reason than merely their wickedness? All of the evidence thus far presented, when taken as a whole, leads us to conclude that the Anunnaki were orbiting earth at 600 year intervals and that this object was an *asteroid* or lost moon from a destroyed planet that served as a place of confinement, a prison of sorts, in the Deep [abyss of space below plane of the ecliptic]. In 3439 BC [456 AM] 200 Anunnaki made the mutual decision to descend to earth from their prison though they were violating the command of the Godhead. 600 years later they descended again the year of Noah's birth as their prison-asteroid passed by the planet, beginning the reign of the Seven Kings. This kingship lasted according to the Sumerian King-list 670 years, though the initial 70 years is merely calculated back to Enoch's ascent to heaven 70 years prior to start of rule of the Anunnaki. Then did the asteroid-prison collide with earth, a massive "star-spear" according to ancient fragments that immediately caused the Flood. The asteroid's trajectory and its own density compounded with its extreme terminal velocity and impact initiated a poleshift away from Alpha Draconis [felling the Dragon], breaking earth's 90° axis and collapsing the marine mesosphere. The antediluvian flawless biosphere was destroyed, human longevity reduced by 90% and the heavens appeared afterward far away because the magnification-effect of the watery firmament [mesosphere] was destroyed. The earth recalibrated as the broken planet passed [origin of Anunnaki asteroid fragment] and the new pole star became [AR]ktos in [UR] sa Major. Incredibly, Arktos lies in the northern heavens above the zodical sign of Leo, the AR UB star group, or fifth house. This is the Great Bear constellation which is commemorated in the Celtic name of the goddess [AR] tio whose companion animal was a bear. (126) The Maya creation myths also remember the Great Bear as being the former pole star [Polaris in Ursa Minor is present polar axis], telling of a deity named *Seven Macah* who was associated to the Seven Stars of Ursa Major. (127) A macah is a bird, a winged creature often used in arcane iconography to symbolize divinities and the fact that the Maya attached the number Seven to this deity exemplifies their remembrance of the Seven Kings of the Anunnaki. The Dragon Star, hybrid kingship, matriarchal society and flood memories are all maintained in the Greek legend of Cecrops who reigned over a kingdom before the Flood, being half dragon and half human. The stories tell that a matriarchal culture took root and for this he sent the Flood to destroy the world. (128)

Evidence that the Great Bear, or Seven Stars, were located in proximity to the pole star long ago is discovered in Egyptian inscriptions. Depictions of a ladder tipped so as to point to the Seven Stars of Ursa Major indicate that the polar axis was once pointed there. (129) The Egyptian Book of the Dead records that the Seven Spirits [Anunnaki] are linked to the Seven Stars of Arktos. They served Osiris, but they were called Sebek "...and his associate who dwell in the water [Deep]." (130) Osiris is a description of a

Watcher, from os [many] and iri [eyes] according to Plutarch. (131) Seneca also recorded that the pole star had been formerly located in the Great Bear before a subsequent poleshift removed it to its present position in the Little Bear called Ursa Minor at the star Polaris. (132)

That there was a poleshift from Alpha Draconis to Arktos seems to be alluded in the writings of the Arabic antiquarian Masoudi who wrote that at the Flood the fixed stars wandered confusedly. (133) Draco is a large constellation extending from east to west in the northern heavens, winding around the Great and Little Bears by a continued succession of bright stars, coiling under the feet of the Little Bear and then sweeping around the north pole and terminating in a trapezium formed of four stars from 30° to 35° from the north pole. (134) A Gnostic text reads, "Know and believe, that the serpent [Draco] at the beginning of creation, was indispensable to the creation of the world, so long as he kept his place; and he was a great servant, created to bear the yoke down *even unto Sheol and Abaddon.*" (135) This final segment of the statement further validates this author's contention that the Abyss and Deep known to the Sumerians and later cultures was in fact the nether regions of our own solar system far south of the ecliptic for Sheol and Abaddon are the same as the Deep and the Dragon's head was the pole star but his tail extended through the earth and far below it into the underworld, a symbol for the earth's *axis*. This concept is confirmed in Gerald Massey's epic work *The Natural Genesis* who wrote that the end of the Seven Headed Dragon [Draco and the Seven Stars] was when the stellar dragon was found to be playing false messiah. Earth's axis changed and all the heaven's revolved around a newer pole star. Thus the Old Serpent was self-condemned and self-dethroned.

We have discovered that the majority of the most popular chronologies from distant times all align at either 1200 years or 600 years to the Flood. But our thesis is only now beginning to unfold. There were 200 Anunnaki that descended in the days of Jared upon Mount Armon and another 200 when the Seven Kings began their rule. When Kingship began there were 600 Anunnaki on earth with thousands of their hybrid Nephilim offspring, fulfilling the NER and overlording over human affairs. The origin of the other 200 Anunnaki not yet disclosed is the subject of the next archive, a topic that will solve the most baffling mystery of the ancients: the origin of Chaos.

Archive II

End of the PreAdamic and PreFlood Worlds

The earth is tilted at 23° toward the plane of the ecliptic today, the axis it spins upon slightly wobbling as the planet orbits the sun while pointing at the pole star Polaris in the Little Bear. But this has not always been the case and many scientists postulate that this tragic inclination was the result of a cataclysmic impact of a gigantic asteroid some time in earth's remote past. (1) We are not without abundant geologic evidence of such massive impacts. The largest known crater in the world is the Vredefort Ring in South Africa which measures 186.4 miles in diameter and not far behind this one is the Sudbury Crater in Ontario, Canada at 155.3 miles in diameter. Also there is a 105.6 mile crater called the Chicxulub Crater near Yucatan, Mexico. The scientists today are right, though they postulate such collisions are random events spread throughout vast epochs of time. But this is far from the truth.

The scientists of today are little different than those of yesteryear. They are a virtual priesthood of knowledge, and from those priests and naturalists long ago we have many *scientific* observances preserved for us even from three and four millennia past. In the Babylonian tablet records there is found accounts of a demon lord called Kingu who was allied to the Chaos Dragon but was abruptly cut off by a "weapon not of war," a *star spear*. (2) The language employed in these texts seems to be the reverse of what we find in the biblical Revelation account where we read that Abaddon [cut off from others] is released from the Deep, or Place of the Lost, by a burning *mountain* that crashes into earth. By asteroid impact was the reign of the Anunnaki ended and the Eighth King imprisoned within the Abyss and by asteroid collision [Second Trumpet judgment] is the Eighth King [who is of the Seven] returned to kingship to *fulfill the Sumerian King-List*.

The crashing of an asteroid of immense size into the earth long ago is supported in the writings of the Sumerians who recorded that the Flood was preceded by a great thunder and large black clouds on the horizon. (3) The Rabbinical traditions hold that the firmament above [marine atmospheric canopy] flooded the earth by the falling of *two stars*. (4) The Revelation account maintains a similar motif with the descent of the asteroid of the Second Trumpet followed by the impact of the burning mountain called

Wormwood in the Third Trumpet of the Apocalypse. The Enochian histories provide us a very scientific clue as to the approach of a planetoid with a strong magnetosphere that preceded the Great Flood causing a poleshift. In the Book of Enoch we read, "In those days Noah saw the *earth became inclined*, and that destruction approached...the earth labored, and [was] violently shaken." The early Hebrew stories tell that God threw down a pair of stars from the Pleiades star system to cause the Flood, and Mexican lore across the planet reveals that it was the passing of *six stars* called the Tzontemocque close to earth that initiated the Deluge according to an old colonial manuscript in the Spanish National Archives at Madrid. Perhaps this is related to the Pleiades, which has six visible stars, and the Aztecs probably referred to this in their festival that commemorated the change of constellations after the Flood. Further, a 3000 year old Egyptian Twelfth Dynasty papyrus describes the Flood and its survivors. Accordingly, a star fell from the sky and burned everything before the Flood. In China a Jesuit missioner named Martinius was told that at the start of the *second* heaven and earth the world was shaken to its foundation and the sky sank lower to the north, the sun, moon and the stars all changing their positions, even the planets altering their courses. (5)

Grecian historical fragments masked in mythical garb tell us memories of poleshifts and their attendant destruction. Older traditions claim that "... Zeus, aided by Eris [Eye: metaphor for pole star], reversed the laws of nature, which hitherto had been immutable. Helios [sun], in mid-career [noon], wrested his chariot about and turned his horses toward the dawn. The Seven Pleiades and all the other stars, retraced their steps in Sympathy; and that evening, for the first and the last time, the sun set in the east." (6) The Greek legend of Phaethon is a preservation of a massive poleshift, the myth itself invented to explain the unprecedented phenomenon. Phaethon was the son of the Sun [Helios] who one day took charge of his father's sun-chariot but was immediately told that he was too young to handle the chariot horses that pulled the sun across the sky. But Phaethon disregarded the warning, the sun began its journey and reached the height of the sky when suddenly the chariot swung wide and even increased its speed. Phaethon struggled but he could not keep the sun from leaving its course as part of the sky grew dark and showed the sun descending upon Scorpio, then over to Cancer [a third of the Zodiac away]. Then the sun went back upward right before plunging down again and setting the world on fire. Valleys and mountains burned, streams turned to steam rivers and shrank as forests were consumed with flames. Then the sun was wrapped in thick smoke and disappeared over the sea quickly. (7)

Grecian historians, playwrights and philosophers also left behind fragments concerning a belief in this mysterious changing of the earth's pole. Euripides in his *Electra* (485-406 BC) states that the stars long ago moved *backwards* and also recalled a change in the sun's movement, which he mentioned in *Orestes*. (8) Herodotus claims that the sun has twice risen where it was supposed to set (9) and in Book II of his *Histories* he wrote that the Egyptians recorded there to have been four changes in the sun's direction. (10) That the sun and stars would cease moving in the heavenly vault was a fear of the natural scientists in Aristotle's day according to his Book IX of *Metaphysics*. (11) Similar stories and facts are recorded by the Roman writer Solinus. (12).

Because of the relevance the subject of poleshift has to our thesis we must endure this tangent only long enough to understand that even in the ancient Americas these scientific phenomena were remembered and passed down all the way to modern times. Truly these memories are universal. It was a common belief among the various cultures of America long ago that the sun was much closer to the earth than it appears today (13), which is what one would expect when a thick marine atmosphere was in place that magnified the heavens, making the moon first and then the sun appear much larger than they actually were. Other traditions hold that the sun was once bound to a huge chain that let it swing from side to side long ago to the amazement of those on earth. The Native Americans of California tell a story from of old that the sun fell by accident from the sky just around sunrise. Early American accounts say that the pillars of heaven broke and the heavens sunk *northward* and the sun darkened as the planets altered their courses. (14) Any deviations in the movement of the sun are *poleshifts*, but with the great migrations after successive catastrophic centuries, after the Flood knowledge was fragmented and lost, diluted into oral traditions with moral attachments. The occurrence of poleshifts was no longer understood and was merely recorded as changes in the sun's course over the sky. But this is not always the case. There are instances where the Native American accounts do appear more scientific.

The natives of Greenland fear a group of evil spirits called the Inguersoit, a species of ghosts of those who died when the world was *turned upside down* in a flood. (15) The Hopi tell of a time called the Dark Midnight. Men learned trade and commerce and all sorts of information which caused the end of the world by greed. The earth *tilted* and all geography changed again and the world was flooded but the Hopi knew it was coming and had prepared a special cylindrical boat and survived. As did Noah of the bible, so too, did the Hopi send out birds to see if any lands had surfaced. (16) Most poleshift memories are affixed to flood myths. The Mayan Book of the Popul Vuh of the Quiches of Guatemala we find that the god Huracan became angry and flooded the earth, killing mankind. This destruction of the earth by water was at the same time as a great conflagration that appeared to burn the heavens. (17) It is to be noted that Huracan is the origin of the modern hurricane, a deadly storm of wind. Several years ago Fred Gladstone Bratton in his Myths and Legends of the Ancient Near East cited the research of A.G. Rooth who studied over 300 myths throughout North America and concluded that they could all be divided into 8 types and that 7 of these categories were also present in Eurasia. Bratton also noted that these myths explain that the Flood was a type of *punishment*. (18)

The most misunderstood aspect of antiquated calendrical systems is that *none* actually span back to the very *beginning*, though many are believed to have done so by those that adhere to them. By all accounts the oldest dating systems seem to universally span back to some distant apocalypse or widespread, civilization-destroying cataclysm. Those that do not start in like fashion begin with mankind, such as the Hebraic system and Annus Mundi, but still found wanting are any stretching back to an alleged *creation*. Our planet's past was *ancient* by the time humanity was created and placed in the Garden of Eden. The four ages of mankind that seem to be embedded in the older calendars may indeed be a corruption of the fact that the 1656 years from Year 1 Annus Mundi [3895 BC] and Year 1 Hebrew Calendar to the Flood of 2239 BC [1656 AM] was exactly *four periods* of 414 years each. This peculiar number was associated to *cursed earth time*, in reference to the earth being cursed by the disobedience of humanity in Paradise. Year 1 Annus Mundi marks the beginning of mankind's exile into the curse of earth. The Annus Mundi and Hebraic Calendar begin a 6000-year countdown to the final redemption of mankind and removal of this curse, ending in 2106 AD [6000 AM]. This 6000 years is divided between 50-year periods the Hebrews call *jubilees*, also known as earth generations. Incredibly, to the credit of Berossus, our learned Babylonian priest-historian, we learn that the history of the world is measured by the *shar*, for 120 fifty-year generations is exactly *6000 years*. That 6000 is the greater of 600 implies that there are yet more NER epochs to discover. And it is a logical assumption that since there were four Cursed Earth epochs then there should also be four NER periods as well.

Already we have identified that the Flood date was a NER point, that the beginning of the Anunnaki kingship 600 years prior to the Flood in 2839 BC [1056 AM] was a NER point and that 600 years before this in 3439 BC [456 AM] was a NER point when the Anunnaki [Watchers] descended. With three NER identified but only covering 1200 years [432,000 days] from 456 AM to 1056 AM when Noah was born during first regnal year of Seven Kings and to 1656 AM Great Flood *we are missing 600 years*. The method by which to find this hidden NER is calculated *backward* from the time when the 414-year Cursed Earth periods collided with the NERs at the Flood. Three NER is 1800 [600 x 3] years *before* the Flood, and 600 years before the Anunnaki descended in the days of Jared [456 AM]. The Flood serves us as a calendrical axis point where the Stonehenge Cursed Earth Chronolithic System of 414-year periods aligns perfectly with the Anunnaki NER Calendar. The particulars of the Stonehenge Chronolithic system will be expounded upon in a later archive. So where is the hidden NER? Astonishingly, it began exactly *144 years* before Year 1 of the Annus Mundi and Hebraic calendars, being 4039 BC. This is 600 years prior to the descent of the Watchers in 456 AM [3439 BC]. This means that mankind resided in paradise on earth for 144 years in Eden before he was exiled by the Godhead for disobedience in the Year 1 Annus Mundi. 144 is the number in the Hebraic Kabbalic system associate to *Adam*. This is the origin of the first 200 Anunnaki. 200 more descended in Jared's day and the final 200 appeared for Sumerian kingship under the Seven Kings that ruled for 600 years over 600 Anunnaki, their thousands of Nephilim offspring and millions of humans until the Flood. The presence of the first 200 evil angels is hinted at in scripture by the presence of a wicked serpent in paradise and a Tree of Knowledge of Good *and Evil*.

To discover this sum encoded between the angelic Anunnaki and human dating systems should not come as a surprise to those familiar with *Lost Scriptures of Giza*, for this is the number of white limestone casing blocks abbreviated from 144,000 of the Great Pyramid, each block a stone symbol of the redeemed that will replace the fallen Anunnaki, blocks covered in inscriptions of the knowledge of good and evil meant for mankind and the histories of heaven and earth. The pyramid is a metaphorical image of the Tree of Knowledge in rock. In the final book of the Bible, Revelation, the prophetic text at the end of the testimony of the prophets written in the language of symbols found only in the *beginning* of the Word of God, or Genesis, we find that there will be 144,000 people of the redeemed who represent the holiest of all the saved from earth, whose names were written in heaven from the very beginning. The Genesis text conveys this idea as well concerning the eternal life of 144,000 redeemed who *cover* the rest of the saved [just as the white casing blocks cover the millions of core blocks of the pyramid], the first verse in Genesis reading "In the *beginning*," a word derived from a root [kedem] that has the gematria of 144 and carries with it the idea of eternalness. (19)

Also in the Genesis record we find that earth was renovated in *six days*, each evening and morning passed until the final climatic event occurred *144 hours* later: the creation of man on the Sixth Day. (20) In the Gospel of Barnabas we learn that God has sent 144,000 prophets into the world that all bore the mark of prophecy. (21) Prophets are keepers of divine knowledge, and they are noted for their *divine nature*, which in Greek is *theion*, a word having the gematrical value of 144. (22) The number 144 will have even greater import later in this study but for the moment it is interesting to remember that this number links the ancient calendars noted earlier in this work. Further, 144 is a product of 12 x 12, and 12 years is 144 months, this span being exactly 4320 days under the preflood Draconian Calendar.

The arrival of the first 200 Anunnaki is best understood by first being aware of the state of the earth at their arrival. It is commonly held that God created the heavens and the earth in six days, this conception of course being that of core fundamentalist Christians and those of the Judaic faith. This supposed creation event was by their reckoning less than 6000 years ago. But the scriptures do not convey this fiction. There was a vast time period between when in Genesis 1:1 the heavens and earth were *originally* created and later in verse 2 when the Anunnaki found the earth covered in darkness in a state of chaos [tehom]. Even Genesis 1 makes the distinction between created [bara] and *made* [asah], the latter carrying with it the connotation of *renovation*. The only new creation in Genesis 1 after the earth was restored from the chaos was *mankind*, the center of controversy between the Godhead and the Anunnaki, and man was commanded to "replenish" the earth. This command is void if the earth had not been filled with life priorly.

This mystery of a preAdamic world was known to the Sumerians and later Babylonians. The Euphratean cultures rewrote the original inscriptions of the Sumerians concerning the creation and changed object nouns and descriptions of phenomena into pronouns, the names of nonexistent deities. In the seven tablet series called Enuma Elish we find a retelling of the same cosmogony found in Genesis 1 in that the world was originally subject to the waters of chaos. The Babylonian redactors literally took the six days of creation story and turned them into six phases of conflict between the Chaos Dragon and these newly arisen gods. The idea behind this manipulation was because the elder traditions concerned a teeming world of paradise prior to humanity that rose up in insurrection against the gods and was destroyed utterly by the Dragon. They merely merged concepts that seemingly belonged together, and while this has been a vex unto scholarship, to their credit, the Babylonians were *right*.

Before the sun and moon were present, in the Enuma Elish text we read, "...Anshar and Kishar were created; they surpassed them. *Long were the days, years were added.*" (23) Though the scribes altered the texts considerably, attempting to place gods where none existed, we see in Anshar and Kishar not deities, but elements of *time*. These are Sumerian personifications of heaven [AN] and earth [KI] time. In fact, as probably already noticed, they are affixed to the Sumerian designation for time period [shar]. The phrase "...long were the days, years were added," reveals to the reader that earth during the epoch of chaotic ruin had virtually ceased rotating, making what should have been 24 hour rotational periods to extend to month-long or even years-long days and nights. And the fact that "years were added" probably infers that it took a lot longer for the planet to orbit the sun.

In essence, the Anunnaki arrived 144 years prior to Year 1 Annus Mundi to a dead planet. There is no other reason for this Babylonian text to have preserved such an unusual statement unless it was the elements of time that brought earth back out of its stupor, the Anshar and Kishar that rescued the planet after a period of divine judgment. Having ceased rotating the earth was dead, probably just another Wanderer [arcane designation for planet] far away from the sun [universal symbol of Deity] and Genesis 1 did not occur until something with a powerful gravitational field passed closely to earth's surface generating sufficient friction to cause the earth to spin again while pushing it back into a trajectory that would then allow it to gravitate back to a stable orbital belt, the passing object [gigantic fragmented planet] forming the appearance of light *before* the sun naturally appeared as shown in Genesis 1 and initiating the first "evening and morning." The Babylonians are to be praised for preserving these elements, however, this restorative process did not begin with Anshar and Kishar but with the appearance of a broken planet that voyages from the vast Abyss that serves the Godhead as a sufficient prison for the [AN]unna[KI]. This broken planet Passover is the origin of the first 200 Anunnaki who descended 600 years [NER] before 200 more descended in Jared's day.

Scholars are at odds concerning the second verse in Genesis 1 but all accounts agree it is a textual anomaly. Though God very clearly commanded man to "replenish the earth," or to *fill it again*, theologians and academics are apprehensive in considering the possibility that this passage describes the result of a planetary cataclysm before humanity. But the evidence, scriptures, ancient textual and even mythological passages and traditions from around the globe are enough to convince the unbiased trier of fact that Genesis 1:2 describes a world lost in space, encased in dark ice and frozen solid until it returned toward the warmth of the sun, defrosted, and then its heating up evaporated the frozen moisture below back into the atmosphere to create a firmament above and below as Genesis 1 describes. The world was one vast ocean until the water canopy was again above the earth, an aquatic atmosphere that again collapsed in 2239 BC [1656 AM] at the Flood.

The chaotic waters were called tehom, from which the Babylonians personified into the Dragon Tiamat. Translators claim that the word tehom is a "...veritable survival from prehistoric antiquity, an ancient word older than the text itself, which was written in Hebrew, derived from hum [to roar: rage]." (24) These translators and researchers have for over a century now held that Moses had access to olden writings when compiling Genesis, and probably studied an "...ancient primeval record of the formation of the world."

(25) It was because of this ancestral memory that Aristotle in Book I of his *Metaphysics* wrote, "…some people think that even those who lived far back in antiquity, long before the present age, and who were the first to discourse about the gods, held this kind of view about nature [regarding earth originally covered in water]. For they made Oceanus and Tythys the parents of all who had come into being, and said that what the gods swore by was water, which they called Styx: for what is most precious is what is most ancient." (26) This seems to be confirmed by Aristotle's learned predecessors Plato and Solon, the latter teaching and the former recording that there was more than one flood—"…remember a single deluge, but there were many previous ones." Even before Solon the famous Hesiod 800 years before Christ wrote, "First came Chaos, and then broad-bosomed earth, the everlasting seat of all that is, and Love." In another part, Hesiod wrote, "From Chaos came Black Night and Erebos. And Night in turn gave birth to Day and Space." (27) The idea of cataclysm was conveyed also by early Hebraic scholars and renowned Church Fathers. The Hebrew Targum of Onkelos, the earliest Aramaic version of the Old Testament passages, translates Genesis 1:2 as "…and the earth was laid waste." Also did Origen [186-254 AD] in De Principiis write that Genesis 1:2 is after the earth had been "cast downwards."

The Sumerians and Babylonians too regarded water as the *uncreated* first principle and source of all from the primordial waste of waters. (28) That water was uncreated denotes that they recognized its preexistence, a former existence predicating the existence of a former world. We have here a confusing admixture of scientific observances cloaked in mythical garments so tangled as to have baffled even the ancients who recorded these events and scenarios. This confusion is also recorded in Vedic Hymn No. 129: "Darkness there was: at first concealed in darkness this All was indiscriminated Chaos. All that existed then was void and formless: by the great power of warmth was born that Unit…Who verily knows and who can here declare it, whence it was born and whence comes this creation? *The gods are later than this world's production.* Who knows when it first came into being?" (29) This very old Vedic description of earth in ruins is so informative and descriptive that we are left with the impression that the Genesis record is actually an abbreviated version of it. The "Unit" that was born by the power of warmth was the *rotation* of earth that restored the "evening to morning" motion of the planet's spinning as it rapidly thawed out.

Early Persian records tell that prior to the creation of earth was the First Creation, before the establishment of time, when "…the sun, the moon, and the stars stood still." (30) The Greeks believed that the world was inhabited before the creation of mankind by all male deities during a Golden Age before women had yet been made. (31) Also, Ovid's *Metamorphosis* holds that mankind was created using certain divine elements which had survived some preexisting catastrophe. (32) Philo wrote that "...the first beginning is quite half the whole," and later in the Christian apocryphal text entitled the *Epistle of Barnabas* we read, "I will show you, how He made us a *second formation* in the latter days." (33) These pieces of forgotten knowledge are incomparable to the immense wisdom of the millennia-old oral traditions of the earliest American cultures who preserved fragments of compelling interest to our thesis.

As shown in *Lost Scriptures of Giza* the Hopi of Midwest America maintained traditions that exhibit a knowledge of the Great Pyramid and its purposes, so it is not a surprise to find that their ancestral traditions tell of an even more remote period in earth history. They tell that the original World was destroyed by *fire* (34) and that "...this world teetered off balance, spun around crazily, then *rolled over twice*. Mountains plunged into seas with a great splash, seas and lakes sloshed over land; and as the world spun through cold and lifeless space it froze into *solid ice*." It remained frozen for many years. Though some may be suspicious that this author has embellished this account, the diligent researcher will find the text unaltered in the Book of the Hopi as presented herein. (35) It was then when the world entered into what the Hopi term as the Dark Midnight after the terrible rains of fire that destroyed the previous world. (36) The Book of the Hopi then concludes that "...with a great shudder and a splintering of ice the planet began rotating again. When it was revolving smoothly about its own axis and stately moving in its universal orbit, the ice began to melt and the world began to warm to life." (37)

The Hopi are not alone in their curious annals. Mexican traditions held that the sun and moon we have today appeared *after* an earlier sun burned out, and left the world in darkness. Venezuelan myths tell of the *death of the sun* and the complete freezing of the sea followed by the rule of the Dreadful Night. In the Cakchiquel manuscript we learn of the arrival of strange beings to earth during an Endless Night, a tradition of Guatemala. Further, American stories from long ago tell that the sun was anciently no bigger than a *star*. The Pawnee said that the Creator whose name was Tirawa, had Four Gods govern the Four Quarters of the world, who created the world by the action of song-making. The Pawnee of North America claim that the creation of the world was actually after *another time period* and that creation beings from the sky had made the earth, which is paralleled to the Japanese stories of sky-beings that created the world out of the materials from an *earlier earth*. Arabic lore has it that prior to the creation of mankind the earth had been inhabited and a great chaos developed, and earth with these inhabitants were tossed about like a great ship, the planet becoming so imbalanced that a great angel had to bear it *upward.* (38) The Mexican legend seems to preserve the right idea, however, this researcher has found *nothing* closer to the Sumero-Babylonian texts than the story of the beginning by the Bungee Indians of Lake Winnipeg recorded in the Journal of American Folklore, VOl. XIX:

"...before the Creation, the world was a wide waste of water, and there was no light upon the earth, the sun being only an *occasional visitor to this world.* Anxious to keep the sun from wandering far, the god Weeseke-jak constructed an enormous trap to catch the sun, and the next time the sun came near the earth he was caught in the trap." (39)

This historic oral tradition parallels the Babylonian writings that were themselves copies of older Sumerian records that conveyed that "...long were the days, years were added," telling how earth was on an eccentric orbit, highly elliptical that took it far deep into space before returning back toward its orbital belt near the sun. Not only do all of these traditions and texts appear to be constructed from the same unknown and forgotten source materials lost to the distant past, but they uniformly qualify as scientific observations made by ancient men that conform to modern astronomical scientific discoveries that establish the veracity of these historical accounts.

Astronomers have discovered a disturbing phenomenon concerning earth's orbital position and distance from the sun. There is a mathematical formula belonging to all the other planets in this solar system [exempting Pluto which is probably a lost moon] that forms a pattern that Earth does *not* fit into. Each planet is about twice the distance from the surface of the sun than the preceding planet. On a scale of millions of kilometers the distances of the planets from the sun are:

Mercury	58
Venus	110 [x2 of Mercury]
Earth	150 [only 40 from Venus]
Mars	230 [x2 of Venus]
Asteroid Belt	440 [x2 of Mars]
Jupiter	780 [x2 of Asteroid Belt]
Saturn	1430 [x2 of Jupiter]
Uranus	2880 [x2 of Saturn]
Neptune/Pluto	alternate orbit

This data shows that earth is an *intruder* fit snugly between the orbital belts of Venus and Mars. Mathematically, earth can be *removed* to make the pattern perfect. Our planet does not belong in this solar system, we are a sojourner here just as men on earth are sojourners through material existence until death.

So where did we come from? Could earth have wandered to this system all the way from another star? It has now become appropriate to introduce a radical new theory that would perfectly explain many astronomical mysteries evidenced within our solar system hitherto unpostulated by ancient or modern scientists. Throughout the rest of this work will be provided mounting evidence that our solar system was long ago a *differential binary system* having a principle star [the Sun] with a lesser star revolving around it far away. This lesser binary also had planets revolving around it such as the Anunnaki home world, some smaller planetoids, moons and even *Earth*. Our planet was orbiting this lesser star during the PreAdamic World and under the perfect biospheric conditions of a Daystar [the Sun] and a lesser sun far away to illuminate gently the night skies the prehistoric creatures known to us as dinosaurs from the alleged PreCambrian to the Jurassic Periods flourished, growing to immense sizes because of the vitamin-nitrogen enriched soil and vegetation, oxygen-dense atmosphere and outer water canopy that magnified the heavens while also diffusing light and deflecting away harmful radiation. Even today under pristine conditions and diet amphibians and reptiles grow to truly astonishing sizes. Even in Genesis there is no mention in the Creation account of a moon, but instead the text reads: "And God made two great lights; the greater light to rule the day; and the lesser light to rule the night; He made the stars also." (40)

Differential binaries are not uncommon. In fact, with over 50% of the stars viewed in the night skies being binary and triple-systems it is statistically probable that our own solar system began as a binary system. Even our closest luminaries, Alpha Proxima and Alpha Centauri belong to a binary system where the former revolves around the latter. Binary systems are more common than isolated stars. The massive damage seen upon the surfaces of Mercury, Mars, Mars' two asteroid moons, the Eye of Jupiter, Saturn's badly scarred moons and billions of rock fragments trapped in its beautiful rings, the anomaly of Pluto's existence and the fact that Earth's own moon is larger in relation to its planet than any other moon in this system and the fact that it is made of an entirely different chemical make-up than earth all serve to exhibit signs that there was a cataclysmic solar system-wide event of massive damage. The Asteroid Belt and existence of comets further allude to this catastrophe.

This author's theory is that the lesser binary [lesser light to rule the night] collapsed quietly [black holes are a theoretical extreme] or with a nova of small proportion. The former idea of collapse seems to support this thesis favorably. Once the small star collapsed our present sun pulled the fragmented Anunnaki home world into our system as well as Earth on the plane of the dead star's ecliptic which happens to run through Mars and Venus. The Anunnaki home world was further damaged by close proximity with a large planet that was destroyed, leaving only the planet's residual fragments in what we know as the Asteroid Belt. The hundreds of comets known to intersect our ecliptic at an extreme inclination are frozen chemical seas from the Anunnaki planet and/or the destroyed one of our own system now reduced to orbiting strewn fields of rock. The lesser binary when still illuminating the system from afar orbited our Sun every 600 years but when it collapsed its weakened gravity field was not strong enough to keep its own planets, however, an Anunnaki planet maintained this 600-year orbit [until the Flood], each passage allowing imprisoned Anunnaki rebels access to earth's surface, our own planet having been trapped in the area between Mars and Venus where the two planes intersected. The origin of this planet and Earth being from hundreds of millions of miles in southern space below our present system is the Abyss [bottomless pit] and Deep of the Sumerians. This is why the Anunnaki were Lords of the Deep.

This theory may never be proven, no attempts may ever be made to validate it, but what is sure is that it was the Anunnaki's presence 144 years before the expulsion of mankind from Eden in Annus Mundi 1 that initiated earth's spinning again as the broken planet kept its trajectory on the dead star's ecliptic when the Earth was kept back by gravitational drag, trapped in our present sun's magnetosphere. This contact between a large celestial body where the Anunnaki remain imprisoned and periodically released every 600 years participated in the *renovation* of earth from a PreAdamic destruction that left it in total chaos, flooded, lost in space and without minimal motion. This same planet passed by earth on the dead star's ecliptic in 2239 BC [1656 AM] after 600 years of Sumerian Seven King's kingship and caused the Flood when one or more of its gigantic fragments collided with earth as it passed by. The key to remember here is the sum of 144 years, which will prove to be an astounding prophetic period in the Last Days, for 144 is the sum of the beginning and end.

This concept was comprehended by the great Kwanzi of China, who wrote that there was no beginning that was not an end. (41) There is much to be inferred in such statements. There was great meaning in Christ's claim of being Alpha and Omega. Recorded in the *Gospel of Thomas* Jesus told His disciples, "Have you then deciphered the beginning, that you ask about the end? For *where the beginning* is, there shall be the *end*...Blessed is the man who reaches the beginning; he will know the end..." (42) In another apocryphal Christian text we read; "...for the Lord hath both declared to us, by the prophets, those things that are past; and opened to us the beginnings of those things that are to come." (43) This is a principle tenet of eschatology. In order to pierce the veil of the future the diligent antiquarian must fully understand how the past unfolded. The ancients were convinced that events reoccurred in great and lesser cycles, and for good reason. In-depth analysis of history has predictive value. All prophets are *first* historians. In this instance the Great Flood was an end, but it was one that was tightly connected to an event in the beginning. The master of posterior analytics himself, Aristotle, student of the great Plato, wrote that "...people assume the end, and consider how they can get to it, by what means. Where it seems that the end can be produced by several means, they consider which means does it most easily and best. Where the end is produced, by one single means, they examine how it comes about, and what will produce it, until eventually they arrive at the *first cause*, which in fact is *last* in the process of discovery." (44) Aristotle could have been referring to this book had his statement not been written twenty-three centuries ago. The *first cause* in this study is the broken Anunnaki planet that periodically passes by to the detriment of all on Earth. The lesser end was the Flood and the greater end is the Dark Star's apocalyptic passover in the Last Days, with several devastating episodes throughout history between these major passovers that will be revealed in later archives.

Our ancestors three and four thousand years ago blamed the Anunnaki for the Great Flood while also accusing the Seven Kings as having a war against the Creator when He created the world in seven stages, the seventh being His rest. Because these Anunnaki divinities were thought to be involved with the creation and the destruction of the earth they are depicted in many texts as a seven-headed dragon at war against a Hero god. The Babylonians wrote the seven-tablet Enuma Elish series and altered an earlier version into a seven-staged battle between Marduk and the Chaos Dragon Tiamat. In the Ugaritic Canaanite Baal Epic we read, "When thou hast smitten Lotan, the fleeing serpent and hast put an end to the torturous serpent, the mighty one with seven heads." (45) The head is the center of intelligence and knowledge; seven heads describes seven *individual* sentient beings all sharing the same purpose and design. This is reflected in a little-known Babylonian tablet: "In the *first days* the evil gods, the gods who were in rebellion, who in the *lower part of heaven* had been created, they caused their evil work, devising with *wicked heads*. (46) In India they are collectively called Sesha, the seven-headed snake contemplating the creation of the world. (47)

A 10th Dynasty Egyptian papyrus entitled the Destruction of Mankind reads, "...God made heaven and earth at their desire [supernatural beings:

angels]. He checked the greed of the waters and made the air to give life to their nostrils. They are His own images proceeding from His flesh... He slew his enemies and destroyed His own children [the angels] because of their plots in making rebellion." This olden story so reminiscent of the luciferian drama was also found inscribed in the tomb of Seti I of the 19th dynasty. (48) The Egyptian annals in the Book of the Dead tell of Sebau the Serpent Fiend and his Sons of Revolt that warred against Ra in a prior Creation. (49) The old Egyptian Building Texts tell of an original world where the gods called the Primeval Ones were destroyed by the Great Serpent. The world was flooded and began anew in another Age where the survivors became Builder Gods, architects of the pyramids. (50) Later in this work it will be shown that the Babylonians mistakenly linked the Seven Kings of the Anunnaki to the building of the large stone monuments around the world when in fact this is untrue. This is especially true in regards to the Great Pyramid, which as *Lost Scriptures* extensively details was built by the antediluvian Sethites after Enoch ascended in accordance with "divine instruction" Enoch was given from patterns already made in heaven.

The evidence from antiquity that our world was remade upon the ashes of a former world abounds. In the Egyptian Creation of Ra text we learn that the creation event is actually *after* the destruction of an earlier creation when men and wise beings existed (51) and a Ritual Text proclaims that "...the time when He made the heavens, creating the earth, creating all the accursed generation, *cannot be found out.*" (52) In the Islamic Quran we read, "And surely you know the first creation. Why, then do you not reflect?" (53) Also, Native American traditions claim that modern man was made *after* a massive flood (54) and that a deity named Quaoar descended from heaven, reduced chaos into order and put the world upon the backs of seven giants. (55) Buddhist legends tell of the Tingheris, divine beings that lived for 80,000 years [compare with 800 motif of prior archive] in a perfect world before they fell from it, lost their wings [ability to travel] and promise of longevity. (56)

Before concluding references to a prior world here on earth we must make mention of the teachings of the Egyptian Gnostics. An old Gnostic record reads "Though all of the gods and men in the universe say, Nothing existed before the Chaos, I for my part, will prove to you that they are all mistaken, for they *never knew the nature of Chaos, nor its root* [beginning]..." (57) No more profound utterance could have been so weighty with inferences. The nature of chaos is the anathema of biblical scholars, especially Christian theologians who cannot grasp the concept of an Earth older than Adam or the fact that we were not the first sentient beings on this rock. Genesis is very specific: we are the first beings made in the *image* of God. There is no scriptural guarantee that we are the first intelligent creatures to have dwelt here. The Gnostics recall the seven-headed serpent and knew the heads represented the Seven Guardians [Anunnaki] (58) originally appointed to protect humanity, *not* to teach them with the forbidden knowledges that earned them their judgment into the realm of chaos.

The Gnostics were learned in the sacred literature circulating through the halls of the Alexandrian Library at Egypt. No doubt some of their sources were Rabbinical works based from older manuscripts like the Book of Enoch, Secrets of Enoch or Adam and Eve books. An Enochian text here contains a reference to Satan having been ousted from his position, thrown out of heaven before "...flying in the air continuously *above the bottomless* [abyss]." (59) The bottomless has a dual meaning, one being the watery chaos of the ocean in darkness [Genesis 1:2] and the other is the depthless expanse of dark space that in keeping in line with this thesis would be the area of the collapsed lesser binary of earth's origin. This imagery calls to mind the prison of the Anunnaki, their broken planet, hurling through the Deep [space] until passing by the frozen waters of the earth as well as the language of Genesis 1:2 where we find that the Spirit hovered over the waters. In the Book of Adam and Eve we learn that God drove Satan and his minions from heaven "...to this dark earth." (60)

An old Gnostic text studied by Theodore bar Konai that unveils knowledge of a PreAdamic World reads:

"Before the beginning of all things, there had been a divinity Who divided Himself in two, and from Whom the Good and the Evil came to be. The Good gathered to the lights, and the Evil the darkness. Then the Evil *gained understanding*, and arose to make war upon the Father of Greatness. The Father of Greatness pronounced a Word, from which the Lord God was created. The Lord God in His turn uttered seven words from which were born seven powers. But *seven demons* set themselves up against the powers He had engineered: after having shackled these adversaries, they stole from the Father of Greatness the principle of the soul. The demons then began to cleanse and scour Adam, the first man, but the Lord God came, and destroyed Adam, and remade him." (61)

These Gnostics were researchers of the oldest writings and beliefs, and this was twenty centuries ago. They had an acute grasp of what really transpired in the beginning between the Anunnaki [seven demons] and the Godhead over mankind [Adam]. El became Elohim as shown in Genesis 1, God dividing Himself into the Father, the Spirit and the Word [Lord God]. Evil *gained understanding* is a reference to the preAdamic prophecy of another being going to be introduced into the creation that was destined to be exalted even higher than the angels, who were first. This knowledge came from the Tablets of Destinies, also called the tables of heaven, which the Tree of Knowledge symbolized. The epithet of *Lord God* is never used in Genesis 1, which was a primordial record of the renovation of earth, but from Genesis 2 onward the title Lord God is found everywhere. This shows that Genesis 1 is truly an ancient record of the creation that antedates the Bible and was used to prefix the Genesis text. This further explains why Genesis has *two* distinct creation accounts and why throughout the entire Bible God is said to have created everything with His *hands* [in the very beginning and He also *spoke* everything into existence [Genesis 1]. The only thing in Genesis that God made with His hands was mankind [image of God] from soil materials of a archaic planet, a new creation. The *seven words* used in creation is a reference to the first verse in Genesis 1, which is exactly seven words in Hebrew: "In the beginning God created [bara] the heavens and the earth."

The seven demons are linked to the seven days of God's restoration of earth as preserved in Genesis 1 because it was then that the imprisoned Anunnaki [shackled demons] were released 144 years before Year 1 of the Annus Mundi Chronology and *144 hours* before the new creation [man] was made on the sixth day of earth's reinitiated rotation upon its axis. Having read the future in the tablets of destinies in ancient heaven the demons sought to alter mankind knowing his seed [offspring] would one day defeat and replace the seed of heaven [angelic Sons of God that rebelled]. Thus, the evil angels impregnated the daughters of men seeking to pollute the genetics of the purely Adamic race on earth. God did not destroy Adam per se, He destroyed the *Earth* which is derived from the same Semitic root: adamu. The first destruction of the world was due to the heavenly rebellion of which earth and all its civilizations [sentient beings beneath the authority of the angels *not* made in God's image] participated in, and second He destroyed the earth with the Great Flood in 2239 BC [1656 AM] because during the reign of the Seven Kings the earth had become tainted with hybrid blood.

Arabic traditions as recorded in the Quran [which actually include elder histories antedating Islam] retell this dateless story. In the beginning Allah created the jinn from spiritual fire, a smokeless fire before mankind. (62) They were originally created to worship Allah and there existed in those times *nations* of jinn. (63) The jinn were ruled by Iblis who led a rebellion against Allah and was later banished from heaven to earth for an allotted time period and destined to end in hell. (64) Later the jinn were guilty, adding to their judgment the act of seducing mankind and provoking humans to worship them. (65)

This story is in the Egyptian Book of the Dead, which calls the Anunnaki the Sons of Revolt. The text reads, "...as concerning the night of the battle, the invasions of the eastern portion of heaven by the children of rebellion, whereupon a great battle arose in heaven and in all the earth." (66) The battle occurred in the late hours of the night, before the dawn. (67) This statement is a metaphor for the *end* of the Angelic Age which gave way to the beginning of the Age of Man with the renovation of earth. It was at the end of this conflict that Sebau and his fiends were fettered. This shackling or fettering is never specific but does not at all preclude an asteroid prison banished into Deep space [Abyss]. Intriguingly, the Book of the Dead mentions that the fiends of Sebau were turned into *animals* (68) which is what we discover in Genesis and Revelation. The Seven Kings and the combination of the Eighth King who is of the Seven is richly described in anthropomorphic imagery as the serpent of Eden that grows in the Last Days into a mighty red dragon with Seven Heads, these heads being that of a lion, bear, four-headed leopard and the Dragon himself.

The history of the Great War before Genesis is also mentioned in the Sumerian records. Such a motif further fulfills the eschatological tenet that what occurs in the future must have a predicate in the past. Armageddon is the end-time war between heaven and earth necessitating a planetary war in the *beginning*. The evil archfiend in the Sumerian texts was ZU [one who knows] who was formerly one of the IGIGI [Watchers] or heaven under ENLIL [Lord Wind], (69) and ZU was chosen to confront Him. But ZU in reality sought the throne of ENLIL as found in a Sumerian fragment recorded by Zecharia Sitchin in his *Wars of Gods and Men*, a fragment having derived from the same parent source as Isaiah 14:12:

"I will take the celestial tablets of destinies;
    the decrees of the gods will I govern;
I will establish my throne,
    Be master of the heavenly decrees;
The IGIGI in their space will I command!" (70)

Later ZU became identified with ZU AB, the Sumerian Deep remembered by the Babylonians as apsu. (71) Note the AB suffix, another example of the survival of this arcane syllable. The Amorites of the kingdom of Mitanni named a city after him (72) and the name is the origin of the epithet attributed to the biblical giants called the Zuzims in Genesis 14. ZU means 'He who knows" and is no doubt related to the fact that the root word for demon comes from the word for *knowledge*. In the Hebraic traditions ZU is remembered as Azazel in the Dead Sea texts and in the Book of Enoch it was Azazel who revealed "...the eternal secrets which were preserved in heaven." (73) The records of Sumer claim ZU did not actually fight Enlil, but that Enlil had a Son who was responsible for defeating ZU in "...a terrifying war, a fierce battle." (74) *Lost Scriptures of Giza* provided ample evidence showing that the Great Pyramid at Giza was a stone symbol of the necessity of evil in the evolution and maturity of *good*, and this idea is what lied behind the image of the Tree of Knowledge of Good and Evil, a tree that is actually known by this very name in Sumerian records. (75)

The Great War in heaven was primarily over ZU's right to divulge the secrets within the tablets of destinies. The tables in heaven contained the eternal past, the present epochs and the secrets of the future on earth and beyond. This olden concept is what the Great Pyramid richly mimicked with its 144,000 white limestone casing blocks covered in minute inscriptions that formed the largest book on earth. These tablets of heaven are also found in Hebraic writings. In the Book of Jubilees we learn that Abraham was told by two angels that he would have a son in his old age, when Sarah was 90 years old. At hearing this Sarah naturally laughed, but was immediately admonished by these angels who told her that this was written in the tablets of heaven, "...and she became afraid and denied that she had laughed on account of their words." (76) Other Hebrew extracanonical works mention the tablets of heaven, but none are like Jubilees which mentions them no less than 50 times. Though ZU was solely responsible for the divulging of hidden knowledge in early heaven, he led a rebellion of a *third* of all the Anunnaki. The decision of the imprisoned Anunnaki to descend to earth and teach mankind forbidden knowledge was partly due to the fact that they were already awaiting judgment for their participation in the Rebellion. Their descent was a *choice* to either remain within their celestial prison [broken planet] or descend to earth [primordial battlefield] and increase their judgment with ZU [the Serpent]. Obviously, 600 of them chose to immerse themselves in judgments and attempt to thwart the plans of God.

The catalyst of the heavenly rebellion was a secret so profound that even today humanity is largely ignorant of it. It is the *identity* and eternal destiny of mankind. Humanity has something the angels do not. In the beginning the angels were created out of divine fire, and for this fact they were very proud, however, mankind was created later from *lesser materials* [earthen soil] which offended the angels and by revelation within the tablets of destinies was it discovered by ZU [Satan: Adversary] that this inferior being was to be made complete by the very Spirit of the Almighty: the breath God breathed into Adam. Humans were going to be formed into the terrestrial *image of God*, being made of 66.6% soil and *created* essence [the soul/mind] but finished with the eternal Spirit of the Living God that the angels were never made from. God Himself would *live in man*. The Holy Spirit is eternal, having no beginning and no end, something no resident of distant heaven could claim. Mankind is 33.3% *divinity* encased in mortal trappings designed to forge the spirit into the image of the Living God. This prophecy in the tablets of heaven was broadcast to all the angels and they were confronted with a choice: to succumb to the Will of the Creator and serve this newer being made of earth or rebel, build their own kingdom and try to abort the plans of God.

Of further note is that the heavenly rebellion was also recorded in the tablets of heaven *before* it occurred and it was made known to those rebellious angels afterwards that humanity would replace them after they had fallen from their former state. Assyrian texts read that after the rebellious gods were ousted from heaven for their blasphemy and insolence, the Godhead made mankind to fill their space, "…in their room He created mankind." (77) Persian Zad-Sparam writings tell that the evil Ahreman infested one-third of the star stations with darkness (78) and in the Bundahish "…he stood upon one-third of the inside of the sky, and he sprung like a snake out of the sky to the earth." (79) That humanity was created to fill the breach of heaven is found in Jubilees where we find that humanity "…will serve to a founding of heaven and a strengthening of the earth and for a removal of all the stars upon the firmament." (80) Stars of course are symbolic of stellar beings.

A fragment found among the Dead Sea scrolls reads that "[God] has chosen [His chosen ones] to inherit the lot of the Holy Ones. He has joined their assembly to the Sons of Heaven." (81) In the Alexandrian writing entitled the Book of Adam and Eve we discover an account of God telling Adam the history of Satan in early Heaven. According to this writing, after God is finished telling Adam the story Satan himself appears to Adam and says, "This is our will, and our good pleasure, that we may not leave one of the sons of men *to inherit our orders from heaven*. For as to our abode O Adam, it is a burning fire; and we will not cease our evil doing, no, not one day nor one hour." (82) The entire Age of Humanity, being 6000 years from their exile from paradise to the Great War of Armageddon that brings closure to the Heavenly Rebellion, is the time allotted to Satan to attempt to fight against God and His people in order that the requisite number of the righteous is not met so the orders of the missing *one third of heaven's hosts cannot be filled*, and by this machination thwart his own judgment. (83)

Gnostic traditions held that Adamas the Tyrant [Satan] and his Aeons [wandering stars] became the inhabitants of the earth after they were defeated in heaven. Not only was a third of heaven emptied, but God took a third of their power as well. (84) The replacement-theory abounds with textual support. The Roman Church accepted this belief that man was made to replace certain angels (85), Enochian records claim that the righteous shall become the *angels of God*, Revelation passages cite that the saved will eat *manna* [angel's food] and theologians, philosophers and mystics such as Paracelsus have long striven to show that like the angels only partially, mankind is actually the miniature of Deity. (86)

The missing third of heaven is 33.3%, a very curious sum that reoccurs in patterns in creation and throughout history. Jesus performed 33 miracles as recorded in Scripture during the 3 years of his ministry (87) and the year of the Flood [2239 BC/1656 AM] was exactly 33.3 Jubilees [50-year earth generations] of antediluvian time from beginning to end. This number has been adopted by many sects and secretive societies as esoterically significant, among them the Masons who divide their Ancient and Modern Degrees within a series of 33 rituals. This number seems to be embedded within time periods linking separate events as well. Jesus was 33 years old. He died at age 33.3 years in 33 Anno Domini, the same age as the Father of Western civilization, Alexander the Great who died at 323 BC.

Even our solar system tells the story of the Fall and mechanics of planetary and lunar motion contain hidden allusions to the rebellion of the third of heaven's hosts. Our moon is scarred, Mars has trace evidence of a ruined civilization of immense antiquity and enormous monuments, several planets and moons show signs of catastrophism and the Astroid Belt screams the death of a former planet now missing. The ultimate base for timekeeping in this solar system is 60 [multiplied by 10 is Great Year: NER of 600], and remarkably there are 60 moons that orbit the various planets of this solar system. As moons are lesser planetoids so also are angelic beings compared to the Creator. The planets in our solar system and their various attributes are clever allusions and astronomical metaphors of the One True God; manifestations of His beauty, magnificence and power. As these 60 moons orbit the multiple planetary extensions of the Godhead exactly *one-third* of them have *retrograde* motions opposing the planets they orbit! (88) If we were to design an astronomical theology we would not be short of other parallels. Earth's actual landmass covers 33.3% of the earth whereas oceans and ice-sheets cover 66.6%. This is made more interesting when reminded that man is derived from the word *earth* and biologists assert that the incredibly complex physiology of humans is merely constructed fronm the same minerals, vitamins, metals and chemical compounds found in a handful of rich soil. Further, earth's mass in relation to the sun is exactly calculated by scientists as 1/333,000th. Thus the mass of earth multiplied by 333,000 would equal the mass of the sun. (89) Even our moon's dimensions direct us to a deeper astronomy. The equatorial diameter of the moon is exactly 2160 miles (90) which is 1/12th of the Zodiac in years. The fascinating mechanics and astro-theological codes embedded within the framework of the Zodiac is the subject of the entire next archive.

In our search for accuracy in the world's oldest calendrical systems and the secrets of the Zodiac we must peer into the histories of the Egyptian historian-priest Manetho who long ago wrote that Seven Gods ruled Egypt for a total of 12,300 years. (91) These Seven Gods are personifications of the seven days of the creative act in the beginning of Earth History as retold in variant ways in most of the world's earliest cosmologies. After the reign of the Seven a second dynasty occurred having 12 gods that lasted for 1570 years, beginning with Thoth. Then a dynasty of 30 demigods reigned for 3650 years followed by ten rulers who governed during a chaotic before Men [Menes: Anam] rose to power. Manetho's record is astounding. This is the history of the Seven Anunnaki Kings of preAdamic Earth personified as the seven creative days of earth's first 144 hours of renovation that happened 144 years before the start of Annus Mundi/Hebraic Chronology. The antediluvians were given the Zodiac, a virtual apocalypse decoder spread throughout the stars on the plane of the sun's ecliptic [equator]. These 12 constellations were often referred to as gods, a mistake Manetho also makes here. The 30 demigods is a vague reference to the Zodiacal sign in power during the entirety of preflood history, the 360° of the 12 constellations being divided into 12 stellar regions of 30° each. The 3650 years is merely a multiplication of the 365 years of Enoch's life, the Egyptian *Thoth*. The 10 rulers before Menes are the ten antediluvian patriarchs of Genesis, Berossus' accounts, Solon's Atlantis, the Chinese records and many other histories. These 10 kings of Genesis [actually patriarchs] according to the Hebraic genealogy in the text lived and ruled for a period of 1656 years, which is only 86 years difference from the 1570 years of Manetho's account. Manetho was heavily influenced by Greek thought and culture. The Egyptian priesthoods had over millennia crippled their own attempts to accurately record history but the rising Greek states and mindset with their insatiable inquisitiveness and diligence, philosophers, antiquarians, geographers, mathematicians and astronomers at Alexandria, Egypt put the world back on the right tracks.

Manetho's 1570 years is very close to the Sumerian record as mentioned by Zecharia Sitchin who cited the Sumerian King-List as reading "...Etana [Enoch], a shepherd, who ascended to heaven, who consolidated all countries, became king and ruled for 1560 years." (92) This is only a 96 year difference from the Hebraic and Annus Mundi date, 10 years from the Egyptian version of Manetho and Sitchin further remarks that Etana is dated to have reigned about 3100 BC (93)...the same time period we find Enoch in our thesis and a date that falls within the 21-year period that aligns the Sumerian King-list, Brahmanic Kali Yuga and both Mayan Calendars. These coincidences [coincidence being questionable] find their match across the planet in early America. Four hundred years ago a man of both Aztec and Spanish descent named Alva Ixtlilxochitl wrote down the history of the Aztecs. A reference is made to the earlier Toltecs that tells that in the Age of the Water Sun before a massive Deluge mankind lived on earth for only 1716 years before "… men were destroyed by very great storms and lightning from heaven, and the whole world was without a thing remaining." (94) It cannot be overlooked that the difference between 1716 years and the Flood date of 1656 Annus Mundi [2239 BC] is exactly *60 years*. The Aztecs mistakenly derived this sum by calculating 33 periods of 52 years each, or 1716 years, instead of 33 Hebraic jubilees of 50 years each, being 1656 years. They got the number of periods correct, but merely made the mistake in calculating how long each period actually was.

So Manetho's account is not exclusive nor without substantiation through other sources, even remotely distant ones. The antiquity of the Egyptians was something they prided themselves on but it was also doubted even by Herodotus, who wrote that they were not the most ancient race of mankind. (95) In 1956 AD a Donovan A. Courville, a Loma Linda University biochemist published an important book entitled *Exodus Problem and its Ramifications* and showed how Manetho had mistakenly overlapped the reigns of Egyptian regents and corrected the error, remarkably showing how its first double-dynasty [Upper and Lower Kingdoms] actually began around 2150 BC. (96) This problem was also discovered over *23 centuries ago* concerning Babylonia's pretended antiquity. An historian and writer named Calisthenes worked for Alexander the Great [ca. 330 BC] at Babylon and reported that the astronomical observations comprehended no more than 1903 years to the start of their history. Calisthenes was with Alexander in Babylon researching these stone tables where Alexander died. This calculation was also supported by Simplicus and Porphry. (97) Amazingly, 1903 years prior to 330 BC is 2233 BC, or 1662 AM…only *six years* after the Flood.

A note on modern scholarship. The academic prejudices so pervasive in all branches of science and research have no bearing on this thesis because all historical and apocalyptic dating found within this book is modeled after what the *ancients* believed and has been set forth as they left these mathematical records to us. Modern scientific speculation on the historic occurrence of a global flood or succession of floods is no more valuable to us than the Gregorian calendar or the innovation of the Julian calendar when they were designed. As these calendars disrupted the continuity of free thought unhindered by knowledge filters so too has contemporary "advanced" learning severed the modern mind from the intellectual precision of his historic predecessors. The unfolding of historical events is simply a matter of cause and effect, but the causes are today censured and we are made to believe these occurrences were randomly effected as a natural course of history. Those entrusted to teach have abandoned the truth so easily seen that all events in history are linked together from start to finish.

Now back to our calendrical study. We have identified a hidden 144-year period by counting backward 600 years [NER] from the descent of the Watchers in Jared's day in 3439 BC [456 AM], making three NER periods of 1800 years from Earth's restoration to the Great Flood 2239 BC [1656 AM]. But we have not gone back far enough. So far we found that mankind was in Eden 144 years, but the earth was found in *ruined chaos*, or cursed. How long was it in a state of ruin? This answer can be alluded to in the construction of the NER.

The Anunnaki NER is made up of *five* 120-year periods [120 x 5 is 600]. This forms the five-pointed Sumerian symbol of the AR UB, or Plough of God which is a pentagram of ten 108° angles. (98) The AR UB, having five termination leads us to presume that the four epochs of Cursed Earth time that ended with the Flood [414 x 4 is 1656 AM] would likewise have a fifth period counted backward to the beginning of the curse of ruin upon earth due to rebellion. As the NER periods are reckoned backward so too do we add a fifth Cursed Earth period of 414 years to Year 1 Annus Mundi [3895 BC] to arrive at a date *270 years* prior to the Renovation of Ruinous Earth 144 years before Adam's banishment. This means that the planet was lost in space for 270 years [90 x 3] without rotating and frozen solid when "...long were the days, years were added." This further means that from the PreAdamic destruction of earth to the Great Deluge ruin of the planet passed exactly 2070 years. 2070 years fulfills the Cursed Earth version of the AR UB symbol in that it spans five 414-year periods that are also calculated as ten 207-year periods.

270 years is how long the Anunnaki remained in their stasis imprisonment wandering through the Abyss within their broken planet. The number 270 when added to 1800 [3 NER] becomes 2070 [207 x 10], which just may be the secret year of apocalypse recorded in the Book of Enoch. In Enoch we read that he "...beheld Seven Stars, like great blazing mountains, and like spirits entreating me. Then the angel said, "This place, until the consummation [end] of heaven and earth, will be the *prison of the stars* [fallen angels], and the host of heaven. The stars which roll over the fire are those which transgressed the commandment of God before their time arrived; for they came not in their proper season. Therefore He was offended with them, until the period of the consummation of the crimes in the Secret Year."

The sum of 270 is not without mystic and numerological significance because it is the product of 9 [judgment] times 10 [completion], or 90 years multiplied by the number for *perfection* [3]: 90 x 3 is 270. Even as far back as the Enochian records the number 9 has been associated to *judgment*. (99) The sum 207 is divisible by *one* number: 9. The result is 23, or the angular tilt of the earth's axis toward the ecliptic presently pointing at Polaris but this was due to the *curse* of ruin upon the planet.

The cataclysmic significance of the number 207 is seen again in ancient Chinese records. These annals assert that Emperor Chueni [2513 BC] in the year 2446 BC witnessed a strange planetary alignment of 5 planets [AR UB sign motif] in conjunction the same day in alignment with the sun and moon as well. Scholars in the early 20th century validated this observation by calculating that they indeed aligned at this remote date in the constellation of the Zodiacal sign of Pisces on February 28th, 2446 BC. (100) It is absolutely amazing that 2446 BC is the year 1449 Annus Mundi, exactly *207 years before the Great Flood* in 1656 Annus Mundi [2239 BC]! In addition to this revelation, this 207-year period did not begin until *9 periods of 207 years each* had come to pass since the asteroid impact that destroyed the PreAdamic World and sent it hurling through space in ruined chaos for 270 years. A five-planet alignment is an AR UB alignment, a unique phenomenon that is said to presage great destruction on earth. This may be why the number 270 has been recalled as such a wicked number. In the Zohar we learn that the *number 270* is linked to the Last Judgment, a sum also identifying the *world*. It corresponds to the numerical value of the word *evil* in Hebrew. (101) And this concept is no less true for the 270th year of the United States of America, the final year of this Last Day's empire since 1776, for 270 years after 1776 AD is the fateful year of *2046 AD* when the entire North American continent will be obliterated by the impact of a comet and the rest of the world will enter into a new calendar as the motion of the earth around the sun is dramatically altered.

The AR UB is geometrically depicted as the five-pointed pentagram, which as we learned earlier three-dimensionally appears as a pyramid. Earth's earliest inhabitants recognized this mystery and the mystical number 1080 and its variants [108, 10,800, 108,000 & 1,080,000] as emblematic of the architectural codified eschatology of the world's end hidden right before the eyes of all who beheld these wonderful monuments. The variants of 1080 emerge over and over in ancient iconography, within dimensions of altars, monuments and statuary, encoded within calendars and as we will see, in many other images and concepts from antiquity and even contemporary times. As Neitzsche would say, this is "...the ancient domain of the faith of former times." (102) A largely misunderstood and prehistoric monument that clearly displays the AR UB of Sumer is found among the megalithic ruins in Britain:

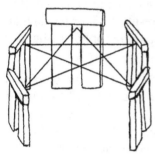

Inner Sanctuary of Stonehenge Encoded Sumerian AR UB

Stonehenge in England is a monumental relic from antiquity that embodied the exact dimensional concepts as the Great Pyramid. The number 10 has long been associated to *completion*, a sum of finality and wholeness by the Pythagoreans, Mystics, numerologists and students of the Kabbalah. Compounded with the fact that the ten 108° angles form five terminations we find that the pentagram exhibits esoterically the sum of the *completion of judgment*. The five 414 year Cursed Earth periods form a 2070-year AR UB from the passover of the broken world that had in its gravitational train a gigantic asteroid fragment that collided with Earth destroying the PreAdamic world to a *fifth* passage when another asteroid broken away to impact Earth and cause the Flood in 2239 BC. 2070 years was of old the *span between two cataclysms*. This epoch dividing two destructions of our planet is linked to the sum of 1080, a fact vital to our thesis.

Exactly half of a NER is 108,000 days and three NER is 1800 years. *Five* Draconian years equal 1080 days. Remember, Draconian years were only 360 days long. A Sumerian AR UB of *five* NER [600 x 5] is exactly 1,080,000 days [600 x 5 x 360] and one *shar* [or a *fifth* of a NER] multiplied by 9 [judgment] is 1080 years. The prophet-king Enoch ruled for 300 years [108,000 days] before he ascended into heaven to exercise kingship over the remaining two-thirds of the Anunnaki that did not rebel. His reign was from 3208-2908 BC [687-987 AM]. Graeco-Egyptian traditions claim that Hermes lived for 300 years (103) and as adequately proven in *Lost Scriptures*, Hermes was just another shadow of Enoch. Enoch's ascent into heaven at Achuzan [Giza] was 1080 days before the Sethites began construction of the Great Pyramid complex in 2905 BC [990 AM]. Interestingly, 990 Annus Mundi is the end of *three* 330-year periods [330x3 is 990]. The Giza, or Achuzan Complex, was completed after 90 years of labor in 1080 Annus Mundi [2815 BC] and the beginning of Giza's constructions before the Flood in 990 AM [2905 BC] began a 1080 year countdown to the year *2070 Annus Mundi* [1824 BC] which was the time when Abraham was living among the Philistines of Gerar spending several years at Giza in Egypt translating the antediluvian Sethite texts [origin of concept of Egyptian Set deity] found inscribed upon the surface casing stones of the Great Pyramid. Abraham's translating and appearance before the Egyptian Court is fully detailed in *Lost Scriptures*.

Abraham's association to the Great Pyramid is the subject of much Vedic esoterica. The Vedic writings of India venerate Brahma as the Creator and a god of remote antiquity, but he is not the oldest in the pantheon. Nor could he be, for Brahma, renowned for wisdom and knowledge of the past and future was A[Brahma]m, translator of the Giza texts known in Vedic literature as the Altar of Agni. The chief characteristics given to Brahma were as Creator, Preserver and Destroyer, which is unusual because Brahma was assigned a very minor role. (104) This disparity is understood by realizing that these characteristics were later attached to Abraham after he had translated the preflood texts that *did* contain the histories and prophecies from the elder civilization. *Lost Scriptures of Giza* serves to show how all of the oldest writings, including Brahmaic, are abbreviated versions of a vast corpus of ancient texts all taken from the surface stones of the Great Pyramid which explains the uncanny similarities in content and syntax of historic cosmologies and apocalypses from cultures thought to have never experienced contact.

The Altar of Agni is a mine of revelations. The word altar comes from a root meaning *knowledge*, just as veda means knowledge. (105) This altar is akin to the Great Pyramid, called by the prophet Isaiah the altar in Egypt at the border to the Lord. The Altar of Agni had 10,800 bricks (106) corresponding to the 10,800 stanzas of the ancient Rig-Veda text, each stanza containing 40 syllables each. (107) The Giza Complex is located at what was long ago called Siriad and was a structure built to warn of the Flood and to warn of an even more remote future apocalypse involving fire. Incidentally, the ancients called the Great Pyramid a *pillar of fire* that contained upon its stones instructions for mankind, which links it to the Tree of Life/Knowledge motif as well as the pillar of fire by night and pillar of smoke by day the Israelites followed out of Egypt. Agni was the Brahman god of Fire worshipped as *Surya* [Siriad].

The confusion over Brahma and Agni both relate to Abraham and his contact with the Great Pyramid's inscriptions after the Flood. The Vedic books tell that Brahma was at the bottom of the ocean [abyss] during the Flood (108) and that Brahma had *four faces*. What was a deity doing at the bottom of the sea? The imagery conveyed is actually of the four-faced Great Pyramid under the waters of the Flood. Depictions of Brahma from India are directly related to Giza correspondences. Four-headed Brahma supports a triune glyph [identifying Brahmanic trinity] and rests atop a seven-petalled lotus [symbol for creative power] with a long stem [planetary axis] that descends to the navel [middle] of Vishnu, who lays on top of a seven-headed dragon in the abyss of waters [ocean and space]. (109) Vishnu covered the Deep much in the same way the Great Pyramid covers the entrance to the underworld. Brahma, Vishnu and Shiva made up the Hindu trinity, Brahma appearing with four faces identifying him as the Great Pyramid, Vishnu was the *coverer* who covered the Deep [which was the symbolic function of the Sphinx] and Shiva is merely a number anciently personified into a deity...*seven*. Scholars of Sanskrit literature assert that the number assigned to Agni was 7. (110) *Lost Scriptures* heavily focused on this number and its relation to the Great Pyramid's interior and exterior angles of 52°. Interestingly, the god Shiva was also represented as having *five faces*, the fifth facing *upwards* and was usually identified with the world axis! (111) The fifth face [surface] would link this imagery with that of the Sumerian AR UB symbol of judgment.

There can be no doubt as to the identity of the Vedic Brahma being the prominent historical figure of Abraham for his consort was Saraswati just as A[Brahma]m's wife was his half-sister Sarah [*Sara*-swati]. Indian traditions claim that Brahma committed incest with his consort because they were related, the same accusation levied at Abraham. (112) The archaic syllables AR and UB are contained in the names [AB]raham and S[AR]ah, the latter also expanded to construct the Sumerian word *shar* [SARah].

Abraham was a man who profoundly impacted the *entire* ancient world of the Near East and Africa from Persia [Elam of Genesis 14], Sumer, Akkad and Babylonia, to Canaan, Aram [Syria and Lebanon] as far as Egypt. There is every chance that Abraham is the reason why the Great Pyramid complex is remembered as *Giza*. Abraham was a Chaldean from Haran, a city right next to the city of *Gozan* in northern Babylonia (113) and he later moved and lived among the Philistines at the city of *Gaza* which was the chief city of the Philistine *Pentapolis* of the Five Lords of the Philistines. Gaza is pronounced GAY-zuh (114) and could easily be the origin of the present Giza. One of the cities of this Pentapolis was called Gath and was home to the famous giant Goliath. Abraham is especially venerated by the Hebrews, Christians, Muslims and indirectly by other names by the Persians as Zoroaster and many other titles by as many cultures. His actual name, Abramu, has been found in some Assyrian writings according to Smith in his Chaldean Genesis (115) and in the Egyptian Sheshonq List mention is made of a Fortress of Abram. (116) Having spent the majority of his lifetime in Canaan we are not surprised to discover his name inscribed within Canaanite Ras Shamra stone tablets of the 2nd millennium BC. (117)

Now we return to our study of the mysteries of 1080. The number 108 is the sacred number of *Brahma*, the Brahmans believing that a man's life was measured in 12 divisions of 9 years each, or 108 years. (118) There are 108 Upanishad texts and in India 108 is important to shrines which are virtually the same as *altars*. (119) 108 is the sacred number for *architecture* in China and Tibet as well as the holy number of *literature*. (120) The number 108 is also the Buddhist number of destiny and customary Buddhist rosaries have 108 beads representing the developmental levels of the world. (121) The Tibetan sacred scriptures called the Tanjur consist of 108 parts and eastern traditions hold that there are 108,000 degrees of reincarnation. (122)

This mystical number and its variants are recorded within the dimensions of cityscapes, architectural monuments and even metaphorically in the myths and legends of various olden cultures. The truly archaic pyramid-temple city of Angkor Wat in Cambodia contains 540 statues along *five* avenues. Each statue signifying a portal or the number two identifies the number 1080 [540 x 2], which is exactly what we find in early America among Mayan ruins where the Maya erected pillars representing units of 20 years, the total number identified as 10,800 years. (123) The five avenues parallel the AR UB terminations and these architectural designs are the same as the Nordic descriptions of Valhalla, the Hall of the Slain, or Exalted Warriors after death which had 540 doors according to the Norse Eddas. (124) Assuming each door was like most historic portals of import they had *two pillars*, fulfilling the 1080 motif. The famous Greek astronomer Hipparchus [190-120 BC] compiled a catalogue of fixed stars numbering 1080. (125) He borrowed this information from the Chaldeans who catalogued these 1080 stars according to their constellations (126) and Heraclitus before him wrote that civilization is destroyed every 10,800 years. (127)

Early residents in Ireland may have incorporated the mystery number 108 in their round tower at Kildare, which was 108 ft. high and *54 ft. in circumference.* (128) The circumference of the stone towers being 54 ft. [54 x 2 is 108] is powerful evidence that the monument was designed to specifically incorporate this concept dimensionally. The Round Towers of Ireland are enigmatic, giving us the impression of lighthouses though most are far from coastal areas. They appear to have had more mystical significance than architectural, for their function is still relatively unknown to scholarship. America's modern AR UB monument depicting geometrically the concept of 1080 is the Pentagon and there are those in modern media in the United States in the entertainment industry who are aware of the coming catastrophe, having subtle clues disseminated through their network shows and movies. The most blatant example is that of the hit TV series *Lost* where the plane crash survivors discover beneath the island a post-apocalyptic scene of bunkers, chambers, galleries and an ominous *countdown of 108 minutes* that must be reset by someone every 108 minutes or something dreadful will occur. Some of the main characters were rescued on the 108th day. Other related examples of seemingly forgotten motifs resurfacing in today's movies are the Deep Impact and Armageddon movies, one of them revealing that the huge comet approached earth from the stellar regions of Arktos, known as the

Seven Stars. There are literally hundreds of other examples but they would unnecessarily burden our thesis.

For those yet unconvinced in the apparent intended design of the Sumerian AR UB as a mathematical and calendrical code concerning planetary apocalypse here are a few more "coincidences" of note. After the completion of seven generations recorded by Josephus, the book of Jasher and the Japanese Way of the Gods tradition to the exact year that a *third* of the human population before the Flood were killed by the arrival of the Anunnaki [Watchers] as the broken planet passed earth causing massive geological upheaval passed exactly *180 years* [90 + 90], 180 being another variant of 108 and 1080. This time span is from 3615-3435 BC [280-460 AM: Jared's birth]. As will be the subject of a later archive, the number 1080 is encoded in America's fate as well when a *third* of the world will be destroyed by a countdown fulfilling the AR UB after a period of exactly *three* 90-year segments of United States history. The amount of years earth spent lost in space after its preAdamic destruction was 270 years, which, if multiplied by four [number of Earth], becomes *1080*. Also intriguing is that if we multiply 1080 Annus Mundi [2815 BC], the completion of the Great Pyramid complex, five a factor of 5 [AR UB] we get 5400 Annus Mundi, or 1506 AD, which *ends* the *108th Jubilee* [50-year earth generation]; also beginning a 600 year [NER] countdown to *6000 Annus Mundi* [2106 AD]!

Thus far our study has taken us back 414 years [207 + 207] to the beginning of earth's 270 years of ruin that ended 144 years before the start of the Hebraic/Annus Mundi Calendars. This fulfilled an AR UB of Cursed Earth epochs to the Flood, being 2070 years between cataclysms. But these calculations only compound our problem. We've only identified three NER periods of 1800 years from the Renovation of Ruinous Earth 144 years before the Edenic Exile to the Great Flood of 2239 BC [1656 AM]. But the Anunnaki's judgment antedates that of the earth, necessitating the existence of yet another NER period of 600 years calculated backward from −144 Annus Mundi. Though many would argue that this thesis has now gone beyond all historical verifications there can be no doubt that simple mathematics here provides the best evidence in the veracity of this theory, for counting backward from 4039 BC [−144 AM] when earth was renovated we arrive 600 years earlier at 4639 BC which is exactly *330 years* prior to the 4309 BC asteroid impact that destroyed the PreAdamic World and started the Cursed Earth Calendar. It was during this 330 years that the 33.3% of the Anunnaki made war and rebellion against God due to the prophecy of the coming of mankind, the terrestrial image of God. The start of the rebellion was before the collapse of our solar system's lost binary when Earth was bathed in light by day and night by greater and lesser lights [suns] exactly

744 years before the start of the Annus Mundi Calendar [4639-3895 BC], this being an Anunnaki NER of 600 years plus the 144 years of Eden. Amazing confirmation in Hebrew of this double-star mystery is discovered in the gematria for "two great lights," which is read in Genesis 1. The gematrical value of two great lights is exactly *744*. (129)

The Cursed Earth AR UB is the concept that the entire megalithic sanctuary of Stonehenge convey, a system of chronoliths that were specifically designed to preserve the mathematics of the AR UB destructions and as we will see in a later archive, Stonehenge was built to commemorate the passage of this broken world in 1687 BC and to be a lithic prophecy of its *return*. This calendar only extends back to the start of the five Cursed Earth periods of 414-year periods, or ten 207 year periods from the Great Flood in 2239 BC. Prior to its start date in 4309 BC [–414 AM] *the earth was not cursed*. These five periods of cursed earth allude to the existence of *five* NER periods, fulfilling the Anunnaki AR UB of 5 NER. This would make the Flood year of 2239 BC [1656 AM] the exact time when the Anunnaki NER Chronology collides with the Stonehenge Cursed Earth Calendar. The Stonehenge calendar ends at the Flood with 2070 years but the Anunnaki dating ends with exactly 3000 years, or 5 NER [600 x 5] from the beginning of the Anunnaki NER Chronology in 5239 BC.

By adding a fifth NER to 4639 BC when the 33.3% of the Anunnaki rebelled we arrive at the original Great Year of 600 years, the first NER that began 5239 BC. This was the start of the Anunnaki themselves, their creation and kingdom when all worlds worshipped the Creator when the Sons of God were One. This first 600 years was the holy foundation, the eternal standard when the Almighty exercised divine kingship over all of His creation. 5239 BC began the 3000-year AR UB countdown to the Great Flood of 2239 BC [1656 AM] and this fact may have been why Herodotus recorded that the Egyptians maintained a belief that the entire period of transmigration "...occupied 3000 years." (130) The Egyptians had preserved many icons and fragments of these antediluvian histories. A prime example concerning the Egyptian memory of Anunnaki kingship is seen in their hieroglyphic determinative for *king*, which is a *five*-pointed star glyph: pentagon without a perimeter. (131)

Five-Pointed Star

Though in Sumerian times, 600 was seen to be constructed from five shars [120 x 5] the builders of Stonehenge encoded their knowledge in the lesser denominator of 40, which is a *third* of a shar. Thus 40 chronolithic pillars at Stonehenge [upright megaliths] multiplied by 15 [number of megaliths in inner ring that forms pentagram], is 600 [40 x 15]. The number 40 is of *trial* and *testing* seen several times in the scriptures, and the original 600 years of trial and testing of the Anunnaki resulted in the fall of a *third* of these beings which fought God for 330 years until their kingdom of light became a *kingdom of darkness* when their sun went out [binary star died] leaving an immense blackened strewn field of billions of fragments of rock and ice millions of miles below our ecliptic that the Sumerians long ago called the Abyss and Deep, origin of the Anunnaki.

That the 600 years of original peace in ancient heaven was actually the beginning seems to be inferred from the life of Adam, who lived for 930 years before dying 60 years before the construction of Giza began. This 930-year time period is encoded within the Anunnaki preAdamic history, for it was 930 years from the beginning of the PreAdamic World and start of Anunnaki NER Chronology to the death of Earth [*adamu*] by global cataclysm that lasted for 270 years. Adam died after 930 of life just as the planet he was made from ended after the same amount of time. Such coincidences hardly seem coincidental at all when taken in light of the whole.

Now we have two separate AR UB dating methods that collide at the second destruction of our planet, the Great Flood 2239 BC [1656 AM]. One calendar ends after 3000 years and the other after 2070 years; the differential between these dating systems is 930 years. What is important to remember here is that the preAdamic apocalypse that left earth destroyed was an *appearance of God upon Earth* which is only barely glimpsed in scripture where we read that in the heavens of old, God rode upon the back of a cherub during a previous unexplained episode of global judgment. These passages, found in Jeremiah 4 and certain Psalms that are older than the psalmists are largely ignored because of their fragmentation and apparent detachment from the rest of Scripture. They convey an earlier apocalypse that antedates humanity, one the angels of God suffered for their insurrection. Though both AR UBs collide at their end of *five* epochs [414 year periods and NERs] they also interface at the beginning and end of the 144 years of Eden with the appearance of Man. This appearance of mankind [image of God] is the link between the NER and the shar and his presence during the 144 years 144 hours after the 144 years began leads us to multiply 144 times the number of Man [6] to arrive at 864.

Why is 864 important to our thesis? The reason is because it forms the key to Sumerian sexagesimal figures. This number proves that earth was restored and set back on track during the 144 years of Eden for 864 is the ultimate number for the *foundation of time*:

1 day	86,400 seconds
60 days	86,400 minutes
360 days	8,640 hours
24 years	8,640 days
72 years	864 months

This system is predicated upon the Draconian 360-day calendar, which probably began at the beginning of the 330 years of Original Earth and was restored when the planet was restabilized 144 years prior to Year 1 Annus Mundi. The number 864 is found within the appearance of the four NER points from the Anunnaki Rebellion to the Flood, for each NER is 216,000 days, but 4 NER is 864,000 Draconian days and the same as one of the Brahmanic Yugas, called the Dvapara. 864,000 days backward from the Flood is the time when heaven and earth time synchronized with the conclusion of the first 600-year period, exhibiting 864s identity as the *foundation of time* number.

The number 864 when divided by the number of man [6] is 144 and if we divide 864 by the number for *new beginnings* [8: see *Lost Scriptures*] we are left with 108. This number is one that will reemerge in our thesis, along with the numbers 120, 144, 270, 330, 414, 600, 1656 and 2070. These sums have amazing historical and calendrical significant and *all* of them appear in countdowns concerning the beginning and end of the United States of America, the destruction of a *third* of the world, and of the Apocalypse soon to be visited upon the sons of men.

But before we delve into the mysteries of the future we are compelled to first peer into the Gizean secrets of the Zodiac, for the Great Pyramid complex is the decoder of the elder prophecies written in the stars in the stellar riddles buried in the constellations of the Zodiac.

Archive III

Gizean Secrets of the Zodiac

The oldest Euphratean cultures divided their ancestral histories between epochs before and after the Great Flood. The most popular rulers after this catastrophe all perpetuated the fiction that they were somehow a contributor to the defeat of the Anunnaki, a claim that served to establish their personal kingship over their people. But these false claims served another purpose: the almost perfect corruption of the antediluvian Zodiac into an anthropomorphical mythos that it was never intended to become.

Prior to the emergence of Babylonia, Assyria, the Aramaic nations and Egyptian dynasties, Sargon of Akkad ruled during what the later Babylonians asserted was during their Golden Age, themselves claiming descendancy from the Akkadians who were themselves a shadow of Sumer. Particularly old Akkadian stone tablets record that Sargon claimed to have fought against hoards of monsters and giants, finally defeating them. These are described as the Seven Kings and their armies, the sons of Anbanini. Only after reviewing the two earlier archives in this book does the translation of these tablets now appear to be a coded version of the Sumerian King-List. Sargon wrote that—

"...one hundred and twenty [120] thousand warriors I sent out, but not one returned alive. As the second year drew nigh, ninety thousand warriors I sent out, but not one returned alive [90]. As the third year drew nigh, sixty thousand seven hundred [670] warriors I sent out, but not one returned alive." (1)

The Shepherd of Akkad, Sargon, lamented, prayed to the gods and listened to their advice, sending forth a fourth expedition that was successful. He defeated the Seven Kings and their armies of monsters. This is no doubt a fabricated account *after the fact* of the disappearance of the Seven Kings. The immense numbers of Sargon's armies are actually cryptographic references to the end of the *shar* [120] dating system of antediluvian time [120,000 warriors died] and the 60,700 warriors defeated is the exaggerated sum of the 670 years identified on the Sumerian King-List [actually beginning with ascent of Enoch 70 years prior to 600 years of Seven Kings]. The mention of Anbanini identifies an *Eighth King* and the 90,000 warriors links the three numbers of armies in a cleverly concealed admission of the scribal knowledge of the apocalyptic number of *judgment,* for 120 x 9 is 1080, the AR UB motif that the Sumerian King-List secretly conveys by its citation of a *pentapolis.* It is quite possible that Sargon himself did not understand these codes, as well as many historic kings who had records written to commemorate their deeds. But the scribes were offended at the insolence and blasphemies of their regents and appear to have cleverly hidden codes disguised beneath these egoistic claims.

Before Sargon was given this throne name he was recorded in history as the cupbearer of Ur Zababa, the last king of Kish. Recall that according to the Sumerian records in archive one Kish was where kingship began after the Flood. Sargon deposed his own ruler and became king himself, assuming the *title* Sargon [Sharru-kin], which means, "The King is Legitimate," an epithet taken because he was *not* legitimate. (2) Sumerian texts remember this figure as Ur Nammu [Nammu of Ur] about 2100 BC because he deposed a king at Kish named Utu-hegal. (3) Ur Nammu developed the first law code and was called the Righteous Shepherd. (4) Nammu is better known by other names such as Nimrod the Mighty Hunter and Hammurabi of Babylonia and in Akkad he was Uz, a regent clad in a goat-skin who was worshipped (5) at Sippar, which was formerly a Sumerian city with antediluvian origin. He was also called the horned one. (6)

Semitic traditions are numerous and extend from distant antiquity to even modern times among Arabic and Hebrew lore that Nimrod the Hunter defeated and then lorded over giants, making them build a tower that was destroyed by God. Because of his pride and the ruin of his tower his people changed his name to Amraphel according to the Book of Jasher. (7) Interestingly, Nimrod later sent some giants still under his command to Lebanon to rebuilt the preflood ruins located at what is called Baalbek. (8) The title Amraphel is very descriptive and deserved, however, Nimrod later corrupted its meaning. Originally it was derived from Amurru-ipul, or "Amurru has answered," (9) and meant that God [Amorites called Him Amurru] answered their king's insolence with the ruin of his tower. Later Nimrod twisted this meaning to claim that his new name was given to be a sign to the people that he was the fulfillment of the prophecy of the Coming One that would restore the kingship of earth back to the Godhead. He even assumed characteristics of Amurru who was a God described as "...the Shepherd who treads on *mountains*." (10) These mountains are divine beings like the Seven Mountains of the Seven Anunnaki. Amurru waged celestial warfare with a bow and arrow. Amraphel is a variant of the Canaanite Ammurapi found among the Ugaritic inscriptions, which is actually the correct spelling of the famous *Hammurabi.* (11)

In December 1901 AD a French scientist named J. de Morgan discovered at the ruins at Susa in Assyria [Iraq] a pillar of black diorite about 8 ft. tall which was covered in 44 columns of lines of text. A virtual book. This has come to be known as the Code of Hammurabi dated about 2050 BC. These laws are thought to have been a compilation of several older codes as old as 4000 BC. (12) In fact, much of the Mosaic laws find their precedents in the Hammurabi Code. Like Sargon, Hammurabi attempted to emulate the divine and rewrite history. The Code begins—

"When lofty Anum, Lord of the Anunnaki, and Enlil, Lord of Heaven and Earth [AN and KI], who determines the destinies of the land, determined for Marduk, the firstborn of Enki [Lord of the Earth: Sumerian Triad], the *kingship* over mankind; made him great among the IGIGI [Watchers], called Babylon by name to be exalted, made it supreme in the world; established for Marduk in its midst, an everlasting kingship."

The Babylonians went to great extents to copy the older Sumerian texts, changing the names of gods and histories, especially in the case of Marduk. (13) The Enuma Elish seven tablets of creation was a Babylonian invention praising Marduk but copied from preexisting texts of greater age that survived from Akkadian and Sumerian times. The Enuma Elish is truly an insult to the earlier cosmologies where Marduk played no part, and as will see, its popularity contributed greatly to the corruption of the original Zodiac. Marduk was not a Babylonian invention but an actual person in Babylon's infancy priorly known as Merodach, or *Rebellious Great One*, derived from a root meaning *rebellion* found also in like names such as Nimrod, Mardon and Marduk. Marduk's history began in Sumer where he was known as AMAR. UDA.AK. (14)

Marduk became regarded as the fulfillment of the Savior motif to the Babylonians, to come and forgive mankind, heal the sick, a mediator between mankind and the gods, defeat the *Tempter* and even raise the dead. He was the one who defeated the chaos [restored the world] in the older writings and he was associated to the Hebrew God Jah. This is evident from the names Babylonians gave their children such as Bel-Yahu [Bel is Jah], which is identical with Bealyah in the biblical books who was one of David's mighty warriors in 1 Chronicles 12:5 and Shamshi-ya [My son is Jah]. (15) Because the Sumerians recorded that it was to be the Son of Enlil [Lord Wind] that was to defeat the Dragon called ZU [thief of the Tablets of Destinies], Marduk & Hammurabi among others all attempted to perpetuate the fraud that they were this promised seed of God.

Marduk gained fame and was regarded in the Enuma Elish texts as having restored a constellation in the heavens after it had *vanished*. The older deities then gave him preeminence and called him the Herder of the Stars. (16) This disappearance of an entire constellation and its reappearance will later prove to be of immense value to our thesis as will be seen, for there truly is something of immense size that reenters the inner solar system every few centuries that could have created an eclipse of this star group before moving on to create the illusion of its reappearance.

The title Herder of the Stars links him to the Shepherd motif of Savior symbolism, God having been likened to a world shepherd who watched over His sheep [humanity] by way of His eye [pole star] over His pasture [earth]. Those dictators and wicked regents seeking to tap into this popularity used symbols such as the Shepherd's Crook, which paradoxically became the uniform icon of the Horned One [Mighty Hunger symbolism]. (17) The Mighty Hunter or Horned One motif derives from the fact that after the diluvian catastrophe the animal kingdoms rose up against the scattered families of earth and many are the ancient reports of wild animals dragging away women and children, even robbing cradles of infants, devouring them. Domestic animals were hunted by their wild counterparts and those men who went out and hunted the wild bears, tigers, lions and wolves became heroes venerated for their bravery. Their chief weapons were bows and arrows further linking them with the idea of saviorship. The shepherd's crook was a merging of the two most powerful images of Sumer: the Shepherd and the Hunter, and kings began associating themselves with both.

In table 6 of the Enuma Elish we learn that an *image in heaven* was made of Marduk with a bow to commemorate his "...shepherding of the blackheaded people," which was a description of the Sumerians, "...that in latter days, lest his deeds be forgotten," his image was eternally stationed in the heavens. (18) This constellation would be the Orion star group in Taurus, a messianic constellation that of course antedates Marduk. Because it was the stars that were blamed for the end of the preflood world in the Enuma Elish tablets Marduk promises to "...uphold the ways of the stars of heaven." (19)

Curiously, Marduk held that the Anunnaki were to serve him and according to these texts he released them from their prison and in return they built for him Babylon and the famous Ziggurat, and Marduk became the Establisher of the Constellations [Zodiac]. He was aided in releasing the Anunnaki by Nannar [Moon] and divided the Anunnaki between the gods of earth and gods of heaven. (20) Nannar may have been constructed from two archaic syllables from Sumer: NUN [abyss] and AR. Not only did he defeat the Anunnaki and lord over them with construction projects and military campaigns but the Enuma Elish texts even go as far as to claim that he also crushed the heads of Tiamat, the seven-headed dragon of chaos to *create* mankind. Of course after reading archive two we know this to be a corruption based off an incorrect association between the arrival of the Anunnaki 144 years prior to mankind's exit from paradise. The weapon by which Marduk defeated the Dragon of Chaos appeared as a *trident*. As god of *life*, Marduk defeated the god of death called Tiamat with a weapon artistically shown as— (21)

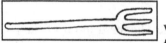 One of the more popular kings of Sumer was later immortalized in Babylonia in the famous Epic of Gilgamesh, a series of twelve stone tablets often theorized to be associated to the 12 signs of the Zodiac. Gilgamesh was likened to a Wild Bull who wore a lion's skin [Hunter's attire] and was a wrestler of lions, tigers and bears as well as other mighty men. He is often shown with a bow and arrow. (22) In the Epic we read, "Go up to the wall of Uruk and look around, examine its foundation, inspect its brickwork thoroughly. Is not even the core of the brick structure made of kiln-fired brick, and did not the Seven Sages themselves lay out its plans?" (23) Uruk is the biblical Erech built by Nimrod in Genesis and the earliest inscriptions claiming Gilgamesh built the wall of Uruk dates back to King Anam or Uruk about 1800 BC. Anam is the subject of mysteries of early Egypt in *Lost Scriptures*, a figure known as Mena [First Dynasty] who was priorly known throughout Sumer as Anam and is recorded above in the Code of Hammurabi as Anum.

Gilgamesh went to the Forest of Lebanon and killed the giant Humbaba who guarded "...the secret of dwellings of the Anunnaki." This is actually a reference to Ur Zababa whom Sargon deposed and there are scores of similarities between Sargon and the earlier Gilgamesh, the latter in fact being Sargon prior to his kingship. The secret dwellings of the Anunnaki are also the Baalbek area of Lebanon where antediluvian ruins were discovered after the Flood. Another epithet of Sumer and Babylonia given to this early treacherous king was Lugal Marad [rebel], who was said to have gone to the Lebanon range in pursuit of ZU, the Dragon. (24) Ninurta was his name in Assyria, where he was known to have rescued the Tablets of Fate stolen from Enlil by the Wind Dragon ZU who was in league with the powers of chaos. (25) He was a famous champion of the people who defeated monsters, giants and animals who attempted to impede the spreading of humanity. A famous Akkadian seal shows Ninurta slaying lions, bulls and a seven-headed dragon. (26)

The Greeks also linked their deities with Anunnaki history. During the reign of Cronus it was the Golden Age for man, when the Good Genie descended from the moon to take charge of oracles, initiatory rites and acted as judges, Watchers and saviors everywhere. (27) The world was originally ruled by Seven Titans who were born from a union of heaven and earth or Uranus and Gaia. (28) The Titans fathered a race of giants (29) and these Seven were called Lords of the Seven Day Week. (30) The several references of the descent of these deities from the moon is a corruption of the actual descent of these divinities from their prison planetoid. The link to the number 7 may be a result of the lunar number being 7, for each quarter phase of the moon is seven days. There are 28 mansions of the moon, or four 7-day weeks. The moon was an obvious link. The fact that the moon is severely pockmarked with craters may be the origin of this idea and it is possible that the bombardment of asteroids upon the surface of the moon in ancient times as seen from earth attended with falling stars [meteorites entering atmosphere] could have given rise to this tradition.

Zeus was thought to be the fulfillment of a prophecy. (31) Interestingly, Zeus *deposed* Cronus in the same fashion Sargon deposed Ur Zababa. In fact, just as the former, Zeus also was the *cupbearer* of Cronus. The Giants rebelled against Zeus and they are described as having long necks. But this is a scribal error for "long-necked" is today thought by scholars to be the translation of *Anak* of the Old Testament, but this is only popular etymology. These Grecians giants are in fact *Anunnaki*. The confusion comes from the fact that the Anunnaki were supposed to be from off of a *divine* necklace of the goddess Aruru and the Greeks merely remembered something about the neck, converging the ideas of gigantic men and necks to come up with *long-necked*. Zeus defeated these giants and banished them to Tartarus [the far Deep]. (32) Tartarus was early on associated with the far west because it was where the sun went down, a place in the ancient mindset where dwelt evil and darkness. But the idea behind Tartarus is that of a place *below* the earth. Zeus did not defeat the giants [Anunnaki], but they appeared and then disappeared just as quickly back toward Tartarus hundreds of millions of miles below our solar system as their broken planet passed by earth on its way back downward into the Deep. Zeus was famous for defeating these Seven Cyclopes, his weapon used to defeat them was the Labrys, or Thunderbolt which is identical to the bolt of Marduk.

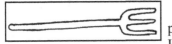 Hercules also was the fulfillment of a prophecy concerning the end of the Giants. (33) He was a wrestler and slayer of giants (34) who wore a lion's skin and fought the Centaurs. (35) Before his name was Hercules it was Palaemon, the Wrestler. (36) This name is very important because it preserves the Sumerian word for *garment* [PALA] used by Ishtar to gain access through all seven gates of the underworld, a garment associated to a *name change* as extensively shown in *Lost Scruptures* that is likened to the biblical promise of the righteous receiving a white garment and a new

name by God. Hercules defeated a Divine Bull, killed a lion and defeated a Dragon that guarded a sacred tree. (37) Like Gilgamesh, Hercules had a best friend [Enkidu and Iolaus], both fell in love with a goddess [Ishtar and Deianeira], both were of semi-divine parentage, descended to hell, killed animals like lions and bulls, both used their garments to sail, found magic herbs of immortality, were associated religiously to the Zodiac and sun. (38) Remarkably, these Sumerian and Greek memories share an unspoken trait that seals these personages together…the fact that history never recorded the deaths of either Heracles nor Gilgamesh, proving these titles were of someone who was later called something else by the time of his death.

Hermes is also a name that is associated to three ancient personalities. Enoch and Abraham are two as shown in *Lost Scriptures*, but the third is Nimrod. The epithet is similar between these people but the histories are quite divergent respecting them. Hermes was born of a goddess and became Lord of the Animals, killing them as sacrifices to God after the Flood. In Homer's Odyssey he is a Giant killer. (39) His Roman counterpart was Mercury, a deceitful *cupbearer* to a king. (40) He created wedge-shaped characters that represented sounds [cuneiform of Sumer and Akkad]. (41) The Arab historian Makrizi, citing even older traditions many centuries ago, wrote that there was a lot of confusion "…about the history of Hermes of Babel: that according to some accounts he was one of the Seven Keepers in the temples whose business it was to guard the Seven Houses." (42)

A very important fact must be recognized. The 12 signs of the Zodiac were so important that the major civilizations after the Flood not only created entire pantheons of deities numbering 12 in commemoration of these stellar mysteries, but their priesthoods even created entire mythos to mask the fact that their gods were merely empty facades derived from the 12 signs of the Zodiac. These nations even remember that prior to the 12 gods lived a pantheon of 8 deities on earth among men. This is perfectly reconciled with biblical records.

The Book of Genesis claims there were 8 survivors of the Flood and one of them was Noah. These 8 people after 250 years seeded civilization, what we know as Sumer today. These people were remembered so fondly because they were of antediluvian stock, living lives far longer than those born under worse climatic conditions after the Flood. The Egyptians called these 8 gods the Ogdoad, and Herodotus in Book II of his Histories wrote that the Egyptians "…say that seventeen thousand years before the reign of Amasis the Twelve Gods were produced from the Eight." (43) This is identical to the Vedic records of the original 8 deities before the 12 appeared. (44)

In the center of the Marketplace at Athens, Greece long ago stood a famous pillar with the inscription "The Twelve Gods." (45) As the center of Greek society all distances were measured from this pillar. Having been dedicated to the Zodiacal divinities [borrowed from Babylon] they were stellar guides used for terrestrial measurements of distance. This may have been the Altar of the Twelve Gods mentioned by Herodotus. (46)

The original preflood Zodiac was a book among the stars and its teachings were openly disseminated by the eight survivors to their offspring. After a few centuries when humanity began exploding populously at an exponential rate the newly arisen cults and priesthoods realized that only by concealing knowledge could they maintain control over the growing masses while also becoming the center of this renewing civilization. This corruption was absolute and continues today, for the Zodiac is still believed to be a hand-in-hand symbolism of a solar mythos. Nothing could be further from the truth.

There is a profound power the stars have over the human imagination. We gaze at the heavens on a starry night, transfixed as if we are supposed to be receiving something that lies at the edges of our memory. As imperfect beings staring into the vast depths of unimaginable distances, the appearance of the night sky and the inspirational currents that pass through our bodies resonate within our being an acute awareness that we are being watched, and called for.

That knowledge was dispersed among the stars is a particularly old idea. Over 125 years ago the mystic Thomas Burgoyne wrote that the revelations of God are "...not lost to us today. The same book lies open before us that faced our ancient forefathers. It is standing out clear and distinct, waiting to be read by the sons of men." (47) The Kabbalists believe that the future and God's divine plan for mankind was written in the stars long before the world was made (48), and this may be due to the Psalmist's passage that "...the heavens declare the glory of God; the firmament showeth His handiwork...night unto night showeth knowledge." (49) In the Book of Enoch we read, "O Enoch, look on the book which heaven has distilled: and reading that which is written upon it, understand every part of it. Then I looked on all which was written and understood all, reading the book and everything written in it, all the works of men." (50) Also in the Enochian records we learn that concerning the final Judgment "...there shall be writings and impressions above in heaven, and the angels may read them, and know what shall happen both to sinners and to the spirits of the humble." (51)

Not only the fixed stars were a part of this stellar alphabet and codified astronomy but also the planets, called by Stobaeus in Physica "Watchful Guardians." (52) The early concepts involved the planets as Watchers, an idea also mirrored in the Book of Enoch where we find that the planets "... behold the earth, and understand what is transacted, from the beginning to the end of it." (53) In Sumer the planets were called lu-bat, or Wandering Sheep or Revealers. There were even seven MASHU [shepherds], fixed stars on either side of the ecliptic to ensure that the planets did not deviate from their paths. (54)

The Zodiac was originally intended as an apocalypse recorder and its mysteries were taught by the Tetramorph, the Four Living Ones called Watchers that have dominion over the four quadrants of heaven. These four were marked by the Four Royal Stars of Aldebaran in Taurus, Regulus in Leo, Antares in Scorpio, and Fomalhaut in Aquarius. In the book of Ezekiel and the Revelation these are the faces of the Watchers that hold up the Throne of God in heaven. Thus, the Bull, Lion, Eagle [Scorpio] and Man are the *zo-on*, or *Living Beings*. (55) The Zodiac refers to these four living beings but the priesthoods early on corrupted this by changing the symbolism and meaning of the 12 signs to confuse the 12 signs with the imagery of the Tetramorph, inventing animal forms and hybrids to conceal the true mysteries beneath. The mythographers made sure that their kings would assume the role of the Sun, and that the new stellar system would serve to convey that the threats of heaven that abide over mankind were done away with by the sun/hero king. Now, as one late philosopher would say, the Zodiac, "...like every skin, betrays something but conceals even more." (56)

The Zodiacal Belt is on the Sun's equator, called the plane of the ecliptic. It is 16° in width and divided into 12 equal houses of 30° each to make a 360° circle. Some constellations are slightly above or below the ecliptic but the sun, moon and planets all move within a 7° latitude on both sides of the ecliptic. (57) The sun only passes through twelve of the constellations in the heavens but the Greeks counted 48 constellations altogether and the Babylonians even more. (58) These 12 signs are not equally distributed and the star groups of each zodiacal house do not in any way conform to the pictures attributed to them by the mythographers, hinting that something is amiss. Because of this unequal distribution there is a give of about three or so centuries from the end of one sign and the beginning of another in the precession of the equinox, which is the birth of the sun in the next sign that occurs theoretically every 2160 years. But these 2160-year houses are entirely theoretical for the actual constellations do not at all conform to such rigid distribution.

Zodiacal constellations appear to go behind the sun and long ago it was thought that the sun passed through these signs to create the effect. The sun traversed the daytime path across six signs in 12 hours and with the planets on the same path across the sky but moving much slower and still relatively in the same place at the next night. This is why the planets, also known as wandering stars, were viewed as much different and inferior to the sun. Every month a new constellation emerges over the eastern horizon. In six months time it vanishes over the western horizon not to reappear for six months, again at the eastern horizon. Except for the pole stars and stars closely in proximity, all the stars move westward across the sky. As the planets moved against the backdrop of stars in the zodiacal signs they were called Lords of the Mansions. (59).

Early on when civilization after the Deluge was still centralized around a single priesthood the Tetramorph was corrupted and mixed up with the newly created facades of animal forms around the Zodiac. Part of the reasoning behind this was to identify the hero-king as the one who would keep the gods of destruction at bay, a ruler who promised his subjects that the world would never be destroyed by water again. A promise literally stolen from God who made it to Noah in Genesis…When this new system was invented to conceal the original some elements were changed enough to forever dilute the meaning of original star-groups while others were altered in similitudes that changed the meaning with such divergent symbolism that the Zodiac's subtexts could scarcely be interpreted, even by the most erudite sage.

The post-diluvian stellar year began with the Sun entering Aries, the Goat or sometimes a Ram, which is a symbol of the Horned King [the Sun]. We are reminded of the Akkadian Uz, which leads us to Azazel, the Hebrew Scapegoat. Interestingly the Greeks regarded this animal as the symbol for deity because of its genitals and fact that goats are noted for their sexual natures. (60) In Aries the Sun became King; Aries is the regnal beginning of the sun's career in the stellar year.

Leaving the throne the sun enters Taurus starting his solar laboring in his pasture [earth]. Most early nations remember the Bull of Creation. Gilgamesh killed the Bull of Heaven in Sumerian stories, a creature called Gugalanna. Mithra of Persian traditions slew the Bull of Heaven (61), Perseus slew the minotaur and many other heroes killed fearsome bulls or bullish monsters. Several historic personages were given epithets identifying themselves with bulls like Gilgamesh, Osiris, Apis, Serapis and many others. In Taurus lies the messianic motif star-group called the Orion constellation, the most brilliant of constellations. The Akkadians referred to this constellation as Sitaddalu, or the Giant/Broad Man (62) and Homer in his Odyssey called him Huge Orion. (63) In Egypt he was Horus (64), which is remotely akin to [ori]on. Interestingly the etymology of Orion is uncertain, some Greek antiquarians asserting that it means "…he who makes water," however, it appears to be constructed of two archaic roots, one in Greek [ion] and the other Semitic [ur]. Orion could simply mean *native [ion] of Ur*.

Taurus is a sign rich with mystical attachments. Herodotus recorded a Greek tradition that reads, "…it is said that Hercules, at the start of the voyage of the Argo to fetch the Golden Fleece from Aea (Colchis), was put ashore by Jason and his companions to get water, and was left behind." (65) This is of course a zodiacal tale concerning Orion, who was also called Heracles. The Argo was the ship that Jason and the Argonauts traveled in on their journey, which was actually earth [a ship called *argo*: company of travelers] through history [Zodiac] to find the Golden Fleece [Aries again: man's search for his beginning and eternal security]. Hercules was said to have been put ashore early on because Taurus was only the second sign and Orion lights up this area of the heavens.

Also in Taurus are the Hyades, giants that aided Zeus that comprised of the V-shaped face of Taurus. But the most intriguing star-group of this sign is the Pleiades, which is variously interpreted as Congregation of the Judges (66) and most nations in antiquity referred to them as *female*. They were the Seven Sisters in the Graeco-Aegean cultures (67), the Virgins of the Spring to the Romans and the Hopi called them the Harmonious Ones, or Stars that Cling Together. (68) The Cherokee Indians believed that their ancestors came from the Pleiades star system and named them the Seven Dancers who were Keepers of the Sacred Light. Even in remote Australia the Pleiades were youthful girls playing to young men [belt stars of Orion]. (69)

Passing from the pasture of Earth the sun moves into Gemini and passes in between the Twins, which are variously pillars, trees or mountains. This is the act of the hero-god passing into an otherworldly realm, where ordinary mortals were not admitted. The mythos successfully concealed this meaning by the creation of myths and legends of the Twins like Gilgamesh and Enkidu who were diabolical opposites reconciled through trials and tribulations, just like Heracles and Iolaus, Castor and Pollux, Oph and Shichim of China, Christa and Balarma of India, Sut and Horus of Egypt, Amphion and Zethus, Romulus and Remus of Rome, and Theseus and Pirithous. Great secrets are unveiled by the merging of the twin souls but the mythographers did this sign damage by creating fictions concerning the Twins. Further complicating the matter was the assignment of certain stars in Gemini area of Zodiac totally vague and variant meanings from their true antediluvian meanings, such as Sirius and his Bow, or the Assyrian Sukudu [Arrow] and Canis Major [Great Dog]. (70) These are Hunter icons serving to hide true Gemini revelations.

After one of these Twins dies or they merge into a single form does the sun move into this forbidden realm known as Cancer, a sign of the Water Domain that lies above part of the five-headed Hydra constellation. This is a dragon defeated by many archaic heroes and because of its placement in the

Water Domain this sign was changed into that of a Crab. Again, this too was a corruption and furtherance in the hiding of this sign's true meaning.

Next the sun enters Leo, an apocalyptic AR UB constellation that has suffered tremendous alteration into a mythos of the lion-slayer hero-king. The imagery of the Bull for Taurus and the Lion for Leo were easy to manipulate by the cults because these are the first two faces of the cherubic Tetramorph or the Four Watchers with bull, lion, eagle and man faces.

After Leo the sun moves into Virgo, the universal symbol of the priesthoods of the Goddess who incidently gave birth to the hero-king Gilgamesh, Marduk, Ninurta, Zeus, Dionysius, Hermes and a host of other divine epithets. The mythographers could not have dealt a worse blow than attributing this sign to a goddess who mothered a hero-god.

The next sign entered by the sun is peculiar. Libra is a vastly misunderstood aspect of the Zodiac and the mythos did little to veil its meaning. As the seventh sign its original meaning just might have been concealed from the beginning. Libra is the Balance, or Scales and the oldest zodiacal writings ever found all detail this sign as being indicative of *judgment*. However, the true meaning of this profound mystery will astound even the most astute initiate into these stellar mysteries. Interestingly, Libra is the only sign not anthropomorphically depicted, being an inanimate object rather than a living being.

That the mythos-designers did not attempt to divert attention away from this constellation is not the case. In the area of Libra was assigned a minor constellation called Bootes, the Huntsman and Herdsman stars, which Arcturus is the principle star. (71) Arcturus is a star of mystery and as we will learn, its significance was never quite lost. Though many cultures remember this star as one associated to hunting, the Shawnee and other Native Americans called it White Hawk the Hunter. (72)

Leaving the Balance, which was also a reference to the equinox of equal day and night which occurs during the latter part of the year, the sun moves into Scorpio which was a Babylonian invention that filtered into many other historic zodiacs such as those in Egypt and Greece. The scorpion imagery was adopted to compensate for the inability of the sages to incorporate an *Eagle* into the pseudo-history of their hero-king. The scorpion was already recognized in antiquity from preflood times as a monstrous being created by the dragon of chaos, Tiamat. (73) In the Sumerian Epic of Gilgamesh the Guardians of the Gate were scorpion men and in the Enuma Elish of Babylonia scorpion men made up 1/11th of Tiamat's army.

A prevailing Native American belief was that the dead repair to the Great Mother Scorpion. (74) The first of the seven powers of Akkad was the scorpion (75), called the Sting-Bearer of Heaven. (76) A large scorpion was said to have confronted Orion (77) which is merely a mythological invention acknowledging Scorpio's opposition across the Zodiacal Circle from Taurus. As Orion in Taurus descends over the horizon Scorpio ascends. The Eagle symbolism as we will see was not entirely lost, but the builders of Giza *knew* that it would be changed and this alteration appears evident in the construction of the Sphinx as will be shown, a monumental guardian of the earthly altar of God in the form of a stone Tetramorph merged into One.

Departing the injured Scorpio the sun enters Sagittarius. The only link between this sign and the later developed mythos is the *arrow*. The Akkadian name for this sign reveals that it was also used to perpetuate the king-motif, which was Nun-Ki, or Prince of the Earth whom the Sumerians called Nergal. (78) Nergal is a personification of the NER[gal] who was also called Ura, the Plague God. (79) The Greeks knew that this was a hybrid sign but they lost the original meaning and invented the hybrid centaur, a horse/man combination linking the imagery of warfare [horse] and king [man with bow and arrow]. The Centaurs were themselves in the traditions symbols for vice and sin, heretics and the devil. (80) But a hybrid fantasy creature is not what this sign actually conveys. The celestial river known as the Milky Way also runs through this sign, which is the original of the myth of Hercules breaking off the horn of the River God named Achelaus in a battle. (81) These horns also leads us to the next sign.

Once the horn is broken it becomes yet another hybrid sign. This is Capricorn, a half goat/fish combination created purely from the symbols adjacent to it; the horn motif from Sagittarius and of a goat and the water symbol sign symbol of Pisces [Fish] and Aquarius before it. The horn is the Cornucopeia, the icon of the goddess Fortuna who rules in autumn holding the Horn of Plenty. (82) The continuation of the goat symbolism renders the constellation an evil facet, but another interpretation is that with the vice destroyed are blessings given. As we will see, the symbolism is rich and deeply masked.

Next the sun enters Aquarius, the Water-Bearer, a symbol little changed from its beginning. As the 11th sign it is the home of the eleven monstruous types of the Chaos Dragon Tiamat. This constellation immortalizes the Flood, but even still much can be gleaned that has been until now remained hidden.

The final sign of the sun's passage is Pisces the Fish and there are no explanations from of old as to how and why this sign was identified as a Fish. Its presence in the Water Domain could be responsible for this elusive fact, however, this sign is *not* a fish at all.

The primary foundation of the sun-mythos is that the sun was born in Aries, became a bull in Taurus, entered through divine portals in Gemini, crossed an ocean in Cancer, slew a lion in Leo, enjoyed carnal relations with a goddess in Virgo, established the law in Libra and judged the dead, fought a giant scorpion or Death itself in Scorpio, became a mighty archer in Sagittarius, was suckled by a goat in Capricorn, traveled through the underworld in Aquarius and became a fish in Pisces before being reborn in Aries from its beginning as a fish. Numerous are the pseudo-historical kings of yore that performed these acts or emulated these types, among them the famous Heracles and Gilgamesh. In the 5th century BC Pausanius observed that the Twelve Labors of Heracles represented the 12 months of the solar year of the Zodiac, a position supported by Hesiod before him. (83) Both Heracles and Gilgamesh fall in love with a goddess [Deianeira & Ishtar], have best friends [Iolaus & Enkidu], were of semi-divine parentage, descended to hell, killed a lion, a bull, fought against giants, used their garments for a sail, found a mystical plant of immortality, battle a serpent-like creature or was confronted by one, and neither suffered a death recorded by history. (84)

Though the post-diluvian stellar mysteries were centrally focused around the supposed labors of the Sun-god the antediluvian calendrical system was based off of 360 revolutions of the circumpolar stars around the Pole Star Alpha Draconis. These were the Seven Stars of Ursa Major that revolved about the Dragon Star and were the principle reason the ancient calendars measured a day as being an *evening* and *morning*. The actual days before the Flood began when the sun went down and the stars appeared and the next day began when the stars around the pole star were seen to begin another circle when the sun set again.

Alpha Draconis was the Eye of the Dragon, the eye motif being a universal symbol for the pole star. This constellation extends over a third of the night sky in the northern heavens around the polar regions, his tail extending over a "...third part of the stars," as the Revelation account reveals. A rather bright star in Draco's head is Ethanim, which means, "the long serpent," and another bright star in this constellation is Al Waid, meaning ".... who is to be destroyed." (85) In the Dragon's tail is the star Thuban, also called the Dragon Star but not to be confused with Alpha Draconis. Thuban in Hebrew means "subtle," (86) which is how the Genesis text describes the serpent. Once the asteroid impacted and caused the Deluge the pole star [Eye of the Dragon] fell and after that the priestly cults that emerged developed a solaric system having little room for recognition of the pole star.

Our entire discourse thus far has merely served to reach this point in our thesis: proof that the original Zodiac was an apocalypse recorder properly decoded by Gizean knowledges, mathematics and architectural anomalies themselves decoded through calendrical geometry. Now we shall delve into the most secretive facets of the Zodiac and unveil what the mythographers tried to conceal, excavating knowledge buried beneath layers of textual and mythological disinformation.

Read herein the Gizean secrets of the Zodiac.

ARIES of the Fire Domain [planet: Mars]

At the height of the Babylonian civilization after the cataclysm Aries began the solar year in the spring at the vernal equinox circa. 2200-1600 BC. Due to the passage of 4000 years in the process of precession Aries has fallen back and now the sun begins each year in the sign of Pisces, the *last* sign. Aries built from the archaic root [AR]ies, which is also found in its ruling planet: M[AR]s. But ARI [watcher] is also embedded within this epithet, which may refer to the fact that Aries begins the first sign of three all in the Bull Quadrant of the Cherubic Tetramorph in heaven.

In ancient India the entry of the sun into Aries was commemorated by the sacrifice of a lamb, a ritual that was also observed in Egypt. (87) The doctrine of substitution is very old, and recognized in Babylonia. One tablet read, "… a lamb has been placed in his hand, opposite him…the lamb, the *substitute for mankind*, he has offered the lamb for his life." (88) This is well connected to the mythographers version of the Golden Fleece stolen by Jason and the Argonauts after many adventures. The Golden Fleece came from a wonderful Ram that rescued two children from certain death from a sacrificial altar. The Ram was sent by Hermes. The boy the Ram had saved then was sacrificed by him and its fleece removed, giving it to King Aetes, the father of Jason who had been sent away and was the rightful heir to the kingdom. When he was grown he searched for this fleece after reclaiming his kingdom. (89) Aries typifies the fleece or lamb's skin from the Golden Ram designed to protect mankind, a garment that hung upon a tree guarded by a terrible serpent. (90) This is the same as the Greek myths of the aegis used by Zeus and other divinities as a shield. This aegis was a goatskin that was given to Adam in Eden to cover his body after he realized he was naked, a skin coming from an animal God killed [act of atonement]. Later according to Hebraic records like Jasher the skin was stolen by one of Noah's sons from off the Ark and ended up in Nimrod's hands who wore it and became a Mighty Huner remembered as Uz, AMAR.UDA.AK, Sargon and several other epithets.

Aries was frequently depicted with a triangle over its head that was supposed to embody the name of God. (91) God has remained invisible behind many historic epithets, one being the *Lamb*. In Hebrew Aries is Taleh, or "…the Lamb." Aries was anciently the Lamb of God when the sun transited during the equinox under this sign, addressed in old litanies as the "…lamb that taketh away the sin of the world." (92) The association is traced back to Akkadian times where we learn that Aries then was called Baraziggar, which is a compound of two words meaning *altar* and *to make right*. (93) To Kabbalists Aries represents the First Divine Word (94) and this sign to mystics and esotericists was that of preparation, prophecy, sacrifice and atonement *in the beginning*; signifying the Fall of Man, emergence of evil through lust [the goat] and God's plan to redeem mankind at a great price [Crucifixion].

This is merely a fraction of the secrets conveyed by the Zodiac, mysteries that exponentially increase with each sign we review. Aristotle understood this perfectly, writing in *Metaphysics* "…everyone has something to say about nature; and though one person's individual contribution is of little or no account, from all of our joint contributions something substantial emerges," (95) and in *Logic* he wrote that individual words or ideas often reveal little or nothing, "…but it is through their combination with one another that a statement comes into being." (96) Aristotle was on the mark for this seems to be an underlying fact not only with this archive, but this entire book.

Taurus the Bull of the Earth Domain [planet: Venus]

The mythographers could not cover the import of the bull-motif and adopted the symbol for this quadrant of heaven for Taurus. Here also is the first of the Four Royal Stars marking the four corners of heaven, called Al Debiran, which is Taurus' right eye. The meaning of Al Debiran [holy place, from *debir*] identifies this area as sacred in the Astro-Theology; the seat of the bull-faced cherub at the foot of the Throne of God.

Taurus is made famous by the presence of the Pleiades, six stars that somewhat resemble the seven stars of Arktos. The principle stars of the Pleiades are Maya, Atlas, Alcyone and Electra. (97) Alcyone in Euphratean astronomy was called the Star of the Foundation. (98) The Greeks held that there were originally seven stars but the Seven Kings [Arktos: Ursa Major] kidnapped one of them named Electra. (99) This tradition is the origin of the current catastrophist theory of a kidnapped planet in our solar system where the asteroid belt lies that they call Electra. The presence of the Pleiades on the ecliptic in the Zodiac and their similarity to the Great Bear [Arktos: Big Dipper] is what led to these six stars becoming an adequate replacement to the Seven Kings. (100) The cataclysm led to the fall of the Dragon and the Seven Kings [stars] no longer revolved around themselves but collectively began rotating around a new pole star. The mythos served to change polar time-keeping to ecliptic *solar* reckoning and the Pleiades were venerated, replacing the Arktos circumpolar stars. As earth and the sun are early on depicted as a ship adrift through the abyss from sign to sign we find it appropriate that the Pleiades derives from the root meaning "to sail." (101) Ancient Mexican traditions held that it was the Pleiades that were connected to the Flood and that these stars would indicate the next world catastrophe. (102) It was during this past event that we suffered a poleshift.

The Taurus star-group is also renowned for its proximity to Orion, the Hunter. It has been noted that Orion may be a variant of Osiris derived itself from os and iri, or Many Eyed (103) according to Plutarch. A Watcher. On Orion's shoulder is one of the brightest stars in the sky, called Betelgeuse, a star 17,000 times brighter than our own sun. (104) The belt stars of Orion are famous for the theory that the Giza complex design of the placement of the three greatest pyramids was *intended* to mimic these three stars, called Rigel, Saiph and Alnitak. Curiously these three stars in Christian times were associated to the three Persian Magi that sought Christ. (105) Orion was the Elder Traditions' messianic constellation, which is why the mythographers affixed relationships between this system and the stories of local deities and heroes.

Also in Taurus are lesser constellations often overshadowed by the presence of Orion and the Pleiades. These are Auriga and Columba, the stable and the dove. The latter is a visual image of the Holy Spirit's purity and the stable is a prophetic reference to the Mansions of the Redeemed who will be fed by the Shepherd in His pasture [New Earth]. The stable was cleverly used by the mythographers as a Labor of Hercules, whose punishment was that he was to clean the impossibly-fouled stables of King Aegeus.

In the Kabbalah Taurus was when God said "...It is good," referring to earth's infancy and restoration in Genesis 1 144 years prior to start of Annus Mundi and Hebraic chronologies. As the second sign Taurus embodies the concept of two becoming one, as a man and a woman. Thus this sign is of procreation, and the bull was a symbol of servitude (106). It was also a popular symbol of fertility, of husbandry, identifying a time when man was starting to multiply on earth, working the fields for sustenance, after God commanded humanity to "...multiply, be fruitful and replenish the earth." The planet Venus' association to this sign infers that it was man's responsibility to fill the earth again for Venus means *newcomer*, and this newcomer [mankind] was to replace the lost positions of the angelic orders.

Gemini the Twins of the Air Domain [planet: Mercury]

The myth of Jason and his 50 companions called Argonauts sailing [Pleiades] through the Zodiac searching for the Golden Fleece [Golden Age of Man's start in Aries] preserves many scattered motifs formerly lost to historians. The connection to sailing through the oceanic abyss of space around the sun is a reference to the early depictions of planets as ships, the ship's mast being a *pillar* [axis] that connects earth to heaven. Jason piloted the Argo [earth] with its 50 companions, said occupants actually being 50 time periods that the Argo would be in motion *led by Jason*, who is called in Hesiod's *Theogany* as the Shepherd of the Folk. These are 50-year periods, or Jubilees. Jason is merely a variant of Jah-son, or Yahso, the Savior and Healer. The Argo was a boat-shaped vessel that contained something important to the pilot [Savior], argo deriving from argha, a cognate of ark or arc. (107) This is like the ark of Noah, preserving humanity, and the ark of the covenant, preserving the stone tables of the Law that foreshadowed the salvation of man. In Latin arceo means "…to protect, prevent," as in the Egyptian arkai [as in ARK-tos] which means *to appoint a limit, fix a decree."* (108) This is the origin of the Greek Archon, a wandering planetary deity that travels the same path as the sun. The root arc in Indo-Aryan means Protector. Interestingly, directly opposing Gemini on the Zodiacal circle is ARC-turus [a gathering together]. (109) Of course, Jason is not God's true name, for the name of the Almighty is concealed in the word *ARCanum* [Protected Name]. This is arc and inum, protected name. The Sumerians held that a god's word was equivalent to the god himself; it was the INEM, the potent name of God. To them the INIM [Word] was the foundation of the creative form. (110)

The ancients held that the mast of the terrestrial ship was a *mountain*, as in Mount Meru of the Hindus which was the mast of the ship of the gods. A mast is a *pillar* with sails [garments] that without them the *ship cannot move*. The ship's locomotion comes from the power of *wind* [spirit] and the ability of the sails [human spiritual garments] to contain these winds. This is reminiscent of why the Sumerians called the High God Enlil by the description of *Lord Wind*. The pillar and mountain symbolism are expounded upon in great detail in *Lost Scriptures of Giza* showing that the two symbols were covered in *knowledges* that were only useful to those seeking a new garment [sail: resurrected glorified body] just as Jason and the Argonauts sought to find the treasured fleece [atoning garment of the forgiveness of sin]. This new garment would give them divine wisdom and information impossible to understand unless the Spirit [Wind] aids one in their sojourning.

The ultimate architectural preflood artifact from the Old World encompassing this lost theology is the Great Pyramid which was long ago covered in millions of tiny white writings. Mount Meru of olden India was the center of the universe just as Giza is the middle of earth's land masses. Maru in Japanese also means protective circle, enclosure (111) reminding us of Eden, and Maru is found in many Japanese ship names. Maru preserves a syllable of great antiquity [MER] which happens to be found in the planet assigned to this sign: MERcury, a planet regarded as a *messenger* of the gods, of knowledges and learning. It also happens to be the Egyptian designation for *pyramid*: MER. In Vedic literature there was an elixir that gave immortality upon the summit of Mount Meru protected by gods in the forms of evil monsters [zodiacal signs]. Indra [covered in garment with many eyes] succeeds in stealing the draught but is attacked by the Archer Krisannau. (112) This exhibits evidence that Gemini truly represents Mount Meru for the Archer here is none other than Gemini's sign in opposition across the Zodiac: Sagittarius the Archer. This same mountain was called *Saphon* in the Ugaritic texts of 2nd millennium BC Canaan (113), which derived from a root [saph] that means *gate, threshold*, and originally having the sense of *holding something*; from an older root connoting *punishment*. But these ideas and concepts were already exhausted in *Lost Scriptures*.

The affinity of this sign to the Great Pyramid is even more stunning. The Argo ship of the Grecian stories is the same as the bark of Rama in Hindu Ramayana text, and upon the brow of this vessel was a *swastika*. (114) The swastika is indicative of something greater to come. In Japanese this symbol stood for the "Ten Thousand Truths," and was universal throughout the early world placed upon doors, above gateways and entrances to walled areas and *gardens*. (115) This is similar to Giza, the Door or Gate to the Godhead inscribed upon its faces with tens of thousands of truths that taught mankind how to get back to the garden of Eden. Incredibly, a swastika was also upon the Chariot of Agni (116) which is merely a rendition of the Argo. Recall that Agni was an altar that had 10,800 bricks with the 10,800 Vedic scriptures upon them; Vedic memory of the Great Pyramid.

While Gemini has proven to be a most esoteric study we are not finished. Two of the principle passengers on the Argo were Castor and Pollux, the archetypal Twins of world mythology. Castor and Pollux were said to live half their lives on earth and half in heaven, and they were the special protectors of sailors. This astronomically concerns their disappearance over the horizon and use as navigational stars. But their identity as protectors of sailors may have been the inspiration for the name of the ship that took Paul to Rome according to the biblical book of Acts, which was called *Castor and Pollux*, a vessel that picked up Paul and the other sailors and prisoners after they shipwrecked on Malta. (117)

Castor and Pollux typify good and evil, further remembered as Jacob and Esau, Cain and Abel, the Chinese Oph and Shichim, Christa and Balarma of India, Sut and Horus, Hercules and Iolaus, Gilgamesh and Enkidu and these last two pairs preserved many particularly early Gemini-related concepts. They are Tammuz and Ningishzida of Sumer and Otus and Ephialtes of early Grecian tales. Tammuz and Ningishzida were guardians of the portal of the Heavens (118). Sometimes Ningishzida is found in an abbreviated form as Gishzida and in *Lost Scriptures* we learn that this title means Lord of the Artifact/Tree of Life. In the oldest Graeco-Aegean stories Otus and Ephialtes are described as the largest giants ever. Their history very subtly alludes to the secret of Gemini. They were accused of attempting to destroy the high heavens and claimed that they were superior to the gods. This tradition is an archaic explanation concerning the twin poles, North and South, which were thought to be good [north] and evil [south pole below equator]. These poles [giants] moved the heavens [poleshift] and shoved the planets over the horizon violently [poleshift occurred at night from Grecian perspective]. The Twins ceased warring against heaven, went hunting and both threw javelins at their unseen prey after they had separated during the chase. Javalins are *axis* symbols, and predictably, the poleshift [war against heaven] ceased once the javelins of the two passed into each other killing them [stabilizing the axis].

Though on the surface it appears strange that our predecessors regarded Castor and Pollux as the patron gods of *horsemen* (119) once we behold its sign in opposition across the Zodiac, Sagittarius the Horse-Archer, we understand. We are reminded here of a sage comment of Neitzsche when we remember how holy the Archer-motif was to our ancestors, a virtual messianic figure who only later turned horridly evil, a Hunter of men: "What a time experiences as evil is usually an untimely echo of what was formerly experienced as good-the atavism of a more ancient ideal." (120)

Castor and Pollux, at least their ideological concepts, were known to the Persians in the Zend-Avesta text as Akam-mano [Evil Mind] and Vohu-mano [Good Mind], the two moving causes in the Universe from the beginning. (121) American Indian stories tell of the Twins, one being evil and the other good (122) and the Gemini sign in China was represented by the Tiger whose stripes were types of good and evil.

Castor and Pollux join us on our journey through life discovering Good and Evil, for it requires *knowledge* to exercise discretion because good and evil, contrary to popular religiosity, are *not* absolutes. There are degrees of good and evil and even exigencies where one action deemed evil would be good in other circumstances. It is religion and its creeds hammered in stone by men and not God that has obscured this ancient fundamental axiom. It is with Castor and Pollux, the chief stars of Gemini as our shipmates, guided by Jason [Savior] that we are made to understand the curious dichotomy of the mystery of the necessity of evil in the maturity of good. (123) In Gemini we come to discern Euripides' statement that "...never is the good separated from the evil; there must be a mixture of the one and the other." (124) Thus with Taurus into Gemini did the Savior of humanity commit the ultimate sacrifice [Aries]: He left Paradise that men might gain *knowledge* [Gemini]. The dual nature of mankind is good and evil—and remember, *both* were already in existence in Eden in the Tree of Knowledge of Good and Evil.

Glyphically Gemini is of two pillars unified into one: II. The Egyptian Copts called Gemini Pi-Mahi, "The United," which is exactly what this sign is called in Hebrew; Thaumin [united]. (125) The Twins of Sumer were collectively called the MASH.TAB.BA (126), the original description of the later words that in Semitic became pillar [matsebeth] and in Egyptian a stone monument [mastaba]. Esoterically the Solomonic pillars Boaz and Jachin before the door to the Temple in Jerusalem represented the same qualities as those of the archaic Great Pyramid complex's two gigantic pyramids [pillars of brick]; creative and destructive powers of God by water and fire. The connection between Giza and Gemini is Mercury, the god of pillars, buried treasure and the secrets of God *hermetically* sealed [Hermes in Greek Mercury]. Though Gemini seems to identify two pillars they are under this iconographic message *united*, which as the third zodiacal sign is geometrically depicted as △, which as we learned in *Lost Scriptures* is also the Egyptian symbol for Set (127) and the symbol for a *door* or *gate*. It was the preflood [Set]hites who constructed the Great Pyramid complex at Giza.

The Great Pyramid was also described as the tomb of Adam, and arca in Latin is tomb. It was built to be an altar [veda] at the middle of the earth mentioned by Isaiah the prophet as standing in Egypt. Adam was promised by God an altar on earth for mankind, and amazingly, the gematria for the word *altar* is 864. This is the *foundation* number seen earlier in this work as the link between the NER [600] and the Cursed Earth [414] dating methods that both synchronized 144 years before humanity's exile from paradise. According to John Michell in his *Dimensions of Paradise* the number 864 esoterically identifies the Rock located at the center of earth that holds down the waters of the Abyss as a cornerstone or Altar. (128) The 144 is no doubt an allusion to the 144,000 casing blocks originally adorning the Giza pyramid.

The Rock [typification of the Savior] is permanent but when the waters of chaos rise up and overcome it the Rock in mystical symbolism morphs into that of an *ark*, which phonetically is an abbreviated rock [the r and k] prefixed with a vowel [a]. Rock and ark are nearly alphabetically identical. They are

One, each preserving divine elements of a former world to a newer civilization after a global ruin: the Ark saves life while the Rock saves *knowledge* of good and evil. The ark is made of the wood of trees while the Rock is a pillar [pyramid] associated in all world mythology as the World Tree and Tree of Life. The Great Pyramid is truly a message to mankind from the mind of God.

Cancer the Crab of the Water Domain [planet: Moon]

This is the fourth sign of the Zodiac, a number corresponding to the number for the *earth* which is further shown by its simple geometry of □. The square has long been the form of the concept of the world. This sign in Latin is called Cancer, meaning "to encircle; holding," and in Arabic the sign is called Al Sartan [He who holds/binds], which derived from the word *to bind together*. The basic idea of Cancer is that of *confinement*, a prison associated to the earth itself and the square is the symbol for the *foundation stone* that covers the Deep where abide those that were imprisoned by the Almighty for their insurrection, a symbolic theology conveyed by the layout of the Giza plateau.

Cancer is in essence a warning of the fate of the Anunnaki, a sign of future imprisonment and evil. The ancients identified it as a crab because it is a sign of the water domain and the creature is known for its ability to grab and hold on to victims with its pincers. Mystics have long thought the crab, being essentially nocturnal, was a lunar animal (129), hence its placement as Cancer which is ruled by the Moon. The shell of the Crab typifies the hard foundation stone that keeps the tides from rising against humanity as the Chaos grows by the passage of time. Its link to the Anunnaki [Watchers] seems to have been the reason why the Chinese represented this sign as the Cat, which to them was a bad omen closely likened to that of the serpent. The Cat is known also for its penetrating and large eyes [a Watcher sign] and ability to escape judgment [nine lives concept].

This sign is evil when conveyed as covering the Deep with a Stone, but it is a good sign when represented instead as a foundation stone that supports the heaven [a circle]. Cancer very mystically embodies the concept of circling the square, to the unification of heaven [circle] and earth [the square]. This sign identifies mankind while under the curse of rebellion [begun by the Anunnaki] and sin, under the artificial light of the moon, a *borrowed* power [that empowered the Anunnaki] that exercises dominion over the seas [chaos] just as the Adversary ruled mankind only by the true powers given to him by the Godhead.

In Cancer begins the darkly infamous Ursa Major constellation, or Seven Kings. Could it be divine metaphor that these Seven Stars begin under the influence of the sign designed originally to warn of the future imprisonment, and that these kings ruled anciently and will do so again in the Apocalypse over mankind [earth], humanity being represented by the Argo constellation also in Cancer? That the Seven Kings rule over earth is shown in the lesser constellations of the Cancer regions, for the ship Argo not only identifies Earth on its journey around the Zodiac but it means "...a company of travelers," (130) otherwise known as *mankind*.

Leo the Lion of the Fire Domain [planet: Sun]

Of all the constellations venerated before the Flood, Leo played most prominently as a sign of the Apocalypse, home sign of the Sumerian AR UB. As the fifth sign of the Record of Heaven Leo is geometrically depicted as the AR UB [pentagram]. Herein we discover the second Royal Star marking a corner of heaven, called Regulus, the King Star. This bright star is nearly on the ecliptic and has participated in a series of fascinating stellar-planetary conjuncts the year before and the year of Christ's birth. These conjuncts are a subject depicted in a later archive. In Leo also is the messianic star Denebola, or the *Judge*. (131)

The Judge star is consistent with what we discovered earlier in this thesis concerning the AR UB being the Sumerian symbol for judgment. The Chinese were aware of this concept for the cross symbol was associated by them to the number *five*, (132) which is unexplainable unless we view the cross glyph three-dimensionally.

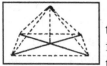 That Leo was anciently the Lion-faced Watcher of the second quadrant of heaven identified with the symbol for judgment is clearly seen in the lesser constellations of the region of Leo. Even in Vedic writings the lion was a instrument for punishment from God. (133) The mythographers did this sign injustice in assigning the meaning of Ursa Major [Great Bear/Big Dipper/ Arktos] the image of a large bear. And it is the Vedic writings and studies of late historians and translators that clarify how this came to be. It has become apparent that the Seven Stars that are called the Rishis [Sages/Kings] of Ursa Major were originally *AR-ishas*, an initial vowel having been worn off either by deceit or time. The idea of this prominent circumpolar star-group was not of a bear at all, but of the *ploughing of the dawn*. (134) Even in the Latin word ursa [bear] we discover it more properly resolved as ur se, or *fire light*. Even today in Great Britain Ursa Major is called the Plough (135) and no traces of

a bear are to be found in the older Chaldean, Egyptian, Persian and Indian Zodiacs. (136)

This sign was not only primordially known as the Plough [a sign of judgment] but also as the *Sheepfold*. (137) Ursa Major, also known as Arktos was additionally known as the flock, which conveys the same meaning as the Sheepfold. In fact, one of the main stars in Ursa Major is Merach, or the *flock*. (138) The Sumerian version of the Plough [version actually being the original] sign is that of a judgment from the sky to the earth [comet] which is what appears to have been remembered vaguely by the Scythians in the days of Herodotus four centuries BC who recorded that these northern peoples thought that a yoke [of Taurus the Bull] fell from the sky. They also recalled that a Plough was in the sky. The Scythians believed that long ago a Plough, a yoke, a battleaxe and a gold cup fell from the sky and caught fire which was interpreted by them to be a sign from God. (139) These symbols are amazingly connected to the Zodiac. The yoke and plough are obvious, but what's more difficult to recognize is the battleaxe, which is the famous Labrys, or Thunderbolt symbol (INSERT K first symbol on far right) and the cup is a reference to Crater, the Cup constellation often called by our ancestors as the Bowl of Wrath over the Serpent in Leo, a lesser constellation. (140)

The Bowl icon leads us to a stunning observation that invokes apocalyptic imagery of the Bowls [ofen called Vials] of Wrath poured out by the Watchers of Heaven over the earth in the last Seven Plagues in Revelation, and in the Zodiac this is conveyed by the presence of the Cup constellation over Hydra, the *five*-headed serpent *under* Leo comprised of *60 stars*. Hydra means *sea serpent*. (141) This may be why the Chinese identified this sign of judgment as the Dragon constellation, the enemy of the Tiger [Gemini]. (142)

Leo conveys to us that *fire* is coming, a dual message for good and evil. The wicked can expect the fires of judgment to consume them and this world they loved and used to their every advantage while the righteous look forward to the spiritual fires of purification that will transform their earthly ore to divine metals. The Plough of God will come and collide with the Earth when the time comes to renew His garden and planet new seed during the Apocalyptic final years of this Age. This Harvest will be the shortest but the most fruitful before Earth is bathed completely in flames before the planet plunges straight into the molten surface of the sun [typologically returning to God].

The Seven Stars of Arktos were supposed to teach mankind these knowledges, for they were "...foretellers of future events," (143) but instead they decided to rule over mankind by the power of their knowledge and later mythographers completed their work by disguising the Record of Heaven behind fantastic fables and lore. Leo as the fifth sign looks toward the *end*, and the archaic symbol astrologers of old assigned to Leo (INSERT modern Leo SYMBOL) is merely a variant of the actual glyph, once universal, that represents the *end*, preserved in the Greek alphabet as Omega [End] Ω, the final letter and opposite of Alpha [the beginning].

Virgo the Virgin of the Earth Domain [planet: Venus]

Though the mythographers largely confused this sign as representing the goddess motif this is far from what it was originally designed to convey. As residing in the Earth Domain it identifies *mankind*, which interestingly is also connected to the Chinese sign of Virgo, which was the Serpent, the symbol in China for the *earth*. To them it was a good sign of resurrection and renewal typified by the molting of the snake in its generation of a new skin. Further linking this symbol to man is that it is the *sixth* sign, humanity having been created on the sixth day.

As the sixth sign Virgo identifies mankind as the unification of the male $\triangle$ and the female ∇ in the symbol for mankind far more ancient than the Star of David ✡, a borrowed emblem. This simple geometry is revealing, but when we view the number six three-dimensionally we unveil the secretive meaning of this sign and its relation to Giza. Note that the very first numerical form that can be three-dimensionally perceived in this thesis is the AR UB, which forms a *pyramid* with four cornerstones and an apex making five points. But this sign as the sixth does not construct to a shape as a pyramid, but merely *one stone* among the many that form a pyramid. The cube ❑ is the three-dimensional form of *six*, like a dice. Because Virgo concerns man in the plural sense then we are confronted with *many* stones:

The link between the idea of people associated to stones and building blocks is a subject covered in *Lost Scriptures*, tradition very clearly evident in the Grecian myths of Deucalion who survived the Flood and planted *stones* in the ground to grow a new human race after the catastrophe. (144)

The Virgo sign to early Christian mystics was emblematic of the soul ready to receive God (145) and the idea behind this symbolism is of humanity being the Bride of God. Because a third of His hosts rebelled and fell man waits for the time when they will be adopted as sons and inherit their former estates. After the Resurrection the elect and redeemed will *marry* God, becoming a part of His family, becoming Sons of the Living God. Both the earth and humanity are often in prophetic literature described collectively as a Woman, and in the beginning of humanity we were made from the *dust* of the earth, a textual clue in Genesis affirming that Earth was already old but mankind was newly created upon it. As Virgo this sign concerns only those who have not committed whoredom with false gods, those having not stained their garments with the vice of this world. Virgo depicts the *holy* seed of humanity as opposed to those led by the Harlot upon the Beast. Ruled by Mercury, Virgo commemorates those who have *received* the divine messages of God and secured salvation.

Libra the Balances of the Air Domain [planet: Venus]

The Balances are Scales known throughout the entire world of old because of their necessity in commerce. They were also religiously employed as symbolic of divine arbitration. In Babylonian times Libra was the time when souls were weighed in the balances, a time for a solemn feast. (146) The Jewish traditions of the Scales of Judgment are believed by some scholars to be derived from Zoroastrian doctrines. (147) Those who have passed on in the Egyptian Book of the Dead also find themselves confronted with divine scales. Further, in the Book of Enoch we read, "I saw all the secrets of the heavens, and how the kingdom is divided and how the actions of men are *weighed in the balance*...and there my eyes beheld the sinners, who denied the Lord of Glory, and whom they [angels] were expelling from thence, and dragging away." (148) The Egyptian designation for Libra was Khi-Ath, or Judge of the Hearts. (149)

The biblical records also preserve this concept. In the book of Job, a man thought by many to have lived as far back as Sumerian times, wrote, "Let me be weighed in an even balance that God may know mine integrity." (150) Proverbs declares "All the ways of a man are clean in his own eyes; but the Lord weigheth the spirits," (151) and the Psalmist wrote that all men are "... to be laid in the balance." (152)

Libra is the only sign not depicted anthropomorphically, but its visage still retains basically what it was intended to convey: divine judgment with absolute *fairness*. The Scales are a fitting symbol for the time of the year important to the ancient timekeepers when day and night were of equal length, called the autumnal equinox. The light and darkness was *balanced*. As the seventh sign it carries the connotation of perfection on earth, and in this instance, perfect judgment. In Hebrew seven is schiba, signifying the fullness of time, which is etymologically akin to the Indian shiva and the number seven in Persian, Saxon, Syrian, Arabic, Phoenician and Chaldean. (153) As the seventh month Libra is the Sabbath Sign and the Israelites celebrated the seventh month as a memorial time and the tenth day of this month was a Day of Atonement. (154) Its relation to the planet Venus reveals that the Scales of Justice will admit *newcomers* into the Kingdom of God, this kingdom typologically found within the image of the Great Pyramid's dimensions.

Libra is truly a Gizean-zodiacal mystery. In *Lost Scriptures* we learned how the Great Pyramid's measurements align perfectly with that of a seven-pointed star, a *heptagram* that produces the elusive 52° angle also found in the exterior slopes and interior angles of the pyramid's facing and passages. The connection between this sign, the Scales, and judgment, is made more profound because this sign literally means *book* [libra] and the Great Pyramid as extensively shown in *Lost Scriptures* was regarded long ago as the *largest book in the world* covered in millions of tiny inscriptions that were defaced when engineers removed the white limestone casing blocks for building materials. The Great Pyramid's dimension's being a gigantic architectural symbol conveying arcane mysteries has probably always been suspected, as Maurice Maeterlinck in 1922 wrote when he stated that "...it is an undoubted fact that the Great Pyramid of Cheops, for example, is a sort of stupendous hieroglyph, which, by its dimensions, its proportions, its internal arrangements, and its astronomical orientation, propounds a whole series of riddles of which only the most obvious have been hitherto been deciphered." (155)

In the Bible we read of visions had by holy men where the Ancient of Days is seen sitting upon a throne while the holy angels search the books kept in heaven for the name of whoever stands before the throne of God. Jewish Midrashic traditions also affirm that books of records of people's lives will be weighed in the scales during the judgment (156) and Islamic beliefs are virtually identical. Libra essentially links the number seven to the concept of divine judgment.

Scorpio the Scorpion of the Water Domain [planet: Mars] (Anciently the Eagle Constellation)

Scorpio has been badly altered by the early priesthoods, only its negative aspects remaining preserved. In Scorpio is the third Royal Star and foundation of heaven, Antares, a bright red star. It has come to be called the Scorpion's Heart and due to its red color Antares has been translated by some as the other Mars, a red planet, (157) and as *Antarus* (158) it may mean "against Taurus." Taurus and Scorpio are signs in direct opposition on the circle of the Zodiac.

The creation of a scorpion being in the Record of Heaven where no scorpion had formerly been may have derived from a desire of the archaic astromancers to include some visual reference to the Anunnaki which in the Babylonian Enuma Elish tablets, Epic of Gilgamesh and several other Akkadian-Babylonian writings and even in the Book of Revelation all have physical descriptions associating these evil beings to *scorpions*. The sign's link to malady and evil is found in that the Sumerians thought it represented the Lawless One and even the Maya called it the sign of the Death God. (159) In the Zodiac of Denderah at Egypt is a monstrous creature with a hundred heads, the infamous Typhon of Graeco-Egyptian lore. (160)

Though a scorpion does basically convey the true meaning of this sign it was actually adorned with the image of an Eagle, the third Watcher of the Tetramorph in Heaven. Near Scorpio lies the constellation Aquila [Eagle] inside the Eagle Quadrant of the Zodiac. The difference between the eagle and the scorpion imagery is subtle, for both are potentially violent and laden with negative consequences. Scorpions are carrion creatures thought long ago to be born from the earth, having arisen from the underworld, their stingers like the fiery pains of hell and their pincers assuring that none can escape their power. In Arabic this constellation is called AL Akrab, meaning, "… wounding, conflict and war," and within it the star Isisdis which means "the attack of the Enemy." (161)

The Eagle too promises of war for it was the mascot of many Sumerian and later Euphratean war deities as well as the historic war-emblem of Roman legions and modern United States symbol for national sovereignty. A freedom marked by rebellion and warfare. Ruled by the planet Mars, the god of war, chaos, ruin and death further identifies the concept behind this sign. But the Eagle itself was not evil, for it was long ago the sky-orientated imagery of the Godhead, a symbol of pride and justice. (162)

If this sign as the eight was made into a symbol like this (INFINITY SYMBOL is a 8 on its side) then it would convey the idea of no beginning and no end. Thus the Eagle and Scorpion both embody the promise of a Great War with *eternal* consequences, of men dying on earth and then *again* in the Second Death. Scorpions are synonymous with dragons and dragons are merely glorified *serpents*. This sign hints that God [the Eagle] will defeat the Serpent, which the Eagle proudly carries off in its talons through the air in countless reliefs and effigies in olden art. Be it remembered that Scorpio is the Armageddon sign of the Record of Heaven.

Sagittarius the Archer of the Fire Domain [planet: Jupiter]

As mentioned earlier the only connection still extant between the altered version of this sign created by the mythos [centaur archer] and the true original antediluvian sign is the *arrow* symbol. The Arrow was its earliest form. (163) After the Deluge this constellation was known to have a dual meaning concerning the fate of an evil god but it was unknown exactly what this fate was and they compensated for this lack of knowledge by creating an image of a hybrid mythological creature, a half horse-man holding a bow and arrow which perfectly fit into the Hunter theology but truthfully only served to bury the amazing significance of this sign.

As the ninth sign this is the constellation conveying the *judgment of evil*. Sagittarius is the Lord of the Earth in opposition against the Lord of Heaven. Ruled by Jupiter we envision a god of earth sitting upon an artificial throne as an artificial messiah with a *bow* upon a horse riding toward apocalypse just as Revelation 6 begins with a false Christ going forth to conquer. Sagittarius is the rider and warhorse *combined*, the horse a fitting symbol of warfare and coming destruction. He will be met in his end by the power of God which is alluded to in the Babylonian name of this sign: Ka-sil, or "opening of the earth," (164), a phenomenon that occurred in the Bible when rebellious people were swallowed by the earth itself as in Korah's rebellion against Moses and especially when the asteroid impact created a hole in earth's surface causing the Great Flood. As a resident of the Fire Domain with Leo we see this being a continuation of the symbolism of the AR UB, which is the plough of God that will smite the earth causing "...earth to go up." As we will see, Sagittarius is very closely related to *cataclysm*. The truth is that the glyphic representation assigned to Sagittarius only ornamentally appears like an arrow but in reality it is not an arrow at all. This symbol is rather scientific, which is to be expected of the antediluvian builders of the Giza Complex, and the symbol of Sagittarius INSERT SYMBOL is that of a cross [of the Zodiac] and that of an *axis pillar* with a *fire glyph* atop it ∧. Further, this symbol is always depicted on ancient and modern Zodiacs as *tilted*, which was done to convey that earth's axis was tilted in a cataclysm. A traditional bow and arrow symbol was very easily manipulated into the Hunter mythos but it is far from its original meaning.

This startling revelation is not without historical verification. An early Chinese practice employed by astrologers was to shoot arrows into the sky when troubled by the prospect of a storm or catastrophe. In an effort to drive away demons they would shoot arrows into *four directions*. (165) This practice was recorded by Herodotus as well who wrote that the Thracians "...will during a thunderstorm, shoot arrows into the sky, and utter threats against the Lord of the lightning and the thunder, because they recognize no god but their own. (166) In the Aegean world a man crowned king had to prove his kingship by first shooting an arrow into all four cardinal directions, then shooting a *fifth* arrow into the sky before performing mock battles with opponents in beastly disguises. (167) The theory behind these practices was that if men could not protect the people from calamity then he was unfit for rulership. Interestingly, if the trajectory of these arrows were traced then a pyramid would emerge:

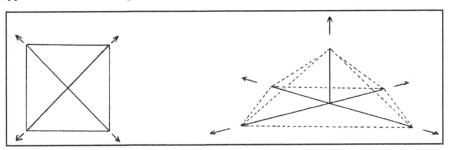

Arrow oracles and divination is called axinomancy and has been found as far from the Near East as ancient America. Thunderstorms were thought to be celestial wars fought in heaven and Native Americans often engaged in archery at the skies to aid God so the world would not be affected by the evil adversaries. (168) The Namaqua Indians, Koi-koi and Damaras all shot arrows into the air whenever lightning flashes, seeking to vanquish it. (169) The arrow symbol identifies the earth's axis which the ancients feared would move again in a devastating poleshit, a concept secretly embedded in the Greek architectural mysteries of pillars adorned with centaurs above their capitals holding bows and arrows. The pillar itself is a symbol of that which supports something else, in this case it is the world being supported. This is further alluded to in the American traditions of the Maya of the Hero Twins and their Triumph over Seven Macah [Ursa Major], which mythologically recalls a poleshift from the polar regions of old [ARKtos] to away from the Seven Stars [Seven Macah] to Polaris. The Hero Twins, also immortalized as Gemini are actually the personified north and south *poles*. The earth's axis has a northern and southern extension into the heavens and when earth stabilized early men interpreted this as a sign of the victory of the Hero Twins over whatever phenomena led to their temporary fall. Because the world could turn and change the scenery of heaven, an event long associated to falling stars, earthquakes and other disturbances in nature, the nations of antiquity aid their gods by shooting arrows into the sky when threats emerged. Herodotus wrote that the Carians "...put on their armor and went as far as the boundary of Calynda, striking the air with their spears and saying that they were driving out foreign gods." (170)

In sum, Sagittarius is a *broken Gemini*, the sign in opposition to it across the sphere of the Zodiac. Gemini alludes to the Great Pyramid, a gigantic *pillar* at the middle of the earth [axis motif] that itself conveys the message of future and past poleshifts that was very long ago called an Altar on earth, one that was attached to traditions of a future cataclysm involving terrestrial fire. Incidentally, in the sign of Sagittarius is also found the Ara constellation, known as the Altar, a group of *nine stars* that to the Greeks connoted ruin and destruction. (171) Another little known fact is that one of the stars of Sagittarius identifies itself as being in the Eagle Quadrant of heaven, for it is Shelyuk, the Eagle Star. (172) Further connecting Sagittarius to this sign in opposition [Gemini] is that the Chinese image of this sign was the Ape, that to them was a *messenger* of the gods and incarnation of the god Thoth [Egyptian Enoch], the messenger of the gods being the officially recognized office of Mercury, the ruling planet over Gemini.

Capricorn of the Earth Domain [planet: Saturn] (Horn of Plenty)

This sign has been covered earlier as to how the mythographers altered its meaning into a hybrid interpretation of the Horn of Plenty on one side and the Sea Goat on the other. This is actually the Zodiacal sign of *inheritances*. The redeemed and faithful will receive divine blessings, all that the earth produces [horn of plenty] while the wicked receive the same lot as their master, depicted here as a half goat/half fish creature.

This sign is ruled by Saturn, planet of misfortune and secrecy, this orb's alchemical metal is *lead* which symbolizes darkness and sin. (173) The goat is the Adversary, the Scapegoat the mythographers also assigned as Aries. The fish is an arcane symbol of the Deep and the merging of the goat and fish reveals that the Adversary's *end* [tail of fish] will be in the Abyss, the blackness of ruin being his inheritance. The goat is also the satyr, an anthropomorphical hybrid representation of Satan.

Aquarius the Water-Bearer of the Air Domain [planet: Saturn]

In this sign is the fourth and final of the Four Royal Stars, named Fomalhaut in the Quadrant of Man. The presence of Aquarius in the Man Quadrant is why the mythographers later personified this sign into the Waterbearer. This sign completes the cosmic Sphinx that identifies the Four Holy Watchers that guard the throne of God in the heavens, a symbol made of stone at Giza that lies 240 ft. long and 66 ft. high of solid rock. It was anciently a representation of the bull, lion, eagle and man, possibly originally painted with eyes all over its body. This was no mystery to the Greek architects who cleverly hid zodiacal crosses [like that of Sagittarius] like this beneath the feet of Sphinx pictures and statuary. (174) This symbol represents the entire Zodiac and the Four Corners of Heaven concept. One of the strangest and most baffling sites it has been found at is called New Grange 26 miles north of Dublin, Ireland at the site of a famous passage grave. It appears 8 times in a row over the megalithic entrance to the passage. (175).

Aquarius conveyed not merely the *prima materia* [origin of world from water] (176) but also that of the Great Flood to the Babylonians. (177) As the eleventh sign it embodies the idea of disorder and chaos, like the 11 different types of monsters in the armies of Chaos Dragon Tiamat mentioned in the Enuma Elish. As the second to last sign in the stellar records it serves as a perfect reminder to humanity of the last days and that the *days of Noah* will soon come upon us as well just as Christ foretold. These times were characterized by the emergence of increased knowledge, the return of the Anunnaki, cometary passage, cataclysm, flooding and poleshift and all those misfortunate things concealed within the secret symbolism of Saturn.

The modern depictions of Aquarius are of two stylized jagged lines forming glyphs for water, astonishing for the sign has changed very little from Sumerian times of 4000 years ago and possibly earlier, which showed the sign for *water* as two stylized jagged lines. (178) One line appearing like water would have been sufficient, like that of the Egyptian pictographic word for water which is a wavy line, but *two* lines were actually necessary to convey that the water of the *firmament above* [former marine atmospheric canopy] and firmament below [oceans/seas] were the cause of the Flood.

Aquarius truly exhibits the earth [and mankind by extension] baptized in the waters of affliction.

Pisces the Fish of the Water Domain [planet: Jupiter]

Pisces is not a fish, this image being conjured by the mythos-creators due to the high antiquity of this symbol, the sign's assignment in the Water Domain in proximity to Aquarius and the fact that this area of the ancient heavens was associated to the Cord. (179) Two fish were usually depicted, a perfect way to divert attention away from the true meaning of this sign for these fish were connected by the Cord. The Cord is associated to the architectural tools like the plumbline and is a symbol for the *axis*. The Cord is presently bent [just like the earth's axis is tilted] but in the future the Cord will be upright and restored to its original position.

Pisces is the last sign in the Record of Heaven and the end of Jason's journey on the Argo and as the 12th sign it is the *testimony* of the 12 signs put together. The 12 apostles were called together to testify of the One; 12 stones of the Urim and Thummim did testify of God's will to men; 12 Tribes united made one nation of Israel and the 12 signs complete the circle of the heavens guarded over by the Four Holy Watchers. The Zodiac is completed after 12 signs each being 30° for a full 360°, a sum that in Hebrew has the amazing gematria for the phrase "Head of the Corner." (180) This is absolutely incredible, for as we learned in *Lost Scriptures* the Great Pyramid was never provided a capstone, the monument merely symbolizing the *future* Kingdom of God that would be made complete once the number of positions of the fallen angels were filled by the elect and redeemed from mankind to finish the building with the final 144,000 Tribulation martyrs who would prepare the way in the Last Days for the Coming of the Chief Cornerstone to descend, the *Head of the Corner.*

Because of Pisces' link to a fish early Christians adopted this symbol as a holy sign because Jesus told the disciples to follow Him and He would make them fishers of men. The Christians in early Roman times were called Pisiculi, or Little Fishes, and amazingly the gematrical value for fish in Greek is 153, the same number for Sons of God. (181) As the final stage of the cosmic drama we see how the righteous will replace the fallen sons of God, known as the Anunnaki.

That humanity [typified by Virgo in opposition] becomes glorified and replaces the angels that kept not their first estate is revealed in Pisces by the presence of the Andromeda constellation in this sign, which means *princess.* Andromeda was left chained to a rock to be sacrificed to the Sea Serpent [mankind left to the Dragon] but she is saved by a hero and married him [the Marriage Supper of the Lamb]. This is actually a spiral galaxy and happens to be the most distant object in space that can be seen with the naked eye. (182) It is associated to the Flood stories and intriguingly one of its principle stars is called *Al Anak* [struck down]. (183) Pisces in conjunction with the Andromeda galaxy tells that the Anunnaki fell from heaven [Anak] but are to be replaced with glorified [princess] humanity. That Pisces refers back to the beginning histories is discovered in that Pisces is the last sign in the Record of Heaven that has become the *first* today due to the precession of the equinox which has caused Aries [the first sign] to retrograde back to the position of the second sign. Pisces is the colophonic end of the stellar records that refers back to the beginning. Heraclitus summed it up best when he wrote that "... on the periphery of the circle [zodiac], the beginning and the end are one." (184)

Mystics have long associated Pisces with the symbol of the swastika (185), attributing to it the sign of completion and reward for past labors. This symbol is what *guided* the Argo as Jason led his companions around the Record of Heaven [history of the world] in search of the Golden Fleece [divine atonement]. The fish conjoined with the lamb [Aries] completes the circle and embodies the mystery of the Marriage Supper of the Lamb cited in the book of Revelation. The swastika is an image of health and happiness (186), the eternal *rest* of the redeemed (187) and as a Sanskrit word it has been translated by Max Muller as "…it is well." (188) To the Buddhist the swastika was the actual Key to Paradise. (189)

While the swastika has long been linked to Pisces it is not the sign anciently used to depict this zodiacal sign. The glyph used has appeared variously as (INSERT SYMBOLS W) and never has this symbol referred to a fish. But this sign is itself incomplete until it merges back into the beginning, to Aries, fulfilling the divine motif that the first shall become last and the last first. This symbol is *fallen*, but when set upright as it was originally intended it clearly becomes the ancient symbol of *man* as seen so abundantly in *Lost Scriptures of Giza*. Fittingly, it is also located in the Man Quadrant of Heaven.

Pisces is the testimony of the Pillar between heaven and earth [axis] that was severed by the Anunnaki who caused the cataclysm and how this breach in the heavens as well as the healing of the earth would be performed when heaven and earth were reunited *through mankind* which was the offensive stumbling block that tripped the angels of olden heaven when Azazel told them what he saw in the Tablets of Destinies. Through pride the Anunnaki refused to relent to a lesser creation, humans, and through mankind did God replace them and undo their follies.

The mythographers took this symbol for humanity and weaponized it, making Marduk hold it as if it were a battleaxe, Baal and Zeus holding the Thunderbolt or Labrys and the glyph has been found in the grasp of numerous deities who battled monsters and dragons. It is the ultimate origin of the Trident as a weapon, however, the trident symbol very early on symbolized the concept of the past, the present and the future; threefold element of *time* as found with the Trident of Shiva. (190) Like the Buddhist vajra symbols many are located and stylized above *pillars* which represent esoterically earth's axis. Many of these pillars have trees of life painted or carved upon them. (191) The Egyptian hieroglyph for Meshkenet, the Japanese mother goddess symbol for Kwan-non, the tridents of Siva, Assyrian glyphs of Marduk and the Hopi symbols all convey a formerly popular knowledge that man was the key to the restoration of the cosmos, a fact that offended a third of the hosts of the Anunnaki.

The Pisces symbol is of a pillar severed through the middle identifying a rift between heaven and earth, but when set upright it becomes the glyph used long ago to represent not only mankind, but the Tree of Life.

The three points upward and downward were explained to Enoch when he looked upon the mysteries of heaven and earth. In the Book of Enoch we read that "…three separations have been made between the spirits of the dead, and thus have the spirits of the righteous been separated." (192) The eternal existence of the called, chosen and faithful elect ψ and the enduring punishment of the Anunnaki [evil angels], their Nephilim offspring and wicked men is the knowledge marvelously concealed within the design of the three Great Pyramids of Giza behind the eternal guardian Sphinx, or Watcher of Heaven.

Conclusion to the Gizean Secrets

We have only scratched the surface of the Gizean Secrets of the Zodiac but more is detailed in the Appendix for those seeking a more penetrating glimpse into the zodical Trigon Codes and the Signs in Opposition and the mysteries they conceal. The original Zodiac taught that provision was made for mankind long ago for his redemption; that the earth was destroyed by the overflowing of water and that it would again be bathed in fire after a comet impacts in the last days. Truly is this record of stellar messages a Star Theology that threatened the early cults and priesthoods who could not maintain a rigid control of the populace with such a predetermined future. They introduced a mythos that rendered these ancestral traditions to the stuff of fable and legend and with the obscuring of the future could they then exercise iron fist dominion over the masses and live luxuriously off of the sacrifices and produce of the people wishing to please deities that didn't even exist. The ancient Mysteries and their symbols veiled the Apocalypse in the forms of images whose meanings they closely guarded, for the future of mankind was concealed beneath a drapery of arcane understanding and associations that the uninitiated remain blind to.

Our excursion into the Stellar Mysteries is not complete, for the stars and planets will prove to be a most astounding study in the next archives concerning the Apocalypse and the history, longevity and *end* of the United States of America. Meanwhile we conclude this study with an illustration of the Galactic Pyramid formed by the geometry of the Four Royal Watcher stars of the Zodiac when connected to the polestar, called the Tabernacle of the Sun in the book of the Psalms:

"The heavens declare the glory of God and the firmament showeth His handiwork. Day unto day uttereth speech, and night unto night *showeth knowledge*...their line [axis] is gone out through all the earth...in them hath He set a Tabernacle for the Sun." (193)

Archive IV

The Anunnaki Chronology

That there was a definitive Anunnaki timeline demonstrative in antiquity has been shown in the first two archives of this work. We have reviewed 3000 years from 5239 BC to 2239 BC, the inception of the Anunnaki Chronology to the total destruction of the world with the great Deluge. But the records of the past are for our future instruction, signifying things to come in types and shadows. This incredible system is based off of the sexagesimal mathematics of archaic Sumer. The Great Years are Anunnaki NER periods of *600 years* each, each subdivided by the periods of *60 years* each. The longevity of the chronology as depicted begins a countdown of 6-year periods to apocalyptic *future* events presaged typologically by those events that transpired in history at the end and beginning of the Anunnaki 600 year epochs.

This system of 600s, 60s and 6s is so precise that it will be revealed herein how the Anunnaki Chronology synchronizes perfectly with the astronomical cycles of planet Phoenix and the Anunnaki homeworld NIBIRU, the start of Earth's Orbital Chronology as encoded in the Great Pyramid's dimensions, the end of the Cursed Earth Chronology and start of the Giza Course Countdown of the Last Days. As the combined numbers of 600, 60 and 6 form the concept of *total authority over men* (666), this is *exactly* what the Anunnaki Chronology seems to mark throughout history and the future.

For those seeking a more exhaustive timeline of this Anunnaki system, the author provides such in his work *Chronicon: Timelines of the Ancient Future*. The following is a more abbreviated version applicable to this work.

Anunnaki Timeline
(600 Year and 60 Year Periods)

5239 BC (-1344 AM)
   Beginning of Angelic Chronology 1344 years (600 + 600 + 144) before Man's 6000 years under the Curse. This begins the 7200-year (600 x 12) chronology to 1962 AD (5856 AM) when Anunnaki (Fallen Angelic beings) permitted to resume abducting human females and males for genetic testing, hybridization and preparation for the Descent of the Seven Kings 90 years

later in 2052 AD. Original solar system a differential binary comprised of a Daystar and Nightstar and the Anunnaki are holy Guardians over the PreAdamic worlds formed by the Word of God.

4639 BC (-744 AM)

First Anunnaki Great Year of *600 years* complete. The Anunnaki instigate a rebellion against the Godhead of a third of heaven's hosts after discovering in the Records of Heaven (Tablets of Destinies: Word of God) that the Creator would one day make a new holy beings, not out of divine fire as were forged the Anunnaki, but out of inferior *clay*. This new creation would be made in the *image of God* as a living Temple of the Holy Spirit and be vested with more *authority* than the angels possessed. As the Divine Plan was acceptable to 66.6% of the residents of heaven, a *third* (33.3%) rebelled and vowed to prevent the Ascension of Mankind. The Rebellion would endure 330 years until the binary system was destroyed in a solar system apocalypse in 4309 BC sending Earth reeling through space for 270 years until it began its orbit around the present sun (former Nightstar) in 4039 BC initiating the Orbital Chronology encoded in the base diagonals of the Great Pyramid's four cornerstones.

4039 BC (-144 AM)

Second Anunnaki Great Year of *600 years* complete. 1200 Anunnaki Chronology. This begins the Earth's orbit around the present sun and the axial rotation of this planet initiating the First Day, as Genesis 1 reads, "… and the evening and the morning were the first day." This year is encoded within the four base diagonals of the Great Pyramid's four cornerstones and was discovered by David Davidson to be the start of the Orbital Chronology of Earth (he was off by a year, for he wrote 4040 BC in his 1924 AD work *The Great Pyramid*). The Orbital Chronology marks the 6084 years Earth will remain on the sun's ecliptic plane, having been drawn off of its original orbit on the ecliptic of the Dark Star (former destroyed Daystar). Earth will be returned to the Dark Star ecliptic in 2046 AD when NIBIRU a draws this planet into a tighter orbit around the sun at an extreme inclined angle vertical to the present ecliptic plane. In this year of 4039 BC the Creator makes ADAM, the first human and gives him *power, authority and dominion* over the world, making him in His image on the *6th day* (144th hour of the Renovation of Earth). Man is commanded to "…be fruitful, and multiply and *replenish* the Earth."

3619 BC (276 AM)

This is seventh 60-year period after 4039 BC. Planet *Phoenix* passes through the inner system unseen from Earth, traveling along the original Dark Star ecliptic almost vertical to the present ecliptic plane.

3499 BC (396 AM)

This is ninth 60-year period after 4039 BC. Planet NIBIRU of the Anunnaki (homeworld) enters the inner system from under the ecliptic after 732 years in the Deep (Abyss) nether regions below this solar system, traveling along the Dark Star's ecliptic plane. NIBIRU travels over the ecliptic and sun for *60 years*.

3439 BC (456 AM)

Third Anunnaki Great Year of *600 years* complete. 1800 Anunnaki Chronology Planet NIBIRU passes close to Earth as it descends back over the ecliptic completing its 792-year orbit, and *200 Anunnaki* (Watchers) descend upon Earth as the planetary Passover causes massive earthquakes and flooding that kills a *third* of mankind. Of the remaining 66.6% of humanity remaining, the Sethites reject the Anunnaki but the Cainite families accept them, begin exogamy and the trading of secrets and knowledges in exchange for the "... daughters of men." Mankind begins transferring *authority* over the Earth from themselves to the Anunnaki. Astronomer Royal for Scotland Piazzi Smyth in the 1870s wrote that the Descending Passage in the Great Pyramid in 3440 BC (he was one year off) pointed directly at *Alpha Draconis*, the Eye of the Dragon, or ancient antediluvian Pole Star. The Anunnaki were characterized as personifications of the Dragon and in this way represented symbolically in the Book of Revelation. Zecharia Sitchin relates that the Sumerian records claim that the Anunnaki descended to Earth 432,000 years before the Great Flood, however, this is exaggerated (at no fault of Sitchins) for the 432,000 "years" are actually *days* on a 360-day Draconian Year calendar, or precisely *1200 years* (600 + 600) to the Flood in 2239 BC.

2839 BC (1056 AM)

Fourth Anunnaki Great Year of *600 years* complete. 2400 Anunnaki Chronology. This begins the 600 years of the Anunnaki Seven Kings, total *authority* on Earth over mankind. In this the first year of the Oppression, Menahem is born, but called *Noah* by God, who will save mankind from ruin and be appointed total authority over the Earth when the Anunnaki are swept away in the Flood. Using their Nephilim offspring, the Giants, as a policing force over men, the Anunnaki enforce their new socio-political schemes and religion upon both Cainite and Sethite lineages. The Elder Faith prophecies of the coming of the Son of God has been perverted into a universal *goddess*-worshipping religion venerating not the Son of the Creator, but the human *daughter of man* that gives birth to Him.

2359 BC (1536 AM)

This is eighth 60-year period after 2839 BC. Exactly 120 years before the Deluge, Noah is given authority from God to begin preaching to the people of the coming of the Great Flood, he receiving immunity from the Anunnaki that would have killed him had not he received the mark of God's protection. This is 2880 Anunnaki Chronology, or 1440 + 1440 years. This year is also *456* Anno Pyramid (completion of Great Pyramid in 2815 BC), and *456* Annus Mundi was 3439 BC when the Anunnaki first descended.

2239 BC (1656 AM)

Fifth Anunnaki Great Year of *600 years* complete. 3000 Anunnaki Chronology. Planet *Phoenix* enters the inner system and transits, *darkening the sun* and causing terrible earthquakes completing the third Phoenix Cycle of 552 years (1656 years) from Man's Banishment from Eden in 3895 BC which began the 6000 years of Mankind. A comet of the *Ancient Earth-Killer Comet Group* collides into Earth's watery mesosphere (firmament above: water canopy) and causes it to implode initiating 40 days of rain. The comet impacts the present Gulf of Mexico region along with a rain of other cometary fragments spread throughout the world. Humanity, the Anunnaki now trapped in mortal bodies and their progeny, the Giants, are drowned and buried and the world's surface materials are literally turned upside down in a series of global geologic upheavals, subsidence and redistribution of surface composition through global flooding. As the world was turned into a planetwide fossil, mankind was returned back into the clay from which he came. Noah survived with his family and he is given the Divine Commission of power, *authority* and dominion over Earth and commanded specifically as were the first humans to "… be fruitful, multiply and *replenish* the Earth."

2119 BC (1776 AM)

This is a second 60-year period after 2239 BC. Cainan, the son of Arphaxad and grandson of Shem (son of Noah and patriarch of Semitic peoples) wandered far and wide and discovered a monument covered in the *inscriptions of the Anunnaki*, said to have belonged to the Giants before the Flood. He did not tell Noah about his find. The writings concerned the motions and cycles of the heavenly bodies.

1879 BC (2016 AM)

This is the sixth 60-year period after 2239 BC. This is the year of the anciently famous *Battle of Kuruksata* when Nimrod (AMAR.UDA.AK) of Babylon met the Elamites under Chedorlaomer (Kudurlagamar of Genesis 14) over supremacy of the Near Eastern *fossil-fuel* resources of the Dead Sea controlled by the cities of Sodom. This was an *international war* involving Sumerians, Akkadians, Babylonians, Assyrians, Hurrians, Aramaens, Amorites, Hittites all against the ancestors of *Persia* (modern Iran) under Chedorlaomer. In the ranks of both sides fought the Rephaim and Anakim Giants. It was the West against the East, which was outnumbered 11 to 7, but despite this disadvantage, the Elamites (East) won, slaughtering the forces of Nimrod (West) and then subduing them and annexing all of Babylonia (Iraq), Aram (Syria) and the Anatolian lands of the Hittites (Turkey & Asia Minor). This is the *360th year* after the Flood and this year's events are a prophetic foreshadowing of what lies in the future for the United States, Iraq, Syria and Turkey, Armenia, Lebanon and Iran. Absolute *authority* over these fossil-fuel resources in the Middle East given over to Elam (Persia: Iran).

1639 BC (2256 AM)

Sixth Anunnaki Great Year of *600 years* complete. 3600 Anunnaki Chronology. Jacob (renamed *Israel* by God) died in Egypt and *authority* over the inheritance (the Birthright of Israel) of Abraham, Isaac and Jacob is given to Joseph's two sons, Manesseh and Ephraim, known as the 13th Tribe of Israel. The descendants of these two grandsons of Israel were destined to become two mighty *Christian* Last Days Empires: the British Empire and the Empire of Adoption known popularly as the United States of America, the latter (USA) prophesied to become the greater of the two. Jacob, before he dies, explains to Joseph that Manesseh and Ephraim will be the last of the Tribes of Israel to inherit their appointments, and that they would take up their positions in the *West*, in the Isles of the Sea and to unknown coasts of the Earth (the Americas).

1099 BC (2796 AM)

This is the ninth 60-year period after 1639 BC. In this year the far-sailing Phoenicians lost a vessel in a violent storm which carried it into alien waters. The ship sailed on to discover the land that would later be called *America*, according to Diodorus Siculus. This is the year 4140 (414 x 10) of the Anunnaki Chronology, or ten *Cursed Earth* periods of the Anunnaki timeline. It is further the 800th year after the Babel cataclysm that divided the Earth into fragmenting land masses and kingdoms, in 1899 BC.

1039 BC (2856 AM)

Seventh Anunnaki Great Year of *600 years* complete. 4200 Anunnaki Chronology. David is born, who will grow up a shepherd and Giant-Slayer (killed Goliath) and become King of Israel whose faith would fulfill a prophetic type later fulfilled again in the role of the Christ, who as the Chief cornerstone would come in the 6000th year (2106 AD) to sit upon the *Throne of David* as a Millenial King over Earth. David was the youngest of all his brothers just as the United States is the youngest of all the *Israelite*-descended empires of the world. Interestingly, this year of David's birth is *1776* Anno Pyramid (completion of Great Pyramid in 2815 BC) which parallels the *1776* Anno Domini (Year of the Lord) year of the birth of the United States of America whose Great Seal exhibits a picture of the *Great Pyramid*. David is born 432,000 days after the Deluge (2239 BC) and typifies the authority of the Christ who would descend from heaven to rule over Mankind, just as 432,000 days (1200 years) *before* the Great Flood the Anunnaki descended from heaven to exercise dominion over humanity in 3439 BC.

859 BC (3036 AM)

This is the third 60-year period after 1039 BC. Assyrian King Shalmaneser III begins his reign as Assyria begins to reassert its already-centuries-old *authority* over the other Near Eastern nations. This is exactly 414 years, or a Cursed Earth period after Assyria became an Empire in 1273 BC. In this year of 859 BC planet Phoenix passed through the inner system.

559 BC (3336 AM)

King Nebuchadnezzar II of Babylon is cursed by God to lose his sanity for seven years, and this is the first year that the king was hidden from the people by his Court. His son Nabonidus reigned quietly in his stead. Nebuchadnezzar II was specifically given all power, authority and dominion over the Earth according to the book of Daniel the prophet, but due to his disobedience, pride and wickedness, the king was humbled for seven years, cursed to suffer lycanthrope. At the termination of the seven years (2520 days: years being 360 days each) the Babylonian king was reestablished upon his throne, his sanity restored.

439 BC (3456 AM)

Eight Anunnaki Great Years of *600 years* complete. 4800 Anunnaki Chronology. The Greeks of Athens finish the famous *Parthenon*, designed by Phidias (490-530 BC) upon the Acropolis. The Parthenon is badly misunderstood. It was designed to commemorate ancient Semitic history of a epic war involving Giants and what the Greeks later equated with the gods, or Titans. The famous and magnificently artistic reliefs known as the War of the Giants upon the Parthenon depicts a war exactly *1440* years priorly, in 1879 BC, the *Battle of Kuruksata* where the ancestors of Persia (Elam) conquered the allied nations of the Near East. The name Parthenon also confirms this, for in this year of 439 BC the realm of Elam, or Persia, was known as *Parthia*, their language being Parsi. Many of the descendants of Athens and Grecia were related to people who had migrated from Asia Minor, Mycenaea, Caria and other domains that were once colonized by *Israelite* peoples who escaped from Assyria when the Empire fell to the Babylonians almost two centuries earlier. The Greek culture has always maintained a strong element of Semitic influence. The Parthenon commemorated this historic and almost legendary battle involving gigantic men long ago as well as symbolized Greekdom's victory against the armies of Persia when the Athenians defeated King Darius of Persia in 490 BC in the *Battle of Marathon* and then again in the *Battle of Salamis* when Themistocles defeated the Persian navy in 481 BC. Thus, the

Parthenon is a Greek architectural *statement* concerning the rise of the *West* (which is the opposite of what occurred in 1879 BC when the East won out). As the *Battle of Kuruksata* was 1440 years (144 x 10) before the completion of the Parthenon, so also *144 years* before 439 BC was the battle between the Medes and Lydians in 583 BC recorded by Herodotus when the *sun darkened* due to the transit of plant Phoenix.

319 BC (3576 AM)

This is the second 60-year period after 439 BC. This year completes the 7th Mayan Baktun, each baktun being 144,000 days and this year fulfilling 1,008,000 days from the start of this amazing calendrical system in 3113 BC. In this year the *Dark Satellite* (former moon of NIBIRU serving as a *prison* for the Seven Kings of the Anunnaki) passes through the inner system unseen from Earth. The Mayan system ends not in 2012 AD, but in *2046 AD* with reappearance of NIBIRU.

259 BC (3636 AM)

This is the third 60-year period after 439 BC. The Ancient Earth-Killer Comet Group enters the inner system for the final time, badly deteriorated in a 19-year long train. It will not be seen again.

139 BC (3756 AM)

This is the fifth 60-year period after 439 BC. The ancient Chaldaei, known also as the Mathematici, astrologers and seers, are expelled from Rome and all of Italy. They were revered during the time of the Seven Kings of Rome (no relation to Seven Kings of Anunnaki) but their ultimate origin lies with the Chaldean astrologer and prophet Balaam who resided in Rome (early Chittim: Italia) in 1555 BC). This was 1416 years. This year is 5100 Anunnaki Chronology and 2100 (700 x 3) after Flood. It is 1308 after Exodus, encoding the number 1-3-8 and exactly *138 years* to the birth of Christ in 1 BC, 138 years being a solar orbit of planet Phoenix. Additionally, 139 BC is *792 years* of the Divided Kingdom, when Israel and Judah split at the death of King Solomon, 792 years being the solar orbital period of NIBIRU.

162 AD (4056 AM)

Ninth Anunnaki Great Year of *600 years* complete. 5300 Anunnaki Chronology. A virtual global epidemic occurred that afflicted first China, lasting for eleven years and then on through the Middle East and the Roman Empire for 16 years. Amidst the massive loss of life the Han Dynasty of China fell, initiating an Asian Dark Age that lasted over four centuries until the emergency of the Tang Dynasty. Even Rome was seriously debilitated, entire provinces depleted of their populations. At this time the Goths and other German groups began migrating into the weakening Roman areas. This is 2400 years after the Flood and 1200 years after the birth of King David.

462 AD (4356 AM)

This is the fifth 60-year period after 162 AD. Planet NIBIRU ascends out of the Deep and passes over the ecliptic into the inner system unseen from Earth after travelling along the Dark Star ecliptic underneath our sun for 732 years. This is 5700 Anunnaki Chronology.

522 AD (4416 AM)

This is the sixth 60-year period after 162 AD. In this year as NIBIRU descends back over the ecliptic and out of the inner system finalizing its 792 year orbital period, planet Phoenix also passed through the inner system completing the 8th Phoenix Cycle (552 x 8 is 4416 AM) since Man was banished from Eden in 3895 BC. Major earthquakes toppled old structures in Greece and Olympia. This is 5760 Anunnaki Chronology, or *1440 x 4*, and this is the *ONLY* year in all of world history and the future that planet Phoenix and planet NIBIRU pass through the inner system at the same time. Additionally, this year begins a *1440 year* countdown to the end of the Anunnaki Chronology in 1962 AD.

762 AD (4656 AM)

Tenth Anunnaki Great Year of *600 years* complete. 6000 Anunnaki Chronology. In the 144th month after the Abbasids began to rule in stead of the Umayyids over Mesopotamia, the Abbasid Dynasty made its seat in this year at Baghdad in Babylon (Iraq), the new seat of the Muslim Empire. As all authority was transferred to Baghdad, this city essentially became a *second Babylon.* As the ancient Babylonians venerated the Anunnaki, we find it remarkable that this is the 6000th year of the Anunnaki Chronology. Additionally, mankind was banished from Paradise on Earth 1244 years (1200 + 144) into the Anunnaki Chronology, in 3895 BC, which *began* the 6000 year timeline to 2106 AD, and this year of 762 AD is exactly *1344 years* to the end of the 6000 year chronology when in 2106 AD the *Anunnaki* are themselves *banished* by God at Armagedon. In this year the Jewish Exilarch Solomon died, the leader over foreign Jewish activities in Persia and throughout the Islamic world. His hereditary successor, his nephew Anan ben David Hassini was rejected by the Elders who opted instead to install his younger brother Chanaya as Exilarch. Anan then fled to Palestine and founded his own synagogue, calling upon Jews everywhere to abandon the corrupt Talmud and obey only the inspired Word of God in the Pentateuch (Genesis to Deuteronomy). His sect grew quickly and became influencial, known as the Karaites, or *Followers of the Text* (Bible), and Anan's view and teachings about Jesus was much more positive than the Talmudic one. He urged Jews to resist the Rabbinate for he thoroughly believed that the rabbis were modern Pharisees bent on propagating the traditions of men rather than the will of heaven. This Karaite movement still exists today, and therein lies the import of this 762 AD event, a date beginning a major rift in the Jewish world. In the world of astronomy, the year 762 AD may have heralded some startling sign, for a Mayan conclave of elite astronomers met and made some important decisions based on timekeeping methods which were published throughout the Mayan cities on pillars for the public to view in the year 763 AD.

1062 AD (4956 AM)

This is the fifth 60-year period after 762 AD. The Muslim Turks invade mainland Greece and commit wholesale slaughter upon the Greek Christians, invading all the way to northeastern Italy. Their occupation virtually ended Greek Christendom. This was 1044 Before Armageddon, encoding the sum of 1-4-4.

1302 AD (5196 AM)

This is the ninth 60-year period after 762 AD. The Vials of Phoenix Comet Group passes through the inner system and largely contributes to the rash of meteoritic storms, comets, earthquakes, plagues, plague-mists and fogs and flooding during the historic period known as the 16 Years of the Seven Comets over Europe (1298-1314 AD). Interestingly, 1302 AD is the year *2046* Post-Exilic Chronology, dating from the time the Ten Tribes of Israel were deported into Assyria in 745 BC. The year 2046 AD is the year the United States, a people descended from Europeans who were themselves the progeny of the Ten Kingdoms that were of ancient Israelite stock, is destroyed by a *comet* impact (see *Anunnaki Homeworld*).

1362 AD (5256 AM)

Eleventh Anunnaki Great Year of *600 years* complete. 6600 Anunnaki Chronology. A Norse-Goth expedition sent out by King Magnus of Norway began exploring North America in the Canadian and Northern States of the USA regions. They left behind the famous Kensington Runestone detailing their misadventures of battles with the local Indians, loss of men and explorations (discovered 1898 AD). The Norse and Goths are the descendants of people that long ago assimilated, people of Indo-Aryan and ancient Israelite stock. This expedition was cursed by its timing, for 1362 AD was precisely one Cursed Earth period of *414 years* before the 1776 AD birth of the United States that the descendants of the Norse and Goths would one day occupy. 1362 AD is 744 years (600 + 144) Before Armageddon and is the year *2106* Post Exilic Chronology (deportation of the Tribes of Israel), the year 2106 AD being the year of Armageddon and return of the Chief Cornerstone when the peoples of God receive their Promise Land.

1542 AD (5436 AM)

This is the third 60-year period after 1362 AD. Pope Paul III revived the dreaded Inquisition calling it the Congregation of the Inquisition, or Roman Inquisition. This was a cover for the elimination of dissidents of both Church and State and the myth of witch hunts were an effective cover masking the true intent of filling official coffers, especially with the wealth of all the well-off widowed landowners.

1602 AD (5496 AM)

This is the fourth 60-year period after 1362 AD. John Greaves is born, the first man to scientifically study the Great Pyramid complex, a mathematician, antiquarian and Professor of Geometry.

1842 AD (5736 AM)

The British defeat the Chinese and through the Treaty of Nanking the opium trade is reinstated. China, which started the war because of oppressive British practices of pushing the drug onto the people, is now forced to legalize opium.

1902 AD (5796 AM)

This is the ninth 60-year period after 1362 AD. This is the *end* of the *Cursed Earth Calendar* (Stonehenge Chronolithic system), marking 15 periods of 414 years each, from the destruction of the PreAdmaic World in 4309 BC. This year of 1902 AD begins a 144-year countdown to 2046 AD return of the Anunnaki, the Passover of NIBIRU, and comet impact upon North America. This year also states the *final* 60 years to the *end* of the Anunnaki Chronology in 1962 AD when these baleful beings will be allowed to continue their genetic programs against humanity. In 1902 AD planet Phoenix passed through the system unseen from Earth, however, comet Morehouse, which orbited Phoenix, is pulled apart by gravitational forces and photographed as it broke apart. 50 tons per square mile of cosmic dust (from Phoenix debris train) rains upon Australia, and much falls upon much of Europe, western Russia, over Britain and the Atlantic. The United States government quietly changes the Great Seal image from the *Phoenix* to the Eagle in 1902 AD. 1902 AD was 138 years (Phoenix orbit) after astronomer Hoffman visually studied planet Phoenix as it virtually transited obscuring *one-fifth* of the sun's surface (not a direct transit). This year is also 138 years until planet Phoenix returns in 2040 AD to *darken the sun* in a direct transit initiating the Sixth Seal of the Apocalypse. 1902 AD begins the Giza Course Countdown of 204 levels of masonry until 2106 AD when the Chief Cornerstone shall descend to make war and defeat the Anunnaki. In 1902 AD the Babylonian Enuma Elish tablets were translated into *English*, these archaic texts detailing a great solar system cataclysm in the beginning (4309 BC) and the history of the *Anunnaki*. 1902 AD is exactly 10 Cursed Earth periods after the Flood in 2239 BC (414 x 10 is 4140 After Flood).

1962 AD (5856 AM)

Twelfth Anunnaki Great Year of *600 years* complete, geometrically forming a *pentagonal dodecahedron,* which symbolizes that *time* has crystallized, assumed a definite form allowing for something to occur. This geometrical timeline began in 5239 BC at the beginning of Angelic History, this being the final and 7200th year, which begins a 144-year (72 + 72) countdown to the descent of the Chief Cornerstone at Armageddon in 2106 AD (6000 AM). This same 144-year period is found in ancient history from 4039 BC when Earth's Orbital Chronology began to 3895 BC when mankind, after listening to the Anunnaki serpent (Instructor) was banished from Eden. As readers of *Chronicon* know, on May 22nd of 1962 AD a secret space probe landed on Mars and confirmed the existence of an environment that could support life, but in the *official* and publicized space program, John Glenn became the first American to orbit the Earth, in a Mercury capsule called Friendship 7. Also, nine astronomers discovered an unnatural bulge at the Martian equator and astrophysicist Dr. E.J. Opik concluded that this bulge may be *hollow.* With the end of the 7200 years the Anunnaki are now enabled to resume their hybridization program between humans and themselves (creating Nephilim) as they did before the Flood. The condition being that humans *voluntarily* agreed to engage in such practices, as before the Deluge peoples traded their daughters for advanced knowledge and secrets. In *Chronicon* is detailed secret US Government treaty between an extraterrestrial race (the guise of the Anunnaki) to do just this: abduction of human females, scientific experimentation including fetal extractions, implant devices for tracking and inducing memory loss of trauma. As UFO researchers can well attest, in was 1962 AD when the first human abductions by UFOs occurred, these causing researchers to create a new class called Close Encounters of the *Fourth* Kind. The most famous UFO abduction of the early 60s was of Betty and Barney Hill. American prophetess Jean Dixon publicized that a great evil was to occur in 1962 AD, her prediction based of a *massive conjunction of planets* that occurred on February 5th. It was the erudite Dr. Carl Sagan who in 1962 urged the scientific community to reexamine the ancient myths and traditions from around the world for evidence of Earth being visited in antiquity by an extraterrestrial species. Amazingly, as the final 60-year period of the Anunnaki chronology began with 1902 AD, which itself initiated the Giza Course Countdown, another pyramid timeline found in the olden ruins of the city of Teotihuacan in Mexico also reveals a perfect *7200-year* pyramid calendar as discovered by Hugh Harleston Jr. The timeline began with the Pyramid of the Sun, which stands *203 ft.* tall (Great Pyramid *203 levels* of stone high) and the 7200 hunabs ends at the ruinous pile of masonry that once formed a pyramidal temple that represented Planet X (NIBIRU). Perhaps beyond coincidence, as the Anunnaki resume genetic experimentation in 1962 AD on humans, Dr.

James Watson of the USA and Dr. Maurice Wilkins of England (Ephraim and Manesseh) were awarded the Nobel Prize for Medicine and Physiology for their 1952 AD determination of the double-helix formation of human DNA. The release of certain Anunnaki in this year of 1962 AD is confirmed in the writings of Enoch, who wrote that the Watchers that practiced hybridization with the daughters of men would be confined for *70 generations* from the Great Flood. As an Anunnaki generation is evidently 60 years, 70 x 60 years is 4200 years. The Flood transpired in 2239 BC, or 1656 Annus Mundi. Adding 1656 + 4200 years in 5856 Annus Mundi, or *1962 AD*.

By now it should be apparent to the reader why the first three archives were so full of information about the world before the Deluge. What happened then is happening *now*. Jesus specifically told us that the Last Days would be "...as the days of *Noah*." During Noah's lifetime he saw how the Anunnaki corrupted mankind, caused him to degenerate by lowering his standards, ethics, morality. They passed newer and newer laws and enforced formerly unknown practices until all vestiges of rights, privileges and immunities were divested from the people. They enslaved mankind without humanity actually realizing it. New social reforms, new sciences, new histories antithetical to the true histories previously taught were introduced and cherished institutions like marriage and family unity were trampled. Those seeking to live virtuously were looked upon with contempt and scorn because they did not fit the new social norms.

As this author has stated in his previous works, the past forms a predicate for the future, and history is a torch we must see by when reviewing what lies ahead. To fully appreciate the mathematical and calendrical genius of the Anunnaki Chronology, we must analyze it further still in its lowest *orbital* denominator: years. We have reviewed all the 600-year periods and many of the 60 year lesser periods within them, but now we must continue the pattern in *6-year* intervals to comprehend the destiny of the Anunnaki in the Mind of the Creator.

The following entries are all extracted from *Chronicon*, and those of the future are derived from the science of calendrical isometrics (explained in Chronicon), cross-calendrical parallels and comparative timelines. Each of the following 6-year intervals measures a *72-month* period, beginning with 1962 AD.

1968 AD (5862 AM)

Apollo completes successful mission to orbit the moon, the astronauts on board taking a spectacular photograph from behind the moon of the Earth beyond while reading the first 11 verses of the Book of Genesis. This is Giza Year 66 and the final 138 years Before Armageddon (orbit of Phoenix), or *1656 months* (414 x 4).

1974 AD (5868 AD)

The Sears Tower is finished in Chicago, Illinois becoming the world's tallest building at *108 stories* (1451 ft.; 1729 ft. with antenna array). The US unofficially acknowledges defeat in Vietnam War and withdraws troops from Vietnam. This is Giza Year 72 (864 months of Giza Course Countdown).

1980 AD (5874 AM)

The Iran-Iraq War begins, these two ancient nations (now both Islamic), constant arch enemies, known better as Persia (Iran) and Babylon (Iraq). The war resulted with over a million dead. As we will see in this archive, the Anunnaki system implicates this year for a very prophetically revealing reason.

1986 AD (5880 AM)

This begins the final *120 years* (120 gematria for Hebrew word *foundation*) to the return of the Chief Cornerstone, the Christ in 2106 AD at Armageddon to vanquish the Anunnaki Seven Kings, this 120 years being *1440 months*. The Lord is prophetically foreshadowed in 1986 AD when the five-mile wide asteroid (a celestial rock) named *Adonis* (Syro-Phoenician for *Lord*) passed 186,000 miles away from Earth, 186,000 miles being the speed of light in a second and Christ being the *Stone* of Israel and *Light* of the World. Halley's Comet passed through inner system and was seen from Earth and the first photographs of its nucleus (a comet's *foundation*) were taken. In 1986 AD the Space Shuttle *Challenger* exploded as it departed Earth killing the Seven Astronauts, their untimely demise recalling the fall of the Seven Kings of the Anunnaki who *challenged* God by attempting to *ascend* into heaven. In this year the renovation project on the Statue of Liberty, a four-year project, is completed. As we will see, this architectural masterpiece is a cleverly encoded *Anunnaki* timeline secretly designed by a French architect. This is the year 4800 Anno Pyramid, or 600 x 8 years after the completion of the Great Pyramid, which also encodes the *same* calendrical information as the Statue of Liberty, as will be shown.

1992 AD (5886 AM)

The Swift-Tuttle Comet passed through the inner system and was closest to Earth on November 7th, at 110,000,000 miles away (sun is 93 million miles away). Scientists discover that the human brain contain trace amounts of *magnetite*, which explains why electromagnetic fields alter brain chemistry and experience. This is dangerous for humanity, for the Anunnaki are capable of lowering their biorhythmic frequencies, allowing humans to perceive their presence. The human senses only perceive approximately 5% of the electromagnetic spectrum, and for this reason the Anunnaki can manipulate our environment around us and create fact or fiction. This is Giza Year 90 (*1080 months*).

1998 AD (5892 AM)

This is the Last Days Epicentral Isometric Year, a year marking the final *108 years* to Armageddon in 2106 AD (6000 AM). 1998 AD is 666 x 3 (1998). Calendrical Isometrics is a unique phenomenon found in the equidistant repetition of historical events linked to an epicentral year. In this case 1998 is the epicentral marker. This system serves to exhibit that the past prerecords the future, that the unfolding of events in history presage those that will follow. Isometric years are like ripples in the pond of time, each wave-ring before the epicentral marker is exactly the same distance in time as the other side of the wave-ring. *Chronicon* goes into explicit detail demonstrating this absolutely full proof and amazing system. In 1962 AD the Anunnaki system ended and John Glenn orbited the Earth three times in a capsule named *Friendship 7* (friendship with what *seven*?), and now in 1998 AD, John Glenn, aged 77, executed his final space mission in the Space Shuttle *Discovery* in a 9-day mission. This was 36 years (6 x 6) later. Also in 1998 AD President Clinton signed into law the Iraq Liberation Act, representing a plan to instigate a regime change ousting Saddam Hussein. This law, enacted during the Isometric Year of 1998 AD will prove astounding. Interestingly, a crop circle appeared in Cuxton, England encoding the number *108*. A simple example of calendrical isometrics is as follows: *three* years before 1998 AD was 1995 when Timothy McVeigh and Terry Nichols detonated a bomb at the Murrah Federal Bldg. in *Oklahoma City*, an American terrorist plot, and *three* years after 1998 was the 2001 AD terrorist attack in America of the World Trade Center Towers and Pentagon in *New York City* (both locations replicate the *State's* name in the City's name). Incidentally, in 2001 AD Timothy McVeigh was executed for the 1995 AD bombing. This is only one of *hundreds* of isometric accounts found in *Chronicon*. 1998 AD is the 222nd year of the United States, from 1776 AD, or a *third* of 666 years.

2004 AD (5898 AM)

This is exactly *one year* after the United States invaded Iraq. This is also *6 years* after the 1998 AD isometric epicentral year, and *6 years* before the 1998 marker was 1992 AD, precisely *one year* after the United States invaded Iraq in Operation Desert Storm. In 2004 AD the astroid *Apophis* was discovered as it passed through the inner system and the world's most powerful earthquake in 40 years occurred beneath the Indian Ocean causing a tsunami that killed 200,000 people. This was Giza Year 102, and also 102 years Before Armageddon (2106 AD).

2022 AD (5916 AM)

The United States forces in the Middle East are terribly defeated by a confederation of Islamic nations headed by Iran after 6 years of warfare, paralleling the isometric year of 1974 AD when the US pulled out of Vietnam after an extended war and humiliating defeat in a Third World nation. The USA loses its Empire status and there is a complete regathering of US forces around the world and the United Nations headquarters are *removed* from New York City as America becomes a virtually isolationist nation, still very powerful but with only limited international interests. This is the 120th year of the Giza Course Countdown to Armageddon (1440 months) and this year is *1400 years* (700 + 700) after the start of the Islamic Hijrah Calendar in 622 AD.

2028 AD (5922 AM)

A manned spacecraft will successfully achieve an unprecedented mission and a famous American/world leader will be assassinated. The United States will demonstrate its continued albeit silent power by detonating a weapon far more powerful than any nuclear device. All of these events occurred in the isometric year of 1968 AD which saw the assassinations of Senator Robert F. Kennedy and Martin Luther King, the Apollo 8 mission and the detonation of BOXCAR by the USA in the Nevada desert.

2034 AD (5928 AM)

This is 72 years after the end of the Anunnaki Chronology in 1962 AD, 1962 being the isometric year for 2034 AD. This also begins the final 72 years until Armageddon when the Anunnaki are defeated by the True King. In this year the presence of the Anunnaki (in the guise of an extraterrestrial species) will be broadcast throughout the world. This will be in conjunction with the destruction of a manned spacecraft from Earth.

2040 AD (5934 AM)

This author has put out an entire book about this date. This is the year of the return and complete transit of planet Phoenix between the Earth and the sun, *darkening the solar orb* and initiating the events of the Sixth Seal of the Revelation in the Apocalypse. Through meteoritic fallout from the debris train of Phoenix many cities of the world will be destroyed. The city of New York will be completely destroyed, this being its 414th year (*Cursed Earth* period) since it was founded as New Amsterdam by the Dutch after a purchase from the locals in 1626 AD. For a complete picture of what lies ahead in 2040 AD, read *When the Sun Darkens: Orbital History and 2040 AD Return of Planet Phoenix*. This is 138th year of the Giza Course Countdown (138 years before a Phoenix orbit), or *1656 months* (414 x 4).

2046 AD (5940 AM)

This author also wrote another work about the events of 2046 AD, entitled *Anunnaki Homeworld: Orbital History and 2046 AD Return of Planet NIBIRU*. Even in *Chronicon*, there is no year in the history of mankind so catastrophic save for that of the Great Flood. A comet will impact the North

American plate ending the United States, most of Canada and Mexico. An asteroid will also collide into Earth and planet NIBIRU will pass so close that Earth will be pulled into a tighter orbit around the sun and completely off the present ecliptic plane and back onto the ancient plane of the Dark Star that both Phoenix and NIBIRU still orbit almost vertical to the ecliptic. This ends the Orbital Chronology began in 4039 BC which David Davidson discovered was encoded in the base diagonals of the Great Pyramid's four cornerstones (the Foundation of the calendar). With the abbreviation of the orbital longevity of Earth and increasef spin-rate reducing the year to 240 days of 16 hour-long days begins the *Condensed Calendar* of the Apocalypse. All of this is fully explained in these other works. An entire *third* of the world's human population is killed, leaving 66.6% left to be ruled or oppressed by the *Anunnaki* Seven Kings. This year ends the 1,872,000 days of the Mayan Long-Count calendars' 13 baktuns (144,000 x 13) from 3113 BC. As Sodom and Gomorrah were destroyed from the sky in *2047 Annus Mundi*, so also is the New Sodom, the United States, destroyed from the sky exactly *2047 years* after the birth of Christ in 1 BC which initiated the Anno Domini calendar, Anno Domini meaning Year of the Lord. This is Giza Year 144, exactly 270 years (90 x 3) after start of the United States and 60 years before Armageddon in 2106 AD.

2052 AD (5946 AM)

In Anunnaki Homeworld this author exhibits truly shocking data on this the 90th year after the end of the Anunnaki Chronology, the return of the *Dark Satillite* after orbiting the sun for 395 years, the *prison moon* of the Anunnaki that formerly orbited NIBIRU but was torn free from its gravitational hold over 4000 years prior. 2052 AD is the key date encoded in the Stonehenge II Bluestone Horseshoe and is found prominently in the chronometry of the Great Pyramid of Giza as revealed in *Chronotecture: Lost Science of Prophetic Engineering*. This is the return and descent to Earth of the Seven Kings of the Anunnaki, the "Secret Year" according to the prophet Enoch when the Seven Mountains are released from their confinement. (Enoch 18:13-16). This year is 54 years after the 1998 AD Isometric Epicentral Year, beginning a 54-year countdown to their defeat by the Chief Cornerstone in 2106 AD at Armageddon, for a total of 108 years. This 54-year period parallels the 54 years of King Sargon of Akkad. One of the most stunning revelations concerning this year is that it was foreseen and encoded by a French architect in 1884 AD when he designed the Statue of Liberty with precisely *168 steps* that ascended to a *54-rung* ladder to the chamber inside the Torch held high above the rest of the statue. This is a calendrical code, beginning in 1884 AD, the 168 years ends in 2052 AD when the Anunnaki Seven Kings *descend* to Earth and divest LIBERTY from men, and the 54 ladder-rungs represent the

54 years of their reign to Armageddon in 2106 AD (6000 AM) when they are themselves defeated by the Light (Torch) of the World, Christ, at Armageddon when He *descends* to Earth and sets men free. The 168 steps and 54 rungs adds up to 222 (a third of 666 years), and the 222nd year of the United States from 1776 AD was 1998 AD Epicentral Isometric Year, which happened to be *54 years* before the descent of the Seven Kings in 2052 AD.

This final 54 years is also subdivided into nine *6-year* intervals until Armageddon, but it is the year 2070 AD that proves to be the most remarkable and misunderstood. In the ancient world, as demonstrated in the first two Archives of this book, 2070 Annus Mundi (2239 BC) was the year God visited the Earth bringing a total global cataclysm. But as with other Cross-Calendrical Parallels, this is *reversed* in the year 2070 Anno Domini. The next Archive, which is the last of this work, will prove to be very rewarding.

Archive V

Charting the History of the Iron Empire

This author has expounded thoroughly on the history of distant and more contemporary antiquity because our knowledge of the past is essential in comprehending the present. There is an empire, a world-ruling and influencing nation today that is descended not merely from the empires of yesterday, but also serving as the fulfillment of the intents, purposes and designs of all of its socio-political predecessors. This is the United States of America and the history of the world is a definitive timeline leading up to the *beginning* and *end* of this American Empire. The events that transpired before the birth of the United States actually identifies *who* in the scheme of the Grand Design, the people of this American Empire are.

We are again reminded of the wisdom of Lewis Mumford—"Time is measured not by the calendar but by the *events that occupy it*." In another way, this is reiterated by the Russian sage P.D. Ouspensky in *Tertium Organum,* "...future events are wholly contained in preceding ones, and if we could know the force and direction of all events which have happened up to the present moment, i.e. if we knew all the past, by this *we could know all the future*." It is because of our blindness to the fact that the future is intertwined with the present that we fail to recognize how connected events today are with those that have passed. Our current concept of *time* is so alien to its true *spatial reality*, both backward and forward, that we conceive history as a motion linearly projected from a starting point to a finish that is the furthest point from its inception. We fail to realize that the phenomenon of time is more like a sphere made up of an infinite number of lines that from any point of the sphere are accessible to any other point of the sphere, and that what is conceived to be an end is merely the return of the beginning and that the start is only the repetition of a finish *already* concluded.

Firmicus Maternus centuries ago wrote that the beginning of anything could be found out by the unfolding of *historical events*. He was a historian, mathematician, chronologist and philosopher; however, this archive will vindicate him, demonstrating that Firmicus was also a *prophet*. We will now relieve the Statue of Liberty of her light, taking her Torch held high above America as we go back in time to the *beginning* of the United States of America *over 63 centuries ago*, a darkened path now illuminated by our chronology discoveries in the previous archives. The synthesis of the following information is provided visually in the calendrical illustration, Charting the History of the Iron Empire to 2046 AD, contained herein.

The Cursed Earth Chronology began in 4309 BC with the destruction of the PreAdamic Binary Solar System and Earth and planet Phoenix were catapulted away from the former Daystar, which collapsed into a *Dark Star*, to their present orbits today around the sun. This ruin of the solar system resulted in the collapse of NIBIRU's atmosphere and initiated its independence upon *earthly* materials and resources harvested by the Anunnaki when NIBIRU approaches its periodic perihelion. The destruction came in the *330th year* of the Anunnaki Rebellion, which began in 4639 BC the *Builders* (designation of Anunnaki as co-creators of the solar system with God) rejected the Chief Cornerstone (Word of God) in the 600th year of the Anunnaki Chronology. The judgment of God was initiated by the sub-nova explosion of their original parent star (our Dark Star binary companion) in 4309 BC which pushed Earth through space for *270 years* until it was captured in its current orbit around the sun in 4039 BC, which was *144 years* before Mankind was banished from Edenic paradise for following the Anunnaki in 3895 BC. Earth's newer position around the present sun began the Great Pyramid's *Orbital Chronology*, a timeline that ends in 2046 AD when NIBIRU nearly collides into Earth and pushes our world into a *different* orbit around the sun. The destruction of the PreAdamic World in 4309 BC that began this series of calendrical synchronizations was exactly *2070 years* (414 x 5) before the 2239 BC total destruction of the Earth in the Great Deluge. It was also 414 years prior to Year One (3895 BC) of the 6000-year timeline to the return of the Chief Cornerstone at Armageddon. These time periods *encode the future*, so be mindful of them as this archive proceeds.

The Annus Mundi (original Hebraic prior to rabbinical corruption) chronology that starts with mankind's expulsion from paradise in 3895 BC (1 AM) began a 1948 year span to the first regnal year of King Sargon I of Akkad, better known to us as Nimrod (AMAR.UDA.AK). This same year of 1948 Annus Mundi was also the year *Abraham was born*, patriarch of all those who by faith become inheritors of the promises of Abraham, Isaac and Jacob (Israel). Incidentally, 1948 Annus Mundi happens to also be *1948 BC*, a virtual calendrical axis, counting *1948 years* to the year 1 Anno Domini (Year of the Lord). As if this was not enough, 1948 years into the Anno Domini calendar, in 1948 AD, the nation of *Israel was reborn* among the nations by an act initiated and supported by Britain and the United States. No other nation in antiquity has been completely destroyed and scattered among the countries of the world and *resurrected* back into its original geographical confines, even relearning its original *language* (Hebrew). The history of Britain, the United States and Israel *as they exist today* began in extreme antiquity, with none other than Abraham.

In the year 1877 BC Abraham followed the instruction of God and traveled to Canaan (modern region called Israel) and the Creator established a covenant with the patriarch, promising that he would be the father of many nations and that his progeny would be as the stars of heavens and sands upon the seashore; uncountable. This promise from God is fully fulfilled today, as will be completely demonstrated herein. The Abrahamic Covenant itself began a *1948 year* countdown to 63 BC when the *Roman* general Pompey conquered Syria and annexed Judea (Israel) as a Roman province. Rome was regarded by the prophets of the Old Testament, such as in Daniel's writings, as the *Iron Empire*. But it was only one of several that have served as world-ruling governments.

The original Iron Empire was that of the Builders who rejected the Word of God, the Fallen Ones who decided to build their own civilizations on the PreAdamic World, which could *never* support the Chief Cornerstone. This Anunnai Empire only endured 330 years, but the entire span of Anunnaki history from the start of the Anunnaki Chronology in 5239 BC to the Banishment of Man from paradise in 3985 BC was 1344 years (1200 + 144). This same 1344 years antedates the fall of Judea to Rome in 63 BC, which counting 1344 years before was the year 1407 BC...the year the Israelites led by Joshua stormed into *Canaan* and took the land as their eternal possession at the instruction of God while the *sun stood still* in the sky for almost an entire day: the Conquest of Canaan. The parallels deepen.

In the year 1407 BC Moses died, who had led the Israelites out of Egypt 40 years prior in 1447 BC in the Exodus after the 10 Plagues devastated Pharaoh's Empire, which, at that time period, having military garrisons all through Ethiopia, Libya, Philistia, Arabia and Canaan as well as Syria, was the Iron Empire of its day. The Israelites in Egypt lived at Goshen near Giza, always under the shadow of the Great Pyramid built and completed *1407 years* before the Conquest of Canaan, the monument finished in 2815 BC (1080 AM). The Great Pyramid is the *Seal of Israel*, and 1407 BC was the year they inherited their Land of Promise as descendants of Abraham. We are not wanting for more evidence.

The people of Israel, a nation of *Thirteen Tribes*, continued as a unified nation for *476 years*, or precisely 68 biblical "weeks," or periods of seven years each. After Joshua died the Elders ruled the Tribes, followed by heroes known as the Judges. Samuel the prophet emerged and the people demanded that a *king* rule over them, which began Israel's decline. Three kings ruled Israel, starting with Saul, then David and his son Solomon until Solomon's death in the 476th year after the Conquest in 1407 BC, the year being 931 BC when Israel descended into civil war ending with the Northern Kingdom of Israel and the Kingdom of Judah to the South, the 10 Tribes of Israel with the 13th Tribe mixed throughout separating themselves from Judah. This began the Divided Chronology, counting exactly *1000 years* to AD 70 when Judea fell to Rome and was totally ruined at the end of the Jewish War which had began in 66 AD. Titus burned the Temple and leveled Jerusalem, salted the fields and carried away the sacred Temple artifacts to Rome after over a million Judeans had been killed and 97,000 people sold in the Slave Markets. Further exhibiting the Divine Synchronicity of Israel's history is the fact that *1407 years* after Israel and Judah split into the Two Kingdoms (foreshadowed in the Two Kingdoms of ancient Egypt) was the year *476 AD* (68 biblical "weeks" Anno Domini) when *Rome fell* to Odoacer the German, the Iron Empire, falling in the first year of the *Ten Kingdoms* of Europe. The Ten Kingdoms were prophesied to come by Daniel in his vision of the Statue of Nebuchadnezzar, made of gold, silver, brass and *iron* (Rome) followed by ten toes of *iron mixed with miry clay* (socio-racial extensions of Rome and some *other* (clay) people. These Ten Kingdoms would endure until the Stone Uncut by Human Hands descended and broke them asunder to initiate the Stone Kingdom of the Millennium. The Stone is at first literal, referring to the gigantic rock that will slam into *North America* in 2046 AD, and the second meaning is figurative for the Chief *Cornerstone* who will descent to Earth to assume total authority of Earth in 2106 AD, the Year 6000 of Man's Banishment since 3895 BC.

So *who* are the Ten Kingdoms? Why is Israel's history intertwined with their beginning? The date of the Fall of Rome is famous. So the calendrical fact that it occurred 1407 years after Israel is divided into two political entities hints that 476 AD begins another timeline to Israel's inheritance of *another* Land of Promise, for it was in 1407 BC that the Israelites inherited Canaan and divided the territories between the Tribes. The answers and explanations to these questions are the keys to comprehending the future, and they are entertained only by looking back into the archaic past.

In 2909 BC, Enoch's final year on Earth, the Anunnaki had grown powerful on Earth and began their oppression over mankind. This year was *670 years* prior to the Great Flood of 2239 BC that ended this antediluvian Iron Empire. The Seven Kings of the Anunnaki before the Flood are the subject of hundreds of cuneiform Sumerian and Akkadian tablet texts that were later copied and adapted by the Babylonians and Assyrians. In this year Enoch left the Sethites complete instructions on how and where to erect the Great Pyramid, a project they began exactly 666 years before the Flood in 2905 BC, which required 90 years to finished in 2815 BC.

After the Flood Nimrod became king and planted the seeds of Empire but in 1899 BC all this ended when the Dark Satellite (prison of the Seven Anunnaki Kings) nearly collided into Earth (see *Anunnaki Homeworld*) and caused earthquakes, flooding and immense flux tube lightning storms. Kingdoms fragmented, the empire of Babel collapsed with its Tower and peoples migrated all over the Near East, Canaan, Africa, Asia Minor, Europe, the isles of the Mediterranean and Aegean, into Asia, India and beyond eventually to the ancient Americas. In 1899 BC the strongest people of all were the *Elamites*, predecessors of the Persians, ancient enemies of Babylon whose descendants are found in the Iranian people. They immediately assumed the role of the Iron Empire, conquering Egypt first, then the cities of Canaan and Babylon. The Sumerians, Assyrians and even Hittites were annexed as well. The Fall of Babel and start of the Elamite Empire began a *670 year* countdown to the most famous civilization of western history: the *Fall of Troy* in 1229 BC. The 670 years of *Iron Empires* continued from 1899 BC with Elam's fall to Abraham and his Amorite allies at Damascus after the attack of Sodom and Gomorrah. The Amorite Dynasty of Babylon brought unprecedented power to Nimrod, then called Hammurabi (Amraphel), and the Amorites conquered Egypt and have been since called the Hyksos by Egyptologists. The Amorites fell to the Hittites of Anatolia in Asia Minor, of which the Trojan and Milesian states bordered.

While the Hittites maintained an Iron Empire over Asia Minor, Armenia, the Near East, the Levant/Palestine regions, Phrygia, Lydia, Caria to the very borders of Ilium of Troy, on the other side of the Euphrates on the Tigris River the Assyrians also became an Iron Empire in 1273 BC the year Phoenix appeared in the inner system. Assyria annexed Babylon in 1273 BC, beginning a 666-year countdown to the Fall of Assyria to Babylon under Nebuchadnezzar II in 607 BC. Assyria's emergence in 1273 BC also began a *670-year* timeline to the Fall of Jerusalem and Judah to Babylon in 603 BC.

The Fall of Troy in 1229 BC (670 years after 1899 BC Fall of Babel) was not merely the end of the Trojan state to Agamemnon of Mycenaea and his immense army of Greeks, but also the end of the Hittite civilization by a strange and powerful series of lightning storms from heaven that vitrified the stone of towns, towers, citadels and roads. The same cataclysm that ended the Hittites was also noted throughout the Iliad of Homer who described the Fall of Troy attended by atmospheric disturbances, a comet, lightning blasts from the sky and earthquakes. The full account found in *Chronicon*. Homer's writings, Virgil's Aeneid and a host of Greek and Roman historical accounts reveal that the surviving people of Troy sailed to the Italian peninsula and after a war with the Latins, Sabines and Etruscans, settled down and built the famous city of *Rome*. The Romans were the descendants of the Trojans, the assimilated Latins, Sabines and the *Semitic* Etruscans that were divided into Twelve Tribes. All of this and more is more properly covered in this author's other works. What is to be noted, however, is that the Fall of Troy was precisely *476 years* before the *Founding of Rome* is 753 BC by the descendants of the Trojan exiles. As Israel enjoyed 476 years from 1407 BC to the split between Israel and Judah in 931 BC, which was 1407 years before the Fall of Rome in *476 AD*, we see in Rome's history the signature of an *emerging* New Israel made of the descendants of the ancient Israelites that were dispersed throughout the kingdoms by Iron Empires.

This history is even more deeply repetitive for 753 BC begins the regnal succession of the Seven Kings of Rome, mirroring the Seven Kings of the Anunnaki before the Flood. 753 BC is *670 years* to 83 BC when the Capitol in Rome burned in a fire and the original Sybilline Books were destroyed, which had been obtained by the Seventh King of Rome. The Romans celebrated the fact they were descended from the heroes of the Trojan War, which ended in *1229 BC*, and the Founding of Rome in 753 BC began a *1229-year* countdown to the *476 AD Fall of Rome* to the Ten Kingdoms under Odoacer the German. This 1229-year period encompassed the period of the Kings of Rome (244 years), the Republic of Rome and the actual *Iron* Empire of Rome. The historical synthesis with Israel occurs in the fateful year of 476 AD. Amazingly, Rome's first king was Romulus, a boy-regent, and in 476 AD the Emperor of Rome was a *boy* named *Romulus* Augustus.

The succession of empires from Babylon was revealed to the prophet Daniel in the interpretation of the dream of King Nebuchadnezzar, these empires being Babylon, Persia, Greece and Rome, followed by Ten Toes of *miry clay mixed with iron* (descendants of *Israel* mixed with Roman people). The Ten Kingdoms fulfill this perfectly. Niccolo Machievelli listed these Ten Kingdoms of Europe as the Lombards, Franks, Burgundians, Ostragoths, Visigoths, Vandals, Heruli, Suevi, Huns and the Saxons. Amazingly, Machievelli left no indication in his works The Art of War (not to be confused for Sun Tsu's text) and The Prince that he was aware of Daniel's prophecy or its meaning. The ancient kingdoms of Europe originally spoke Germanic dialects and could all understand one another, but as centuries passed, they developed standardized languages for their independent rising nations and these Ten Kingdoms have today become the *main body of European nations*. These Ten Kingdoms were comprised of the descendants of the 13 Tribes of Israel who had been deported into the Assyrian domains annexed in Asia Minor and Armenia and forcibly mixed with Germanic colonies of the Cimmerians and Scythians that had already been settled into the regions by the empire-building Assyrians. The deportation and integration program caused the newly arrived people of Israel to adopt the regional language, which was

Germanic (Indo-Aryan), which began when the first Israeli deportees arrived under the direction of their Assyrian overlords in 745 BC. The Ten Kingdoms were racially descended from the admixture of the ancient Germanic nations and Israelis enslaved by the Assyrians, though other Indo-Aryan cultures to the far north never had contact with the Assyrians, such as those that were later known as the Norse (Nordic cultures). These descendants were of all 13 Tribes.

The Old Testament prophets foretold that Israel would be entered into a New Covenant, and that the Word of God would come to them in an alien language in the future. Incredibly, this was literally fulfilled when, over a thousand years after their deportation in 745 BC they had thoroughly adopted the Germanic dialects and in the third century AD the New Covenant spread like wildfire throughout the European kingdoms in the form of the Gospels, for Christianity *erupted* and was firmly established in many of the European kingdoms even prior to the Fall of Rome in 476 AD. We are not bereft of more historical evidence.

In the 666th year since Assyria became an Iron Empire in 1273 BC when planet Phoenix passed through the inner system, King Nebuchadnezzar II in 607 BC defeated the Assyrians and annexed their nation. Hundreds of thousands of formerly displaced people of Israel living among the displaced Germans in Armenia, Asia Minor and northern Assyria made their escape, migrating deeper into Europe (origin of Celts, Gauls and some Transalpine nations). Assyria's emergence as Iron Empire began with appearance of Phoenix in 1273 BC, which orbits the sun every 138 years, and the fall of Assyria to Babylon was exactly *138 years* after Assyria deported Israel in 745 BC, or precisely *1656 (414 x 4) months*. This year, 745 BC, happened to be the 324th year (108 x 3) of the Divided Kingdom Chronology, which began when Israel and Judah became the Two Kingdoms. Though many formerly deported nations escaped Babylonian dominion, still there were other Israelite peoples mixed among the Assyrian population that did not leave. Some were already firmly settled in the Persian realms.

To more accurately understand this thesis we must comprehend who Jesus was and what He instructed His disciples to do after He departed. In the start of His ministry, Jesus spoke before the synagogue in Nazareth, proclaiming, "The Spirit of the Lord is upon me…to preach the acceptable YEAR OF THE LORD, and the Day of Vengeance of Our God." (Luke 4:18-19, Isa. 61:1-2). The *beginning* of Christ's ministry alludes to the END of His ministry in the YEAR OF THE LORD, or Armageddon, when He will descend to make war and vanquish the Anunnaki in the year 6000 (2106 AD), demonstrating that the year of these events was never meant to be hidden (only day and hour).

(See *Chronicon*). Whoever Jesus actually is, when He returns in 2106 AD it will be as an avatar of war.

The scriptural mother and father of Jesus were Galileans, a distinctly non-Jewish metropolis referred to by the prophet Isaiah as "Galilee of the *nations* (Hebrew-*foreign people*)." (Isa. 9:1). The origin of Galilee derives from the massive influx of European, Asian and Near Eastern peoples that settled the area when the army of Alexander the Great of Macedon took up residence in the region. After conquering Mesopotamia and the East the Greek army (with numerous other European auxiliaries) settled in this virtual garden realm barren of people due to longstanding history of Arab raids and violence. They built ten cities in the exact geographical region of ancient *Israel* in western Galilee and Samaria, these cities collectively called the *Decapolis* (Ten Cities), ten thoroughly Greek, international cities, sophisticated and prosperous. This is the cultural-racial pedigree of Joseph and Mary, the Galileans being descendants of the pureblood *Israelites* that became the Ten Lost Tribes after the Assyrian deportation of 745 BC and again in 721 BC exactly *8640 days* later (745-721 is 24 years: 360 x 24 is 8640). Through Greek dominance, many of the descendants of Israel migrated *back* to their ancestral homeland in Israel, now called the Decapolis. The Galileans, (from Gaul, as in Galatia) were of pure Hebrew ancestry having adopted the Greek and Aramaic language. Joseph and Mary were actual blood descendants of the Royal House of Judah, *not* the Edomite tainted post-Exilic Judeans calling themselves Jews after leaving Babylonia.

When Jesus was born, Joseph and Mary were travelling during the Census and in the Judahite city of Bethlehem they could find no lodging and Mary had Jesus in a stable, fulfilling Isaiah's prophecy: "For unto us a child is born, unto us a son is given; and the Government shall be upon His shoulders; and his name shall be called Wonderful, Counselor, the mighty God, the everlasting Father, the Prince of Peace...the Lord sent a word unto Jacob, and it hath lighted upon Israel. And all the people shall know, even *Ephraim* and the inhabitant of *Samaria* (reference to Decapolis)..." (Isa. 9:6-9) The name Ephraim refers to the greatest of the 13 Tribes of Israel, and by the time of Isaiah and the prophets the *prophetic* name mentioned almost a hundred times in Scripture for the name of Israel is *Ephraim*.

The inception of Christ's ministry offended the Jews, for Jesus taught and revealed only ancient Israelite (Hebraic) revelations, quoting Israelite prophecies and nothing of Jewish context was mentioned by Jesus unless in *condemnation*. The Jews of that day practiced a tainted religion they brought out of Babylonia, an admixture of Hebraicism and Talmudicism never before acknowledged in Israel or Judah. When Nebuchadnezzar II took the Judahites into captivity in 585 BC they still held on to the Torah and maintained the Temple as the epicenter of their worship, but when they returned from Babylonia they brought an alien religion taught through the *Talmudic* literature in *synagogues*. Though some among these Jews were still holy unto God, their culture and creed had degenerated into what before God had become defiled and unacceptable. The raging controversy caused by Jesus is casually mentioned by a Roman statesman named Valleus Paterculus who, after 16 years of military service, was on his way back to Rome at the age of 51 when he passed through Judea. A close friend of Caesar from a notable equestrian family, Paterculus wrote that he met a certain man named Jesus of Nazareth, the most amazing man he had ever encountered, who cured disease, made the blind to see, raised the dead and helped the poor. Paterculus specifically mentioned in his writing that the Jews of the region were involved in a controversy over who Jesus was, but that as for himself, ".... was more afraid of Jesus than of a whole army." This amazing account was found in the Vatican Archives. (2) The account is said to be a old forgery, that the Vatican now hides it because its forged discrepancies are now obvious.

In their defense against the accusations of Jesus the Jews focused on where Jesus was from, Nazareth (in Galilee), rather than what His message was, saying sarcastically, "Can anything good come out of Nazareth?" (John 1:46), or as when some cynically asked, "Shall Christ (the Anointed One) come out of Galilee?" (John 7:41) The Galileans were particularly despised by the Jews. Jesus, to their exasperation, chose His disciples from among the people of Galilee, only Judas (the Betrayer) being a Jew. The Galileans were considered to be Gentiles (non-Jews). The rift between Jew and Galilean was not only in character, but genetic as well, and the Jew prejudiced against the Galileans merely continued the more historic animosity of the contention between Judah and Israel which caused the tribes to split into the Divided Kingdom of Judah and Israel, in 931 BC Jerusalem being the capitol of Judah and *Samaria* the capitol of Israel. The Galileans were descendants of Israel, the Jews being correct in that they were non-Jewish, but absolutely blind to the fact that they were of Hebraic ancestry.

Having taken up residence in the Decapolis, the many among the Galileans *relearned* Hebrew and adopted Judaism. Among these were Joseph and Mary. The Jews, despite their animosity, accepted this because this additional multitude of people from Samaria and all of Galilee brought tremendous revenue to the Temple every Passover to Pentecost, 50 days a year. Though the Jews reasoning was financial, God used this to raise the Christ in Israel among those He would expose and redeem, a true descendant of the Royal House of Judah who would return to sit on the Throne of David the Jews believed was exclusively theirs.

The Jewish leaders scorned Him, saying "Art thou also of Galilee? Search and look: for out of Galilee ariseth no prophet." (John 7:52) What the Jews used in ridicule, was actually a *virtue*, for being Galilean gave the disciples of Christ and later the Christian missionary easy access to the rest of the world the message was to be taken to. Galilee was still an international arena of trade, commerce and intercourse.

Christ's ministry objective was very clear, for He stated, "...I am not sent but to the Lost Sheep of the HOUSE OF ISRAEL." (John 10:2) This is a direct reference to the *lost Israelites* called *Ephraim* by the prophets, the name of the 13th Tribe which had become the most populous and dominant in Israelite times before the Deportations. Ephraim was the collective term for all 13 Tribes, including the Judahites, found scattered among the nations as well as those who through *faith* become *sons of adoption* according to the promises given by God to Abraham, Isaac and Jacob. Remember, Jacob (renamed Israel) *adopted* the sons of Joseph in Egypt (land of the Great Pyramid) in 1639 BC, which was a major period aligned with the Anunnaki NER Chronology 600 years before the birth of King David in 1039 BC. These sons, named Manesseh and Ephraim, were named by Jacob (these were *not* their original Egyptian names), for Manesseh means *forgetful* and was a prophetic reference to the future *Ephraim* (13 Tribes of Israel) *forgetting* who they were.

The Jews (of Judahite, Babylonian and *Edomite* pedigree) assumed that Christ would come as an immediate conqueror to subdue all nations under Jewish dominion, and that the covenants belonged only to them, for they still possessed Jerusalem. They in their national pride were totally oblivious that the hundreds of millions of people even in those days dispersed throughout Asia, Asia Minor, Galilee, Samaria, Persia, Europe, the Mediterranean and Aegean, Arabia and Africa (Abyssinians of Ethipoia) and other Africans as well as those of the Americas and the *entire world* not possibly related by blood to the descendants of Israel, were still by *faith* heirs to all the promises of Abraham, Isaac and Jacob and that the entirety of the Holy Scriptures belonged to them as well. By excluding the whole world from the promises of the Word of God, the Jews cursed themselves and reconfirmed their curse by proclaiming as one to Pontius Pilate, the Roman Governor over Judea, "May His blood be upon us and our children."

Prior to His crucifixion, Jesus commanded His disciples, saying, "Go not into the way of the heathen, and into the way of the Samaritans, enter ye not, but go rather to the LOST SHEEP OF THE HOUSE OF ISRAEL." (Matt. 10:5-6, 15:24) The word *lost* here is the Greek (New Testament written in *Greek* not Hebrew) APPOLUMI, which is comprised of root words meaning "separation" (APO) by *punishment* (OLLUMI). This is a direct reference to the judgment of God against Israel's 10 Tribes and their deportation by Assyria for worshipping false gods. The evidence of *where* the Lost Sheep (Israelites not living in their geographical allotments) were located is clearly seen by the ministry of the Apostles after Christ resurrected and ascended, for the followers of Jesus took up the Divine Commission taking the Word of God into *Asia Minor and Europe.* That the Lost Sheep no longer resided in Palestine is further evidenced by the statement of Jesus when He said "Ye shall not have gone over all the *cities of Israel*, till the son of man be come...." If Israel only referred to the geographical confines of Palestine, then the Apostles could have spread the word in only months or years. Even Paul, a converted Jew and Roman citizen, obeyed the Divine Directive, and after preaching in Phrygia and Galatia he imagined to turn toward Bithynia, but he was "...forbidden by the Holy Ghost to preach the word in Asia," for the "Spirit suffered them not." (Acts 16:4-6). Paul then had a vision of people crying his name in *Macedonia*, so he took the Word of God to Greekdom and later to the Eternal City, called Rome.

When Christ ascended an angel of the Almighty appeared before the people, the Apostles and about 500 followers, saying, "You men of *Galilee*, why stand here gazing at the heavens? This same Jesus will also *return* in like manner." On the Day of Pentecost the Holy Spirit descended upon the gathered Christians and each one began speaking the wonderful works of God in *foreign languages* amazing all present, who marveled, saying, "Behold, are not these *Galileans?* And how hear we every man in our own tongue, wherein we were born?" (Acts 2:6-7) It is this author's personal theory that these were the languages now spoken by the Lost Sheep of Israel in the nations they had become, absorbed, or integrated with. When the city of Rome burned in AD 64 the Emperor Nero was largely believed to have caused or at least permitted the city to burn without offering any assistance in putting out the flames. His wife was the beautiful *Jewish* actress Poppaea who is believed to have offered Nero a perfect scapegoat by claiming that the people who would cause such a disaster were called *Galileans* (earliest name for *Christians*), a people vehemently hated by the Jews. Christianity spread through the Roman Empire so fast that Jews in the Roman cities from their synagogues took every opportunity to disparage and conspire against them. This AD 64 event is what caused Peter and his wife and multitudes of Christians to suffer horrible deaths.

The western migration of Israel's tribes is attested also by Flavius Josephus in his *Antiquities of the Jews*, written almost 2000 years ago. He wrote that once the Tribes were free to return to Israel only two tribes returned, the other ten or eleven tribes, according to Josephus, were an *innumerable multitude,* who did not return. (3) Josephus wrote that they remained first in Asia and Asia Minor but later migrated into *Europe*. These people would have descendants from all thirteen tribes, as the Israelites were always intermarrying among themselves, and amazingly, in the apocryphal book of 2 Esdras chapter *13* we discover that the Israelites travelled for a year and a half to a distant country no men yet dwelt in. (4) This began the founding of the Eurasian nations which became the *Ten Kingdoms* of Europe composed racially of the stock of the 13 Tribes of Israel integrated with those Germanic deportees they lived amongst in Assyria, the Iron Empire of its day, fulfilling the dream of the *ten toes of iron mixed with miry clay*. Ten *Christian* nations descended from ancient Israel that succeeded Rome but through the course of their histories carried on the legacy of Rome's culture, language, political structure and philosophies.

Now we have come full circle in our thesis to that transitive year of 476 AD when Rome fell to the Ten Kingdoms under Odoacer the German, and the calendrical motif of *1407 years,* which carried with it the theme of the people of God receiving their *Land of Promise*. As the ancient standard formation of the Tribes of Israel around the Tabernacle had Manesseh and Ephraim to the *west* of the center of the moving formation, so too did the Israelites (Ephraim) migrate to the far west and first inherited the fertile domains of Europe under their prophetic heritage as Manesseh (*forgetting* who they were). But their inheritance time as starting in 476 AD merely begins a more profound timeline to the inheritance of the 13th Tribe of Israel and being the greatest of all the tribes of Jacob, the *Empire of Adoption* which includes descendants of all 13 Tribes that first began as 13 Colonies of England in the *west* in a New Israel (New American continent) that became the United States of America (*Israel*) in 1776 AD exactly *1300 years* after the rise of the Ten Kingdoms in 476 AD!

It is this profound history of both Israel and Rome that identifies the prophetic nation of North America. King Nebuchadnezzar's dream interpreted by Daniel the prophet is the key to unlocking America's identity and decoding the symbolism of the Great Seal of the United States. This dream dealt with Four Empires that would rise and fall all affecting Jerusalem and Israel until many *Israelite nations* (miry clay mixed with ten iron toes) would arise and endure until world governments would end by a stone from heaven. This prophecy began fulfillment in 603 BC with King Nebuchadnezzar II sacking Jerusalem and taking hostages to Babylon, like Daniel. From this year Babylon ruled 66 years (792 months: NIBIRU's orbit in months) until falling to Cyrus of Persia in 537 BC, the Persians reigning *207 years* (half a Cursed Earth period), or an abbreviated 2070 years. This 207-year period was 2484 months (414 x 6), until Alexander the Great conquered Darius III of Persia in 330 BC. The Greek culture flooded the east and south, Egypt, divided, and the Romans emerged on the world scene to defeat the Macedonian kings in Greekdom, Syria and Egypt. In 63 BC the Romans annexed Syria and Judea, this being *540 years* (half of 1080) after the beginning of the fulfillment of this prophecy. Amazingly, Judea's fall to Rome in 63 BC is the start of Rome's final *540 years*, for Judea's Israelite brethren among the Ten Kingdoms of Europe would end the Roman Empire 540 years later in 476 AD. This prophecy and recorded history identifies Israel by the sum of *1080 years* (longevity of Nebuchadnezzar's II prophecy), from 603 BC to 476 AD further linking Israel to its Great Seal of the Great Pyramid in Egypt which was completed in the year 2815 BC, or *1080 Annus Mundi*/Hebrew Reckoning.

The United States' geographical landmass in North America is also the land of origin of the Maya, the celebrated culture of Mexico that claimed they had migrated from the north as *13 Clans* under their 13 Heavens. They believed that after the 13th Baktun of their profound Mayan Long-Count calendar, their land (America) would be drastically changed as will *time* itself. The USA established a Roman-like government with a President, Senate, elected offices, courts and even employs *Latin* in its political, legal, medical and scientific vernacular. The USA is the *first* and only nation on Earth that declares in its Declaration of Independence and Constitution that the rights of men come from *God*, not government. In fact, the United States was *born in faith*, for the Declaration of Independence is a totally unique document and act of man, for the nation declared its sovereignty and purpose long *before it secured it by war*. As *Ephraim*, the USA adopted the Seal of Israel, the *Great Pyramid*, and is chief among the nations of the world in *adopting foreigners* into her national body and making citizens of them, fulfilling the role of the Israelite Cities of Refuge. In fact, it was not without design that Edward Gibbon of England published his monumental 6-volume work, *Decline and Fall of the Roman Empire* in this fateful year of 1776 AD, perhaps a coincidence to Mr. Gibbon, but deliberately timed by God. The year 1776 also marked the year of the start of the modern *Illuminati Order*, its structure based off of 13 old royal families of Europe traced back several centuries. They have taken an oath to see the Antichrist sit upon his throne. (5)

Further calendrical confirmation of the birth of New Israel (United States) in the new Land of Promise (North America) in 1776 AD is found in that 1776 AD (5670 AM) is exactly *2520 years* (360 x 7), or seven prophetic Great Years of 360 years each, after the Ten Tribes of Israel were deported by Assyria in 745 BC (3150 AM). The sum of 2520 years is the same encoded in the writings of Daniel that appeared on the wall in Babylon as MENE MENE TEKEL UPHARSIN which was interpreted as "…weighed, weighed, numbered and *divided*," referring to the *empire* of Babylon which fell that very night in 537 BC to Persia. In the Israelite context, this is the 2520 years that the descendants would be *divided* nationally because of *judgment* until after 2520 years when they will be *united* in *empire* after their judgment was over in *1776 AD*. The original national effigy for ancient Assyria was the *Phoenix*, and the original bird of the United States was also the Phoenix, which was changed quietly in 1902 AD to the Great Eagle, 1902 AD being the beginning of the Giza Course Countdown of 203 levels of stone to the top of the pyramid which indicated the 204th space to 2106 AD, the Year 6000, when the Chief Cornerstone will descend upon the Monument of Mankind and defeat the Anunnaki: see *When the Sun Darkens*.

What is truly shocking is this historical coherency. The year 745 BC which started this period of judgment against Israel was precisely *2070 years* (414 x 5) after the completion of the Great Pyramid in 2815 BC (1080 AM) by the preflood Sethites, ancestors of the Israelites. The pyramid was built to survive the coming of global quakes and a world-killing flood in 2239 BC. This diluvian disaster was itself *2070 years* (414 x 5) after the total ruination of the PreAdamic World in 4309 BC caused by the rebellion of the Anunnaki. Throughout human history the Anunnaki have employed human agents in their machinations against the people of God (all those adopted by faith into the Kingdom), especially the actual blood descendants of Israel. In antiquity their rebellion against God lasted 330 years until *judgment fell from heaven* and destroyed their PreAdamic civilization, sending the world into a blackness of frozen migration for *270 years* until the planet restabilized in a newer orbit around the sun. But God as Architect of History has reversed these events in human timelines. In 1776 AD New Israel is born exactly *330 years* before the War of Armageddon in 2106 AD when *judgment* in the form of the Chief Cornerstone will *descend* from heaven to defeat the Anunnaki, who also in 1776 AD, orchestrated through the human vassals the beginning of the *Illuminati*, an international cryptocracy funded through world banks designed to infiltrate all levels of all governments. Though through controversy the Illuminati went underground, they still exist in the highest levels of international government, in the United Nations, US Congress and especially in their daughter organizations known as the Trilateral Commission and Council on Foreign Relations.

In the world of the Anunnaki before mankind, Earth was frozen and dark fo 270 years to 4039 BC, the start of the Orbital Chronology encoded in the Great Pyramid as discovered by David Davidson and published in 1924 AD (see *Anunnaki Homeworld*). Now, starting in 1776 AD, the United States of America's timeline progresses for *270 years* to 2046 AD when NIBIRU, the Anunnaki homeworld, passes close to the planet, when a comet impacts the North American continent *ending* the United States and also the Orbital Chronology encoded in the pyramid. This occurs 2047 years after the birth of Christ in 1 BC, and in the year 2047 Annus Mundi (1848 BC) Sodom and Gomorrah were destroyed in *judgment from heaven* as fiery cometary detritus rained on the cities for their *rebellion* against God. As revealed in detail in this author's other books, 2046 AD is the *true* end of the 13th baktun of the Mayan Long-Count, which does *not* end in 2012 AD at all. The global cataclysm of 2046 AD also initiates the events of the 13th chapter of the book of Revelation.

It is during the longevity of the United States of America that the Cursed Earth Chronology (Stonehenge Chronolithic system) ends in 1902 AD and the Giza Course Countdown begins, the Anunnaki Chronology of 7200 years ends and as readers of *Chronicon* and *Anunnaki Homeworld* can attest, scores of historical events transpired paralleling exactly events that already happened in ancient times. With the end of America is the final appearance into the inner system of NIBIRU, the end of the Mayan Calendar, the end of the Orbital Chronology on the Great Pyramid as well as so many other synchronicities that they cannot be listed herein. (see *Chronicon*).

Archive VI

2052 AD Return of the Fallen Ones

History and its lessons are for our present instruction. The history of a date-specific timeline like the Anunnaki Chronology serves not merely for the present, but is a tool in *reading* the future. We time-travel into the future by analyzing our histories—the more precise our timelines the greater distance we can see. Our predecessors maintained this belief and were meticulous historians.

In the young Egyptian's tomb, Tutankhamen, a golden inscription reads, "I have seen the past; I know the future." (1) Sitchin cites an Assyrian tablet text of King Esarhaddon that read, "The future shall be like the past." (2) Perhaps even older than this is the Old Testament Solomonic writing in Ecclesiastes—"That which hath been is now; and that which is to be hath already been; and God *requireth that which is past.*" In the New Testament apocryphal *Gospel of Thomas* we find Jesus saying that "where the beginning he, there shall *be the end*...the man who reaches the beginning, he will *know the end.*"

As the beginning of anything was to be found out by the unfolding of historical events, according to Firmicus Maternus, so too must historical events have predictive value. Time runs (or is a phenomenon) in *all directions* because it is a *spatial* occurrence in our fourth-dimensional existence. This does not infer that there is not a fifth dimension. In fact, the Anunnaki are fifth dimensional beings, but this aspect of their nature is not relative to the present thesis. The visionary Ouspensky wrote that, "future events are wholly contained in preceding ones, and if we could know the force and direction of all events which have happened up to the present moment, i.e. if we knew all the past, by this we could *know all the future.*" (3) This is simply because "time is not measured by the calendar but by the *events that occupy it,*" in the words of the historian Lewis Mumford.

The Anunnaki Chronology is not just a calendar, but it is a *rhythm* in the space-time occurrences that through its continuum of unfolding events, tell a story of what is to transpire in 2052 AD and beyond, a mathematical framework of *events* in fixed positions within a matrix of 600-year and 60-year fragments confined in four dimensions. Each historical event contributed to the ultimate outcome of the timeline, like pieces of a puzzle that will all come together at one definitive point in the future. This will occur only once a *solid* is formed in the space-time structure, for once a timeline is finished a geometrical solid actually creates the unfolding events and their conditions (which are building another solid) that were foreshadowed by their historical predecessors. The embedded inferences of what is to come within a finished solid define how these events will unfold again in the beginning of the construction of the *next* space-time solid.

At any given time of day there are infinitely uncountable amounts of space-time solids being constructed and the future multiverse is solely dependent upon this continuity of *creation*. Space-time solids are fractions of the geometrical fourth-dimensional universe that serve as our *where and when reality*. But the Anunnaki are *fifth*-dimensional beings able to traverse between space-time solids—they are literally "beyond time" as we understand it (time is actually *spatial*) and not impeded by our physical dimensions. Height, depth, width and where (when) do not confine fifth-dimensional intelligences.

The Anunnaki Chronology began in 5239 BC and terminated in 1962 AD in its 7200th year, or precisely twelve 600-year periods, forming an amazing three-dimensional geometrical space-time structure. Anciently, the Pythagoreans taught that if something exists as a mathematical concept, it exists in reality (4), and they believed that there were four principle geometrical forms. They were completely unaware of a *fifth* geometrical form, discovered by Hippasos—the dodecahedron. (5) Plato speculated that this was the geometrical form of the universe. (6) The Anunnaki timeline of history in 1962 AD formed the space-time structure of a *pentagonal* dodecahedron, a twelve-sided solid, each plane being a pentagon. Twelve AR-UBs.

The pentagonal dodecahedron has *60 points* (7), each of its twelve planes being a 600-year period, each plane a pentagon having five terminations represented as 120-year periods (120 x 5 = 600). Amazingly, the original crystalline structure of our planet Earth, according to Russian scientists was that of a *dodecahedron* before it expanded into a sphere. They claim that the twelve pentagonal slabs can still be detected covering the surface of the globe. (8) Recently, a space satellite took photos of a continental-size pentagonal shadow on Saturn at its northern polar extremity.

The end of the Anunnaki Chronology in 1962 begins the final 144 years until the end of Man's Exile, the 6000-year curse that began in 3895 BC, *144 years* after Earth was renovated and began its present orbit around the sun in 4039 BC. The sum of 144 has long been associated with *beginnings* and *endings* by numerologists and mystics. With the calendar now fixed within the pentagonal dodecahedronic space-time solid the Anunnaki and human worlds merge in a sequence of events during these 144 years on earth in the creation of another space-time structure constructed from the *shadows* of its progenitor. These are the events of the Anunnaki prophetic geometry that we can expect to reoccur in the immediate future, in 2052 AD, and until 2106 AD (6000 AM).

The author chose to go into explicit detail in the first archives of this work because it is the historical details that permit us to perceive the design of what is to come. The Architect of Time, our Sovereign Creator, set laws in place that by diligent study we can comprehend—chronological strictures that even He obeys. Truly there is deity in the design. Every event is a milestone and the scenery about the milestone in the Anunnaki Chronology contributes to the end picture until all planes and angles become a *closed system*, a geometrical solid otherwise known as *fate*. So in determining the fate of the Anunnaki and mankind, let's review the combined "planes and angles" of this chronological geometry.

The Anunnaki Chronology began in 5239 BC and they were co-creators with God who created a sentient life form that initially served them, the PreAdamites. Then 600 years later the Anunnaki rebelled against the Godhead in 4639 BC and transgressed the commandments of the Word, even enslaving the PreAdamites. A war transpired for 330 years and the daystar burned out after a series of detonations that catapults planets Phoenix and Earth along the new Dark Star's ecliptic to their present orbits around the Nightstar, our sun, which was from Earth's original position in this binary system, very far away. The solar system catastrophe ruined NIBIRU and obliterated the planet that occupied the space between Mars and Jupiter we know as the Astroid Belt today. This was 4309 BC and Earth wandered in space for 270 years until 4039 BC when it began to orbit the present sun, initiating the Great Pyramid's Orbital Chronology discovered by David Davidson. This concluded two 600-year periods, or 1200 years (432,000 days), to a calendrical change.

In 4039 BC earth was renovated and the Anunnaki were on Earth but remained distant and unseen as they conspired against man, who was commanded to "replenish" the earth. Six hundred years later the Anunnaki homeworld NIBIRU entered the inner system in 3439 BC and many of them descended to earth as the world was in a ruined state of chaos from earthquakes and flooding that killed a *third* of humanity. Though originally appointed as Guardians over Man, they quickly manipulated men and induced them to trade their daughters in exchange for scientific and technological knowledges, their sole intent being to thwart the Edenic command to replenish earth by contaminating the pure Adamic gene pool with *hybrids*. Knowing that a savior was going to be born and hoping to prevent it. As time passed they began abducting the daughters of men and upon the earth were raised a nation of giants and hybrids called the Nephilim. By this act the Anunnaki sealed their fate, their descent from NIBIRU beginning many of the world's oldest calendrical systems, a fate that would be suffered in the Last Days. This seal was the AR UB, which revealed that they would be *shackled, imprisoned.* Thus the Fallen Ones, also called the Watchers in antiquity were recorded by the Sumerians as the kingship that "lowered from heaven," texts that hint that the Anunnaki were shapechangers. This descent to earth began a 1200-year (600 + 600 or 432,000 days) countdown to the Great Flood in 2239 BC that exterminated the Nephilim.

In the following 600 years from their appearance on Earth the Nephilim became *nations* and humanity increased under the guidance of the prophet-emperor Enoch. When Enoch *ascended* from earth in 2909 BC at Achuzan (Giza) the Sethites erected the Great Pyramid complex, completing it after 90 years of construction, or exactly *1080 months.* This completion was in the year 2815 BC, or *1080 Annus Mundi.* During this period of building the Seven Kings of the Anunnaki descended on Earth in 2839 BC and began to rule a human race almost already servile to the Anunnaki and their Nephilim offspring, which had quickly filled in the power vacuum left behind by Enoch's departure, exactly 670 years before the Deluge. Though the Sethites erected the pyramid complex, Newgrange and Stonehenge (see *Anunnaki Homeworld* and *Lost Scriptures*) human memory attributed this to the Anunnaki later on when the ancients remember them as the Builder Gods, though this epithet was actually more ancient. The Anunnaki were the Builders that rejected the Stone (Word) known as the Head of the Corner, the Savior. He is the Chief Cornerstone of the Monument of Man the pyramid symbolizes, its your base cornerstones representing the Divine Tetramorph, or Four Living Ones—the zodiacal Keepers of Apocalypse.

This Elder Faith in the Stone was originally held by the Ten Patriarchs of Genesis, from Adam to Noah, their families and communities. These men were according to all accounts Ten Kings opposed to the Anunnaki, the kings of the Sethites at the continual war with the Cainite and Nephilim nations. That the promise of His coming had yet to be fulfilled, the Sethites left the apex of the Great Pyramid flat, a 20 x 20 foot platform, symbolizing the resting place of the Chief Cornerstone when He descends from heaven.

During the last 600 years of antediluvian history the Seven Kings ruled over mankind in a society that grew so chaotic and lawless that it collapsed. Even the Nephilim nations became unmanageable and revolted against the Anunnaki and each other. Humans were eaten, enslaved and killed for sport. Only after securing authority and control over humanity did the Seven Kings come to be regarded as totally wicked, enemies of God and mankind and fathers of monsters, mutants, hybrids, progeny of the Abyss. In the 600th year since 2839 BC, in the reign of the Eighth King, who was one of the Seven come back to reign again, planet Phoenix entered the system and transited, darkening the sun seven days before massive impacts caused the Great Flood in 2239 BC. The Deluge was caused by the falling down of *two stars* to earth and a constellation that fell from the sky. Intriguingly, in the context of 7200 years, planet Phoenix enters the system 45 times, and although the Anunnaki Chronology in this work targets only 31 dates (12 periods of 600 years and 19 periods of 60 years), planet Phoenix appears in 5 of these Anunnaki dates (3619 BC, 2239 BC, 859 BC, 522 AD, 1902 AD). Out of *thousands* of year-dates this synchronicity is stunning. But even more astonishing is the appearances of NIBIRU. The Anunnaki homeworld passes close to earth 13 times in this 7200 years, and yet 4 appearances of NIBIRU align perfectly with 4 of the 31 Anunnaki Chronology dates (3499 BC, 3439 BC, 462 AD, 522 AD). Amazingly, *both* Phoenix and NIBIRU pass through the inner system in 522 AD, which is the *only year in world history both planets do so*, and this is aligned with the Anunnaki Chronology. The orbital chronologies of Phoenix and NIBIRU and the Anunnaki dating system are all related.

The Great Deluge resulted in the confinement of the Seven Kings, these Anunnaki lords imprisoned within a lost moon of NIBIRU called the *Dark Satillite* that shares an orbital history that also traverses through the milestones of the Anunnaki Chronology. Their confinement ended their 670 year long dynasty, the first *Iron Empire*, from 2909-2239 BC. In 1899 BC the Dark Satillite would pass close to earth and initiate the Babel cataclysm and Fall of Akkad and ruin of Sargon's empire, which began a 670 year countdown to the catastrophic end of both the Hittite Empire and the Fall of Troy in 1229 BC. Planet Phoenix entered the inner system in 1273 BC at the start of the Assyrian Empire, which began 670 years to the Fall of Assyria and its holdings in Babylonia and Fall of Jerusalem in 603 BC. The city of Rome was founded in 753 BC and was famous for its original rulers, the Seven Kings of Rome. 670 years after 753 BC was 83 BC when the Capitol in Rome burned and the prophetic books of the Sybil were destroyed which had been purchased by Tarquin the Proud, the seventh and last king of Rome.

The preflood chronicles completed, we now venture into the ancient world. In 2119 BC (120 years after the Flood), an Anunnaki artifact was discovered by Cainan. It was an antediluvian relic covered in the scientific instructions of the Watchers concerning the astrological sciences. Some texts read that these were writings of the Giants, or of the Watchers. Exactly 240 years (120 + 120) after this was the international war known as the *Battle of*

Kuruksata involving Elam (Persia), Babylon and all their satellite allies and vassals and the post-flood offspring of the Anunnaki, the Giants, 360 years after the Flood. This was 1879 BC and was a conflict over the rights to the Middle East's fossil fuel byproducts, mineral and natural resources of the Dead Sea. Another 240 years brings us to 1639 BC when Jacob (Israel) died after adopting Ephraim and Manesseh, Joseph's sons. The descendants of these men would become mighty European and ultimately *American* nations. Counting 600 years after this NER date in the Anunnaki Chronology we arrive at 1039 BC, birth of David, slayer of the Giant, a shepherd who became king of Israel establishing the Throne of David. This year is 1200 years (432,000 days) after the Deluge.

Moving along the timeline of 600 and 60-year periods we come to 859 BC when Phoenix entered the inner system and King Shalmaneser III begins the Neo-Assyrian Empire in what is modern Iraq. Now 300 years after this King Nebuchadnezzar II of Babylon (also in Iraq) is cursed by God to suffer lycanthrope in 559 BC for seven years. A great shar (120 years) afterward, in 439 BC the Greeks complete the Parthenon at Athens which commemorates the War of the Titans and Giants, which actually refers artistically to the Battle of Kuruksata *1440 years* earlier (144 x 10/360 x 4). The ancestors of the Greeks, as well as most of the nations participated in that epic conflict.

Counting 120 years further was 319 BC, the conclusion of the 7th Mayan baktun (144,000 days), or 1,008,000 days from its start-date in 3113 BC. This year begins six baktuns of 144,000 days each (864,000 days) to 2046 AD return of NIBIRU and Anunnaki invasion as well as comet impact destroying North America (origin of Maya). Also in this year the Dark Satillite (Anunnaki prison-moon of Seven Kings) passes through the inner system. In 139 BC the archaic order of astrologers and mathematici called the Chaldaei in Rome were expelled, an order founded under the Seven Kings of Rome. This event transpired 792 years (oribital longevity of NIBIRU) after Israel and Judah split into two separate nations beginning the Divided Kingdom Chronology in 931 BC.

762 AD was 1200 years before the end of the Anunnaki timeline in 1962 AD. It was the year the Abbasid Dynasty relocated to Baghdad (Babylon). Also in 762 AD a very important meeting of astronomers from many different Mayan cities met at the historic city of Copan. What the sky watchers determined must have been very important for the year 763 AD (the Mayan equivalent) was inscribed on reliefs in several cities, and on Altar Q of Copan. (9) Astronomers of Mayan civilization were the official *chronologists*. Also begun in this year was the Jewish Kairite movement, a critical *rift in Judaic faith*. Anan ben David called on Jews everywhere to

abandon the corrupt Talmud and only obey the inspired Word of God in the Books of Moses. Resisting the Rabbinate, the Kairites maintain a favorable view of Jesus. (10)

In the year 1062 AD the Muslim Turks invaded Greek Christendom and nearly exterminated it. This marked the start of the Turkish invasions into Europe. In 1302 AD meteoric storms, plagues, comets, earthquakes and flooding devastated Asia, Europe and the Americas, all in the 2046th year of Israel's Post-Exilic Chronology which began in 745 BC when the Ten Tribes of Israel were deported by Assyria. This series of disasters literally *depopulated* North America. Sixty years later in 1362 the Norse and Goth descendants of those Israelites forcibly integrated among the Scythians, Cimmerians and early German peoples subdued by Assyria now explored a sparsely populated North America for King Magnus of Norway, leaving a record on the Kensington Runestone.

Pope Paul II revived the dreaded Inquisition in 1542, which led to the excruciating deaths of countless victims. In 1842 the British defeated the Chinese (Kings of the East) to reinstate the Opium trade, an oppressive military-sponsored program. The end of the Cursed Earth Chronology was in 1902 AD, the last year Phoenix passed into the inner solar system, also being a milestone in the Anunnaki timeline. Phoenix blankets earth in millions of tons of cosmic dust and also in 1902 the Babylonian *Enuma Elish* tablets concerning the Anunnaki were translated into English, ancient records about the destruction of a primordial Earth and its renovation.

The end of the Anunnaki NER Chronology in 1962 AD begins the global Nephilim program of transgenics testing on abducted humans (Close Encounters of the Fourth Kind) in their Anunnaki master's plans on raising a hidden Fifth Column of human-like supporters that wll aid them in the apocalyptic times to come. 1962 AD ends the 70 generations (70 x 60 = 4200 years) of the Anunnaki's imprisonment and restraint from the Flood. In 1962 the first American orbits earth in a capsule called *Friendship 7*. The pentagonal dodecahedron is complete, Anunnaki time (events) *crystallize* into a space-time solid of their own making. Their fate as well as humanity's in the collective, is sealed. This has been 7200 years filled with events (planes and angles) that will directly reflect the next *72 years* to the beginning of the Apocalypse in 2034 AD, and then the following *72 years* to 2106 AD which is the year 6000 Annus Mundi when the Anunnaki will be defeated by the Chief Cornerstone at Armageddon. The beginning and the end of Anunnaki contention is over the right to *kingship* over mankind—themselves to rule or another—ever blind to the eternal destiny of redeemed humanity. A nation of *kings* and priests that will rule over all of God's future kingdoms.

The first three archives of this work were absolutely necessary because the histories detailed mathematically and conceptually presage everything you are about to read. The past indeed repeats itself and after reviewing the following material it will be blatantly obvious that science at its best seeks most to keep us in this simplified, thoroughly artificial, suitably constructed and suitably falsified world. (11)

This author is absolutely convinced that a Greater Intellect beyond human comprehension has been long at work behind the scenes of world history. It is because of this that historical analysis has predictive value, caused by a Grand Designer whose intention from the start was to end His world by the same mechanics extent at its beginning.

Our analysis of the Anunnaki Chronology will be a two-part review. We will now isolate the *themes* attached to the events. The first part of this study concerns the *beginning*, which would encompass the preflood histories, a span of 3000 years from 5239 BC or 2239 BC. The history of the beginning sets the stage for the end, the Last Days, which is confirmed by the prophecy of Jesus who said that the End Times would "...be as the days of Noah." In the construction of our calendrical geometry the first pentagon of our dodecahedron began with the Anunnaki, as co-creators and 3000 years later the Great Flood ended with their imprisonment. Thus we see in the Last Days the Anunnaki coming as *destroyers* after they are released.

Here are the elements of the beginning that will reoccur in the end times. The Anunnaki—

contribute to ruination of earth

create a nonhuman sentient species

create hybrids of this species and humans (transgenics)

enslave their own minions

war against own minions to deceive humanity

cause Apocalypse altering Earth's orbit (NIBIRU Passover)

conspire against man

descend to Earth during catastrophe

appear after one-third mankind killed

trade knowledges for human females

abduct human females

father the Nephilim (Giants)

fill a power vacuum after human government falls

oppose Ten Kings and subdue them

Eighth King will reign, one of the Seven Kings

world destroyed by falling of *two stars*

This is the framework of Apocalypse, and as readers of this author's other works have found, this is precisely how the Last Days unfolds. The Anunnaki Chronology merely validates what has already been discovered through studying biblical prophecy, calendrical isometrics, comparative timelines and cross-calendrical parallels as clearly revealed in *Chronicon*. This 3000 years is five NER, 600 years each. This means the pattern is firmly established, being *five pentagons* of our dodecahedron. But there is 4200 years of events (lines, angles and planes) remaining until this chronological solid is formed in 1962 AD. These Anunnaki chronological markers provide us additional details illuminating our dodecahedron of Apocalypse. Here are these elements gleaned from the timeline.

planet Phoenix will enter the inner system

planet NIBIRU will pass close to earth

Mayan Long-Count will end (Time Collapses)

natural disasters and calamities

North America depopulated

Dark Satillite will pass close to Earth

"Kingship" will be "lowered from heaven."

Anunnaki artifact discovered-interpreted

major architectural project venerating Anunnaki

new dynasty founded in Iraq

new Order founded in Iraq

"Throne of David" set up

major war won by Anunnaki

the West subdues the Kings of the East

nations descended from Israel (10 Kings) in peril

major rift in Jewish world

global persecution of innocents

state-church sanctioned genocide

By combining all these two categories of motifs together a synthesis emerges that startling synchronizes with modern contemporary events. Because this is a synoptic review of the End Times we cannot possibly reiterate this timeline, which has already been done in minute detail within this author's other works. The following dates and events are proven in *Chronicon* and demonstrated thoroughly in *When the Sun Darkens* and *Anunnaki Homeworld*. Astonishingly, this Last Days timeline was already complete in manuscripts prior to this author's discovery of the Anunnaki Chronology's future-past themes priorly listed. Now we will voyage through time and space in the following two sections, *What Has Come to Pass* and *What Shall Come to Pass*, and see how every element of the Anunnaki Chronology has already, or is about to be fulfilled.

What Has Come to Pass

The Last Days began in 1902 AD, the end of the Cursed Earth Chronology encoded in Stonehenge and the start of the Giza Course Countdown. 1902 AD is Year One of the End Times countdown to 2106 AD, Armageddon War and the return of the Chief Cornerstone (Savior) Who will descend upon the Monument of Man and defeat the ancient Anunnaki rebels. This 204-year period parallels the 203 (gematria for HE CREATED) levels, or courses of the Great Pyramid, which is missing a topstone. This flat apex represents the 204th course, the throne of the *Stone the Builders Rejected*, which has been made *Head of the Corner* according to Scripture. This 204th year is the year 6000 from Man's Banishment and curse in Eden in 3895 BC.

The Cursed Earth system ending in 1902 AD was 60 years before the end of the Anunnaki Chronology in 1962 AD, 60 years being an Anunnaki generation. In 1902 the Babylonian Enuma Elish tablets were translated into English, the modern universal script, texts describing the Anunnaki and the PreAdamic cataclysm they caused. The beginning and end of this *204 years* featuring the Anunnaki.

On schedule in 1902 planet Phoenix passed through the inner system and deposited millions of tons of cosmic dust around the world and a comet orbiting Phoenix disintegrated. Phoenix was last seen and studied by astronomer Hoffman 1656 (414 x 4) months priorly in 1764 when the planet nearly transited, obscuring one-fifth of the sun on a north-to-south trajectory over the ecliptic plane. This new comet remained a mystery to astronomers and was named Morehouse. Remarkably, in the year before, 1901, The Cincinnati Astral Society, published a list of predictions, among them one declaring that a *new comet* would come into view, an unusual comet that *orbits an unknown planet.* They claim that this object would ascend out of the *southeastern sky.* (12) This was Morehouse orbiting Phoenix. Also in 1901 the Babylonian *Code of Hammurabi* was excavated, a text venerating the Anunnaki.

In 1902 the world was introduced to the famous Antikyathera Computer, an astounding precise and advanced differential-geared device used for computing time both forward and backward employing astronomical cycles, a relic of unbelievable sophistication designed to pinpoint the year 583 BC as a specific reference point in calculations—583 BC being the final year in the Age of the Phoenix when the planet transited darkening the sun during a battle between the Medes and Persians according to Herodotus. The Phoenix cycles of 552 years were aligned astronomically with the Cursed Earth system of 414 year periods, 552 being four 138 year orbits of Phoenix and 414 being three orbits. In 1994 members of the Italian National Library in Rome discovered buried in the archives a formerly lost, unknown and unpublished manuscript, fully illustrated with paintings and text by the prophet Nostradamus. After studying the prophecies, Roman researcher and Nostradamus expert Ottavio Cesare Ramotti published in his book, *Nostradamus: The Lost Manuscript*, that the following passage of Nostradamus refers to the year *1903*.

Many will die before the Phoenix dies,
Until six hundred and seventy,
His dwelling shall endure…

This prophecy is in his preface to the 20th century (Prophecy 11 53). He admits ignorance over the 670, but readers of this work will understand its significance in relation to the collapse of an *existing empire* (United States), and readers of *Chronotecture* will also understand that this is a Millennial timeline of 670 years beginning at the end of the King's Chamber 330 years after the War of Armageddon in 2106 AD (6000 AM). 670 + 330 is the 1000-year millennial period when God Himself will rule earth until the Final Rebellion in the year 7000 (3106 AM).

Insiders in the United States government seem to have understood the significance of 1902, the year officials removed the image of the Phoenix from the Great Seal of our nation and replaced it with a picture of the Eagle. Just as the Assyrians, Hittites and Romans did. This begins the USA's Iron Empire status and 144-year timeline to total ruination of the North American continent by comet impact in 2046 AD, the year of NIBIRU's final Passover and Anunnaki invasion. In 1902 the U.S. Census Bureau is founded and the city of Washington DC was planned out and the capitol scheme reworked employing a construction-street design concealing a gigantic pentagram (AR UB). Lastly, also in 1902 transpired a little-known event in the Gulf of Guinea in the South Atlantic. On October 28th at 3:05 AM sailors aboard the SS Fort Salisbury watched as a colossal and apparently metallic plated object about 600 feet long slowly descended into the sea only hundreds of feet away. This sky vessel had a light at each end and was silent except for the sound of the seawater being violently disturbed upon contact with it. (13) Of course, this author purports this to be an Anunnaki ship. There is no guessing how many others have arrived unseen.

In 1903 mankind began his mastery over land and air locomotion. Henry Ford founded the Ford Motor Company giving rise to an international automobile industry and the Wright Brothers succeeded in their first manned flight at Kitty Hawk, North Carolina, fulfilling the prophecy that in the Last Days "men will fly." (14) In 1908 a small comet exploded over Tunguska, Siberia on June 30th, the blast heard well over 500 miles away, damaging and toppling trees 300 miles away, and knocking people off their feet 100 miles away. The pressure of the explosion affected barometers in England and was seismically recorded in Irkutsh, Turkey, Tashkent, Tbilisi and Jena. This was a divine warning to the Northern Hemisphere, for the comet was 1656 months (414 x 4), or 138 years (Phoenix orbit) to the comet impact of 2046 AD that will end North American civilization.

An intensely black object measured approximately 250 miles long and 50 miles wide passed over the surface of the moon in 1912. On April 8th over Wiltshire, England near Stonehenge were witnessed two triangular shaped UFOs almost concealed in rapidly moving clouds. The continuous stream of clouds moved but the dark triangular objects remained fixed in the same area for about a half hour. (15) In 1913 a tremendous procession of objects was seen all across North America passing three miles above the surface of the planet, seen from Canada, the USA, over the Atlantic and from Bermuda. Many described this train of objects as a fleet of battleships, attended by cruisers and destroyers. (16)

On April 8th, exactly a year after the April 8th sighting of a UFO near Stonehenge, the shadow of another object was seen passing over the moon from Forth Worth, Texas. (17) In 1915 a Professor Bernard studied the strange region of space around the constellation Cephus and discovered a vast black object near the star Al Gol (the Ghoul, or Blinking Demon), considered by the ancients to be the most evil of all stars. (18) In the following year in the Astrophysical Journal he revised his observations to "dark nebula." This 1915 AD date serves as a cross-calendrical parallel of 1915 BC when the Anunnaki homeworld NIBIRU passed Earth initiating a series of disasters.

In 1917 the British defeat the Turks and the Balfour Declaration recognizes Palestine as an Israeli state and Iraq (Babylon) falls to the British. The following year has the British defeat the Turks again in the Valley of Megiddo (Armageddon). Iraq is officially recognized as a kingdom seated at Baghdad (origin of Abbasid Dynasty) by the British starting a 70-year countdown to the Fall of Iraq to the United States in 1991. President Roosevelt in 1935 had the Great Seal published on US currency of the Great Pyramid on one side and the Eagle on the other exhibiting 13 levels of bricks, 13 arrows, 13 olives, 13 leaves—the insignias of the 13th Israelite tribe (Ephraim) that was born in *Egypt*. This is the Last Days inheritance of Israel, America's 13 colonies coming together as ONE NATION UNDER GOD as read in the scroll in the Eagle's beak in 13 Latin letters—E. PLURIBUS UNUM, or, *one out of many*.

The Nazi Germany government in 1936 retrieved a downed UFO. This began a reverse-engineering project not discovered until US forces raided the complex in World War II. (19) In 1938

The Nazis instigated the Kristalnacht Riots, which resulted with the intended detention of 200,000 Jews confined in concentration camps. In defiance of the Treaty of Versailles, Hitler annexed Austria to Germany and invaded unopposed. The Nazis looted and burned Jewish-owned businesses and synagogues.

Also in 1938 on October 30th Orson Welles dramatized H.G. Wells science fiction story *War of the Worlds* for his Mercury Theatre radio program. The seemingly "live" broadcast terrified millions of people and a Princeton University study later revealed that six million people had listened to the broadcast. 1.7 million had believed that extraterrestrials from Mars were invading earth, and 1.2 million people actually *acted* on this belief. (20)

A stunning planetary augnment in 1940 of five planets form a ladder in the night sky: Mercury, Venus, Mars, Jupiter and Saturn. This same planetary augnment was seen in 2446 BC exactly *half* a cursed Earth period (207 years is half of 414) before the world was destroyed in the Great Flood in 2239 BC. Five planets geometrically form a *pentagram*, the dimensions of the inner sanctuary of trilithons at Stonehenge. The pentagram forms the ancient Sumerian *AR UB* sign, the comet representing the *Plough of god* that strikes the earth in *judgment*. Amazingly this planetary alignment is precisely *207 years* after the founding of America's 13th colony: Georgia, in 1733 AD. Perhaps not coincidentally, in this year the United States (13th tribe of Israel: Ephraim) began construction of the gigantic architectural *AR UB* known around the world as the *Pentagon*, the seat of America's Iron Empire status. It is located in Ar-lington, Virginia.

In 1947 occurred one of the most famous UFO sightings in recorded history. Pilot Kenneth Arnold witnessed clearly a visible UFO near Mount Rainier in Washington on June 24. In this same year happened the most celebrated and widely publicized of all UFO crashes, in Roswell, New Mexico, which began a publishing phenomenon of speculative books and documentaries about Area 51 and Hanger 18. This began the Anunnaki campaign to provide the elite human governments with ultra sophisticated hardware for reverse-engineering programs.

Concerning the Anunnaki and 1947 we find that the Dead Sea Scrolls were discovered at Qumrum, which contained a text called the *Testament of Amram* [4QAmram] which contains references to shape changing reptilian beings known as the Watchers, dark entities that can assume the faces of Addars. Anunnaki. The Watchers took the daughters of men in exchange for knowledge and the women gave birth to giants, hybrids and monsters. As the Dead Sea is located in a valley, so also is *Death Valley* in California where also in this same year archeologists discovered gigantic human skeletons that had stood *nine* feet tall. (21) The Dead Sea texts are full of references to the Sons of Darkness (Anunnaki) and the Sons of Light and the Great War that will go on between them. Armageddon.

In 1948 Jews from eastern Europe, Russia and its satellites strengthened by Soviet armament from the Jewish Bolsheviks invaded Palestine and drove out about 880,000 Palestinians, both Christians and Muslims. Some Special Forces from the United States participated. The modern state of Israel was begun by British Mandate amidst an enraged Arab world. The reappearance of Israel after over 18 centuries since the entire nation was enslaved and dispersed by the Romans in 135 AD, is a national miracle, a first of its kind. Never before have a people suffered so terribly in destruction and for so long a time period spread around the world to reassemble as one sovereign nation in their original homeland, even resurrecting their formerly *extinct* language—Hebrew.

In 1950 a meteorite fell near Murray, Kentucky and two scientists of the Arizona State University independently examined the rock and detected the presence of all eighteen of the known amino acids as well as pyramidines from the nucleic acid of what were once living cells. (22) This is only a fraction of the evidence that terrestrial life has an extraterrestrial origin, as seen in *Anunnaki Homeworld*.

In 1952, on June 2nd, EBE died, a chlorophyll-based sentient creature captured in 1947 in New Mexico. EBE maintained communication with U.S. scientists for five years. (23) In July UFOs were visible over Washington, DC and tracked by radar. Air Defense was initiated and the event was broadcast around America in headlines. This was July 26th, exactly *50 years* before the *July 26th* appearance of the UFOs tracked by NORAD in 2002 heading for Washington, DC. (24) Perhaps not coincidentally, 1952 is also the *50th year* of the Giza Course Countdown that started in 1902 when the Cursed Earth Chronology ended. Fifty years is a Hebrew *jubilee*. After the 2002

UFO incident, counting *50 years* we arrive at *2052 AD* return of the Seven Anunnaki Kings. All four dates are UFO-Anunnaki related. Also in 1952 President Truman created the National Security Agency (NSA) initially to investigate the alien (Anunnaki) presence on Earth as well as to contain all data and censure it from the public as well as redistribute false information to lead researchers down false trails. The NSA was also originally used to set up a dialogue with these extraterrestrials. (25) By this time 16 UFOs had been retrieved from crash sites in the United States (26), these being *gifts* from the Anunnaki expected by U.S. officials for their agreement to allow the Anunnaki agents to engage in their clandestine abduction-transgenics program involving unwilling human females. As human consent was required before the Flood for the Sons of God (Fallen Ones) to abduct the "daughters of men" to produce hybrids and giants, so too was human consent required in our generation.

In 1953 astronomers discovered a group of large objects moving toward Earth in space. Believing them to be astroids the find is reported to government officials. These objects near Earth then assume a geosynchronous orbit around the equator and their presence as occupied vessels is discovered and kept secret. A dialogue between elite U.S. officials and the Anunnaki commanders (not the Seven Kings) results with an alliance for the exchange of goods (knowledge for genetic material) (27). In the following year, 1954, these officials and the Anunnaki ratify the alliance of '53 with a formal treaty. (28) This year came 1998 years (666 x 3) after start of Roman Julian calendar and 1332 years (666 x 2) after the Islamic Hijrah Calendar began in 622 AD.

In 1955 astronomers of the Carnegie Institute discovered radio signals coming from Jupiter, a phenomenon predicted by Velikovsky but spurned by the scientific establishment. This was rerpoted to Einstein who vowed to use his influence to have Velikovsky's theory of planetary intrusion put to the test. Unfortunately, nine days later, on the 108th day of the year, Einstein died, a copy of Velikovsky's *Worlds in Collision* on his desk.

In 1958 a powerful broadcast was picked up by hundreds around the world and people listened in awe for two and a half hours as someone identifying themselves as *Nacoma* from the planet Jupiter spoke about Earth's impending ruin by atomic destruction if testing of nuclear bombs was not discontinued. He spoke in English, German, Norwegian and a strange dark musical language, as found in John Keel's book, *Our Haunted Planet*.

On April 12, 1961 Russia put the first human in space, named Yuri Gagarin, for exactly one hour and forty-eight minutes, or *108 minutes*. Also in this year in September the first modern alien abduction case involved Betty and Barney Hill, involving alien medical-scientific procedure. (29) This may have been preparatory staging for 1962. However, the Anunnaki years are not likely to have begin dates in January or March like human calendrical systems. The 7200nd year of the Anunnaki Chronology could have begun as early as August-September 1961 AD.

Hugh Harleston Jr. at the ancient city of Teotihuacan in Mesico discovered an amazing *pyramid timeline* in units in antiquity known as *hunabs*. He found that by starting at the gigantic and world famous pyramid of the Sun (203 ft. high parallels *203 levels* of Great Pyramid) there is a distance of *7200 hunabs* to a ruinous pile of architecture he believes represents Planet X (NIBIRU of Anunnaki). (30)

On February 5th, 1962 the world of astrology was in a frenzied state over a massive conjunction of planets. On May 22nd a secret space probe landed on Mars and confirmed the existence of an environment that could support life (31), long suspected John Glen orbits the earth in *Friendship 7* and radio telescopes were detecting strong X-ray activity coming from the Cygnus constellation, catalogued as Cygnus-1. Other sources emitting x-rays were later discovered, now known as pulsars. (32) However, Cygnus-1 in 1971 underwent a change revealing to astronomers that they were dealing not with a pulsar, but possibly a Black Hole (33), a collapsed star also called a Dark Star.

Moralists are in agreement that it was at this time that America, and by extension the world, began a rapid moral decline, a tailspin into degeneracy socially and spiritually. This weakening of our spiritual foundation is a direct reflection of the past before the Flood when the Anunnaki engaged in hybridization and transgenic programs, fathered hybrids and *made* sentient species, also teaching mankind more effective methods of metallurgy, murder and mayhem. They instructed women on how to brew spermicides that would render them barren (contraceptives) as well as artificial beauty enhancements. The Anunnaki even taught women how to kill an embryo in the womb (abortion). America has been a proverbial refuge kingdom where the persecuted and downtrodden could become naturalized and make a good living, a sanctuary to destitute people around the world who seek to raise their children in a environment free from the cultural and political tragedies of poverty, war, civil unrest, ethnic cleansing and oppression in their own homelands. The United States has been the closest thing to a Millennial Kingdom mankind could ever build. But despite all this the nation has fallen from its pedestal among the peoples of the earth and turned its back on its Maker. God's hand was with America from its beginning, so says ANNUIT COEPTUS on the Great Seal (He has favored our beginning). But this proximity to the Godhead this nation has enjoyed has only amplified our judgments for our national and personal disobedience.

On May 15th, 1963, astronaut Gordon Cooper's voice from space was drowned out on a channel reserved for spaceflights by a strange unintelligible unknown language that has never been identified. (34) Also in 1963 the U.S. Supreme Court ruled that the reciting of the Ten Commandments, the Lord's Prayer or Bible verses in public schools was *unconstitutional* despite the fact that the Constitution is the first document of any nation declaring that rights come from God, not man. On November 22nd President John F. Kennedy was assassinated in Texas in an automobile with Texas governor John B. Connolly. The real bullet killing Kennedy exited his head and penetrated Governor Connolly's leg. The Texas governor refused to allow the bullet to be removed despite it being a federal investigation. This refusal actually granted him because the conspirators knew the ballistics would not match Oswald's weapon. John Connolly was later commemorated by having a famous maximum security prison named after him, the John B. Connolly unit where the Texas Seven escaped in 2000, this prison located at *Kenedy*, Texas. Incidentally, this is the author's current address while writing this book.

A triangular-shaped UFO appeared over Madrid, Spain on September 4th, photographed and witnessed by thousands of observers. (35) In 1970 a meteorite dubbed the Murchison Meteorite fell to earth. Studied by the Ames Research Center at NASA and the scientists of two universities it was determined to have contained within it definite traces of amino acids. (36) Two years later in 1972 the NASA Mariner 9 probe took pictures of Mars' surface at what appeared to be pyramidal structures fifteen degrees north of the Martian equator in the Elysium Quadrangle. It would be a decade before these shapes would be officially recognized.

In the 11th year of America's spiritual decline, 1973, the U.S. Supreme Court in *Roe v. Wade* ruled that the human fetus is not a person, and therefore has no constitutional or human rights. This is in direct contravention of Sacred Law, which reads, "Thou shalt not destroy thy conceptions *before they are brought forth*; nor kill them after they are born." (37) From 1973-74 the world experienced the greatest wave of UFO sightings in recorded history. (38) Top Soviet scientists in October of '73 reported that *extraterrestrial intelligent* radio signals were recorded from *within* our own solar system. It was concluded that the transmissions were of artificial origin by very sophisticated transmission equipment. (39) Disturbingly, this year Otto O. Binder wrote that "It is an established fact that more than 100,000 people utterly *vanish* from Earth each year. No trace is ever found in missing person's bureaus nor by the best detective hunts. Many Ufologists surmise that these people are *abducted* and whisked away from Earth *alive*. (40) Dr. Bartholomew Nagy in

1975 published his controversial research on the existence of microbiological fossils on and within meteorites from Mars. (41)

In the year 1976 the Jewish scholar and expert on Near Eastern studies, translator of Sumerian, Zecharia Sitchin, published the first of his famous Earth Chronicles, entitled, *The 12th Planet*. This began a prophetic ministry and countdown of 70 years to the return of the Anunnaki and their planet NIBIRU in 2046 AD.

In 1982 the National Aeronautics and Space Administration (NASA) announced its conclusion that there exists another *large planetary body in our solar system* as yet undiscovered that is the cause of the unusual perturbations in the motions of the outer planets. (42) In the following year the Jet Propulsion Laboratory claimed that their infrared telescope on the spacecraft IRAS had discovered beyond Pluto an extremely far "...mystery celestial body." It was said to be about four times larger than Earth and *moving toward us*. This author believes that this is planet Phoenix, which had been gone 81 years since 1902 and was due back in this year in 57 years in 2040 AD. This belief is supported by the fact that this discovery was made in *207th year* of the United States since 1776 AD Independence, half a 414 year Cursed Earth period. The University of Chicago scientists gathered evidence from past catastrophes noting mass extinctions at regular intervals, their research and conclusions finalized in 1984. (43) In 1984 two independent research think tanks of astrophysicists and astronomers took the research findings from the University of Chicago made in 1983, both groups deriving the same conclusion—our solar system either once was *binary system* (having two stars) or still has a sister star, which would be a Dark Star commonly referred to a frozen or compressed stars. This they dubbed Nemesis or the Death Star. (44).

In 1986 Halley's Comet is clearly seen from earth, this being *120 years* to Armageddon in 2106 AD. NASA's Space Shuttle explodes ascending into the sky killing the Seven Astronauts, a terrible omen paralleling the fate of the Seven Anunnaki Kings that will descend to earth. In this same year the Statue of Liberty renovation project is finished, originally erected in 1884 with 168 steps leading up to 54 ladder rungs to the Ascendant Torch. This is 1884 + 168 steps to 2052 AD when mankind loses his *liberty* to the Anunnaki, and 54 rungs +2052 to 2106 AD (6000 AM) when the Light of the World (Torch represents the Savior) defeats the Anunnaki at Armageddon.

The Temple Institute in Jerusalem in 1987 began, dedicated to preparing all necessary Temple sacraments, artifacts and procedures. This is integral to prophecies concerning the return of the Temple and ritual sacrifice, as well as to others declaring that in the Last Days the Antichrist will sit in the Temple as a god.

NASA and European Space agencies support a Soviet mission in 1989 sending satellite probes called Phobos I and II to investigate Mars' moon Phobos. Phobos I simple vanished. Phobos II made it to Mars and sent back photographs from a normal camera and an infrared one. The last pictures sent by the probe were of a cigar-shaped UFO (same as those reported often around Earth). The probe was destroyed and subsequently written off officially as an accident or mechanical failure. This moon has been a source of profound mystery ever since it was discovered by Asaph Hall in 1877 to the astonishment of the astronomical community. Hall discovered two asteroid-shaped moons orbiting Mars and named them Deimos and Phobos (Fear and Terror). Initially this report was unbelievable because Mars had been the object of study for *centuries*. These anomalous moons appeared only recently and many believe them to be hollowed-out lunar bases, as astronomers have reported seeing strange lights coming from Phobos.

In 1996 a long-period comet named Hyakutake passed within 22 million miles of the sun (Earth is 93 million miles away) putting off an extremely long tail. On April 11th the comet passed over the star Al Gol in the Perseus constellation. (45) Al Gol is the evil star, *The Ghoul*. Scottish scientists clone the first official mammal. The very next year Comet Hale-Bopp is still visible as it departs the system, having arrived in 1996. Hale-Bopp like Hyakutake passes over the star Al Gol and on the *same day*, April 11th, 1997. (46) This concerns the birth in 1996 of one who will deal treacherously with humanity, an Evil One who can be described as *undead*. (Ghoul). This is the Antichrist who will come to power 40 years later in 2036 AD.

The year 1998 is the Last Days' epicentral marker measuring Earth's final 108 years until Armageddon *forward and backward* from 1998 (666 x 3) AD. This amazing system allows a chronologist to verify his timelines because of their conceptual synchronicity. This is the science of calendrical isometrics, a unique system found in the equidistant repetition of historical events linked to an epicentral year, in this case 1998. Isometric years are like ripples in the pond of time, each wave-ring anterior to the epicentral marker is exactly the same distance (length of time) as the other side of the wave-ring (geometric reflection). These concentric rings in the space-time structure permeate throughout the unending creation. Here are but a few brief examples:

a. Terrorists in America in 1995 destroyed the Murrah Building in *Oklahoma* City, OK (city & state name the same) and U.S. government passed the Anti-terrorism and Effective Death

Penalty Act which harshly and secretly abbreviated the rights and privileges of ALL U.S. citizens. This was *3 years* before 1998, and *3 years* after terrorists in America destroyed the World Trade Towers in *New York City*, NY (city & State name the same) and U.S. government passed the revised Patriot Act, legislation that is actually *against* U.S. citizens. Further, Timothy McVeigh who participated in the 1995 bombing was executed in 2001 before 9/11.

b. In 1993 NASA's Mars Observer was lost entering the atmosphere of Mars *5 years* before 1998, and *5 years* after in 2003 the Space Shuttle Columbia was lost entering Earth's atmosphere.

c. In 1988 Vice President George Bush, Sr. initiated the Bush family's 144 months (12 years) of Presidency over the USA *10 years* prior to 1998, and *10 years* after in 2008 was George Bush, Jr.'s final year in office, replaced by Barack Obama, a black president elected exactly *144 years* after the 1865 Emancipation Proclamation freeing the blacks in America was enforced after the Civil War.

There are many more isometric projections as demonstrated in *Chronicon*. Even the year 2052 is an amazing isometric year, as we will see. Calendrical isometrics is a window into the future. The internal geometrical dimensions of the Great Pyramid display a perfect chronological timeline of world history and what is to come. Further, mystical traditions assert that the Great Pyramid's prophetic timeline an end of a beginning in *1998 AD*. (47) A crop circle formation appeared in Cuxton, England that encodes the sum of 108, demonstrating an awareness of this 108 years remaining until Armageddon in 2106 AD (6000 AM). Edgar Cayce, the mystic prophet, predicted that 1998 was the start of the preparation for the coming of the Master of Earth (Chief Cornerstone). 1998 is the 222nd (third of 666) year of the United States from 1776.

In 2000 scientists of an international project announce the completion of the mapping of the human genome, isometrically foreshadowed by the 1996 cloning of a mammal. The next year in 2001 scientists of the Ames Research Center released data on the discovery of carbon-rich meteorites found on Earth loaded with organic compounds, including amino acids and *sugars*. (48)

Astronomers took the first direct photograph of an *exoplanet*, a strange planet twice the size of Jupiter and about 100 AU's distance in 2005. An AU is an Astronomical Unit, about 93 million miles, the measure of Earth's distance from the sun. An exoplanet is a world that doesn't orbit a star. The most distant official planet in our solar system is Neptune, approximately 30 AU's from the sun. The closest star to our own sun (official luminary) is *4.2 light years* away, Alpha Centauri with its orbiting companion luminary Alpha Proxima. This means that this newly discovered exoplanet *is in our own system*, probably NIBIRU which is only 36 years away from passing close to Earth in 2046. European scientists announce in 2008 that they have begun to build the largest telescope in the world to search for *exoplanets*, a facility employing a 138-foot mirror (Phoenix orbit *138 years*) and standing 21 stories high. This telescope is located in the *southern* hemisphere, which is the only region NIBIRU can be seen from. In another case for synchronicity, NASA's *Phoenix* Lander touched down on Mars taking soil samples and signs of life, further, the world-televised Superbowl occurred in *Phoenix*, AR-izono and on April 21st over the city of Phoenix were filmed four UFOs nationally televised. Lastly, in 2008, this author finished *When the Sun Darkens: Orbital History and 2040 AD Return of Planet Phoenix.*

This sums up our study of the ancient world up to the present, exhibiting abundant parallels to the Old World histories we focused on in the first three archives of this work, the times up until the Flood. Now, in this final archive we shall peer into the future…which shall verify the past.

Archive VII

What Shall Come to Pass

The following material is of necessity an abbreviated chronology of end-time events already explicitly covered in *When the Sun Darkens*, in *Anunnaki Homeworld* and in *Chronicon* as published on www.nephilimarchives.com. This archive is provided to exhibit how the apocalypse is merely the *fulfillment* of events already transpired in antiquity.

2012 AD (5906 AM)

This is the popularized end-date for the Mayan Long-Count calendar, however, this date is derived by butchering the system from its original 5200 years of 360 days a year (total 1,872,000 days) to the modern "vague" year of 365.25 days—a year unknown prior to 713 BC when the Dark Satillite (Anunnaki prison-moon) nearly collided with Earth pushing our plant less than .01% further away from the sun increasing its elliptical orbit by 5.25 days. Mayan Long-Count ends with "collapse of time" in 2046 AD on the 1,872,000th day from 3113 BC. For entirely *different* reasons (though the 2012 adherents will scream that this fulfills the Long-Count) 2012 AD may herald the publicized discovery of planet Phoenix, NIBIRU, or that of our Dark Star binary, with the Last Days epicentral year being 1998 (108 years before Armageddon), 2012s isometric year was 1984, the year independent scientists from two groups determined that our solar system was or still is a *binary* system with the Dark Star. Also note that a manmade manufactured event can serve as the "fulfillment" of the 2012 expected event, though it will be artificial.

2022 AD (5916 AM)

U.S. forces based in Iraq are terribly defeated by an alliance of nations with Iran, paralleling the defeat the U.S. ultimately suffered in the east in the Vietnam War by 1974, this years' isometric date. United States loses its Iron Empire status and begins *Sodom Time* as military supremacy passes to *Israel* and the Muslim Confederation. The U.S., still powerful, becomes isolationist and degenerate into a stunningly wealthy, hedonistic society until its cataclysmic end by comet impact in 2046 AD, just as Sodom and Gomorrah were destroyed *2046 years* after mankind's first year of banishment from Eden, in 1848 BC (2047 AM). 2046 AD is 2047 years after the birth of Christ in 2 BC (1 & 2 AD are same year), the Anno Domini calendar referring to Jesus (Year of Our Lord).

2036 AD (5930 AM)

The Apocalypse begins 70 years before Armageddon when the Antichrist emerges as a world leader who by military force has all Muslims expelled from the regions claimed by Israel. His seat (capitol) is in Iraq and he becomes a messianic hero to the Israelis. There is a major division in the Jewish world as to this figure's identity when he forges peace covenants with all of Israel's enemies. This begins the First Seal of the Tribulation, setting the stage for a *counterfeit* Armageddon.

This apocalyptic beginning was commented on by Jesus, who said that this period we find in Revelation as the Seven Seals would be very chaotic, but merely the *beginning*. The original Greek text reads—

And there will be signs in the sun and moon and stars; and on earth anguish of nations in perplexity of the things coming on the habitable; for the *powers of the heavens* shall be shaken. (1)

This final statement links us directly to the Book of Revelation, for the "powers of the heavens" are found in Revelation as personified into the Divine Tetramorph, the Four Living Ones, Keepers of the Apocalypse representing the Four Corners of the Zodiac. Combined these beings form the Sphinx which protects the Monument of Man (Great Pyramid). The Bull, Lion, Eagle and Man.

The Seven Seals unlock a book that unveils the future, guarded by the Four Holy Watchers in the court of heaven.

"...and in the presence of the Throne and the sea of glass like crystal; and in the midst of the throne and in a circle of the throne *four living ones* full of eyes (the Watchers) before and behind. And the living one and the first like unto a *lion*, and the second living one like unto a *young bullock*, and the third living one had the face of a *man*, and the fourth living one like unto an *eagle flying*. And the four living ones, one by one of them had a piece, *six wings*, round about and within they are full of eyes." (2)

The "Circle of the throne" is the planet Earth and the Four Living ones form a square in the Zodiac Belt around Earth as the Four Royal stars in the Bull, Lion, Eagle and man *quadrants*. These are the foundation of heaven and the four corners of a cosmic pyramid that has for its apex the Pole Star. This pyramidal geometry is confirmed in the Revelation vision prior to the opening of the Seven Seals—

And I saw in the midst of the throne and the Four living ones, and in the midst of the Elders, a young lamb having been standing as having been slaughtered (sacrifice of crucifixion); it had *horns seven*, and *eyes seven*, they are the seven spirits of God, those having been sent forth into all the Earth. And he came and took the scroll (Book of the Apocalypse with Seven Seals) from the right hand of the one sitting on the throne." (3)

John Mitchell in *Dimensions of Paradise* demonstrates geometrically what a seven horned image with seven eyes would look like. Amazingly the lamb of God (*beginning* and *end* of the Zodiac): Aries) appears as a seven-pointed star with *eyes* inside seven 52 degrees angled *pyramids*. (4)

This seven-pointed star, or heptagram, was believed to have no beginning and no end because no two geometrical forms can combine to produce it, and it refuses to couple with any other geometrical forms. Trigons can merge to become six-pointed figures and squares coupled become octagons, but the origin of the heptagon and heptagram was a source of profound mystery to the ancients. (5) This seven-pointed star is exhibited in *Lost Scriptures of Giza* as the primary architectural component employed for the geometrical angles of the Great Pyramid's interior and exterior slopes.

The Apocalypse was written among the stars some distant time in the eternal past in the heavens prior to the PreAdamic World. Before there was a beginning for mankind the *end* was already known and written down. The Christian mystic Thomas Burgoyne who provided us with knowledge on the existence of the Dark Satillite prison (see *Anunnaki Homeworld*) in the 1880s asserted that the hidden wisdom from olden times was veiled in terms of astronomy and deciphered through a knowledge of the Great Pyramid and Sphinx. The Sphinx as a symbolic representation of the Zodiac is a stellar record of the combined messages of the Zodiacal Bull, Lion, Eagle and Man quadrants, an astroprophetic warning of the coming of a Stone from heaven that will follow after another stone strikes the Earth in an act of *judgment* (cataclysm North America). The Sphinx has the body of a Bull, feet of a Lion, face of a Man and was anciently depicted with the wings of an Eagle. Additionally, it was thought long ago that the Sphinx did not face east at the sunrise, but looked upward in that direct for the *coming of stars*. (6)

This Tetramorph plays a vital role in the Revelation account. The *First Seal* is announced in heaven by the *Bull* cherub concerning the White Horse, or imposter messiah emerging in 2036 AD. The Second Seal is announced by the *Lion* cherub concerning the Great War (Gog & Magog: Islam in WW III) fought against the Antichrist in 2038 AD. The Third Seal is announced in heaven by the Eagle cherub concerning famine, inflation and global economic collapse. Remarkably, the Revelation depicts a Black Horse with a Pair of Scales (Balances) in his hands, and incidentally the Scales of Libra are indeed located in the Eagle Quadrant (Scorpio). The Fourth Seal is announced by the *Man* cherub concerning the deaths of a *fourth* of the world's population. Strangely, the Fifth Seal (AR UB) is not announced, but conveys that there will be a global persecution of those refusing to exercise faith in this False Christ for the altar in heaven begins filling up with the slain spirits of the righteous. It is to be noted that in *Lost Scriptures of Giza* this author showed that the ancients called the Great Pyramid as *God's Altar*, each stone representing a soul of man.

The Sixth Seal is the subject matter of this author's entire book, *When the Sun Darkens: Orbital History and 2040 AD Return of Planet Phoenix*. This Seal is of the *Phoenix*, the planet causing a cataclysmic pole shift in 2040 AD, felling many of the cities of Earth, including the total ruination of New York City in this the 414th year (Cursed Earth period) from its founding with the purchase of the region by the Dutch from the Manhatta Indians and beginning of the settlement New Amsterdam in 1626 AD, later to be renamed New York. Planet Phoenix, last in inner system in 1902 AD will now *darken the sun* and redden the moon and cause global quakes, attended by meteoric fallout. All Four Living Ones participated in this Sixth Seal and their positions the Four Corners of the Heavens in this text now changes to the Four Corners of the *Earth* and the *Bull, Lion, Eagle and Man Watchers* are given power by God to "…injure the earth and the sea," after God *seals* a mark of spiritual protection upon 144,000 believers. (7) This participation of the Tetramorphic Keepers of the Apocalypse is supported by a passage in the *Book of Enoch* where we read that the Four Archangels will in the Last Days be strengthened against Azazel's (Adversary) hosts. (8) Enoch wrote that these were the Four Voices of God and that the Bull represented His mercy and patience, the Lion is suffering and every wound of the sons of men, the Eagle being the power of God and the Man-cherub symbolizing repentance and the hope of those who will inherit life eternal. (9)

It is during these judgments that God will reduce the world's population by 25%. At the following Trumpet judgments it will further be reduced by 33% and ultimately to 50%. Though this is difficult to conceive, this mass-death rate is an act of *mercy*, mankind dying enmasse by natural disasters and war, violence and plague by the Creator "…to keep them from the *evil to come.*" The world after this will not be a place anyone would want to live in. The forfeiture of human life to protect people from future evils is not a new act exercised by the Creator. He has been exercising this discretion from the beginning. Not only with cataclysmic episodes but even by the little-understood deaths of infants born perfectly healthy, with children crossing a street struck by vehicles, innocents caught in crossfires, the random bullet from blocks away that kills a sleeping woman, victims of terroristic acts and homicide, the unexplained drowning's of people who have lived in water all their lives, plane crash victims, heart failures. He knows their futures and understands that their *eternal* security on the balances of salvation mandate their exit from the world before they are endangered with worldly or carnal corruption that will stain them forever. A concept difficult to grasp but nonetheless operating as you read these words.

The episode of the Seven Seals is a deliberately planned deception by God, a judgment against *surviving* humanity for their continual disobedience and blindness specifically mentioned in 2 Thessalonians 2:1—

"And then shall that Wicked one be revealed, who the Lord shall consume with the spirit of His mouth, and shall destroy with the brightness of His coming; even him, whose coming is after the working of Satan with all power and signs and lying wonders, and with all deceivableness of unrighteousness in them that perish; because they received not the love of the truth, that they might be saved. And for this cause God shall *send them strong* delusion, that they should *believe a lie*: that they might be damned who *believed not the truth.*"

The Antichrist will assume the Throne of David, King of Israel, and the nations of Islam will assemble the greatest jihadic war in history in 2038 and be annihilated in the valley of Hamon-Gog and this artificial savior will be credited with their ruin. Meteoric impacts, quakes, famine, epidemics and general chaos will ensue and the Phoenix-induced poleshift will alter the geography of the world and stir multiple *millions* of people to migrate to the Iraq-Israeli kingdom of this figure who offers refuge to all people...a safe haven soon-to-be-turned-snare. Many in North America and Europe will join ranks with the Antichrist, descendants of the Ten Kingdoms descended from Israel and identified as the Ten Horns of Revelation.

As millions flock to his kingdom the peace and safety promised does not come. While the Antichrist's domain is relatively unscathed, the Americas, western Europe, northern and eastern Asia, Africa and India suffer numerous calamities. The socio-political dimensions of the nations of the world virtually return to their biblical Old Testament parameters. The only true power apart from the Antichrist is the confederated Asian Kings of the East.

2044 AD (5938 AM)

The First Trumpet judgment involves meteoric rain striking earth and setting fires.

2046 AD (5940 AM)

This single year is the focus of this author's book, *Anunnaki Homeworld: Orbital History and 2046 AD Return of Planet NIBIRU.* 2046 AD is--

• "when time collapses" according to Mayan prophecy, and Mayan Long-Count ends on 1,872,000nd day from 3113 BC (144,000 x 13);

• 144th year of Giza Course Countdown which began in 1902 AD at conclusion of the Cursed Earth Chronology;

• End of Astronomical Chronology encoded in base diagonals of Great Pyramid's *four foundation stones* (Tetramorph) that started 6084 years priorly in 4039 BC when Earth's orbit stabilized after wandering *270 years*;

• comet impacts North America ending United States in its *270th year*;

• ancient American calendrical unit was 52 years (Olmec, Mayan, Toltec, Aztec), and 52 years before 2046 AD was 1994 when *comet* Shoemaker-Levy 9 slammed into the planet Jupiter.

2048 AD (5942 AM)
A second comet terrifies the world, a nightly spectacle seen clearly because artificial lighting around the globe has ceased to function. The Earth has been darkened. This comet approaches and enters the atmosphere detonating at high altitude, its composition combustible and toxic. This contaminates the planet's oceans and lakes.

2052 AD (5946 AM)
The lost moon of NIBIRU, the Dark Satillite, deposits the ancient Seven Kings of the Anunnaki upon Earth. Accompanying them are the legions of Anunnaki soldiers and the Nephilim (who we refer to as little grey aliens). 2052 AD is--

• "The Secret Year" the Anunnaki Kings are released from their confinement since the Flood as written in the Book of Enoch 18:14-16;

• The calendrical fulfillment of the Anunnaki necklace represented by the chronometry of the Bluestone Ring of Stonehenge II, and the 1996 "pointer" crop formation (see *Chronicon*: 1996 AD);

• This began the final 54 years to Armageddon, paralleling the 54 years of Sargon I of Akkad. This is the Eighth King, who is of the Seven. Enoch calls these kings the Seven Mountains. (10) This was the same title used by the Sumerians.

• Physical appearance and massive invasion of Anunnaki soldiers parallels this year's Isometric counterpart of 1944 AD, D-Day, the largest naval-amphibious military invasion in *history* executed by the United States (Iron Empire) and known as Operation Overlord, exactly *108 years* before 2052 AD (54 + 54). Enoch wrote in the *54th chapter* of the Book of Enoch that

"Hell shall be opened," and come forth destroying (11), and in the Islamic Quran we read that in the Last Days the angels "shall present Hell to unbelievers, plain to view!" (12)

• As already cited, the French architect that designed the Statue of Liberty encoded the calendrical secret to the return of the Seven Anunnaki Kings in 2052 and return of Christ in 2106 AD. Designed in 1884 AD, the 168 steps up the giant statue ascent to the arm which ends in a ladder with 54 rungs. 1884 + 168 is 2052 when the Anunnaki depose mankind, assuming power, authority and dominion (demonic Operation Overlord) over the world wielded by the Seven Kings and the ante-diluvian AR UB curse [to shackle; to imprison] now afflicts humanity. The combined Anunnaki Chronology periods of 600, 60 and 6 (666) form the concept of absolute AUTHORITY over man. The ladder in archaic symbolism represented the concept of *ascending to heaven* [the attempt of the primordial Anunnaki in the PreAdamic Rebellion] and its 54 rungs are 54 years to the Torch, the Light of the World, the Chief Cornerstone that will vanquish the Anunnaki darkness at Armageddon in 2106 AD (6000 AM) and dispel the Curse of Man (AR UB), for as Scripture declares, "He came to set the captives free."

At the height of the Seven Kings' power in the Apocalypse imagery of the Book of Revelation they are depicted as a red, seven-headed dragon, which is what over this 6000-year period the "subtle serpent" of Eden has become. Our ancestors believed that long ago the beginning of our world was secured by the slaying of a seven-headed dragon of chaos…alas, *in the beginning* has not ended at all.

The End Was an Ancient Science
The disparities remaining unreconciled between earth's most archaic calendrical systems remain elusive and seemingly unfathomable to historians and scholars because the existence of the Dark Star and its rogue planets, Phoenix and NIBIRU, so prevalent in the annals of the ancients, has not yet been admitted by the learned of our own civilization. These chronologies and dating systems preserve the arcane mathematics of a formerly lost global time-keeping system that measured history by the intervals *between cataclysms*. This period in antiquity was 2070 years, or five Cursed Earth epochs of 414 years each.

In 4309 BC the PreAdamic World and NIBIRU were destroyed by the visitation of God to earth on the *back of a cherub* (Tetramorphic image), a theme of obscure origin found in the Psalms. Judgment in heaven was pronounced against the Anunnaki and their sentence was to be carried out 2070 years later when they were confined upon the Dark Satillite in 2239

BC when the Great Deluge drowned their gigantic Nephilim sons. The 8 last righteous people on earth, Noah and his immediate family were preserved, blessed and *delivered from death* to begin a whole new world. Man inherited what the Anunnaki originally controlled, the Earth, and their ultimate future judgment was to suffer *replacement* by resurrected humans who would inherit the one third of the heavenly positions the Anunnaki fell from. This Flood disaster and imprisonment was the 3000th year of the Anunnaki Chronology. As these events set the stage for a repetition of history, we are duty-bound in this endeavor to search for a future date that synchronizes both a 2070-year and a 3000-year period relevant to our timeline.

In order to comprehend the thematic concept of the sum of 2070 years some further circumscription is required. It will prove to be fascinating. In the year 2815 BC the Sethites after 90 years (exactly 1080 months) had completed the Great Pyramid and Sphinx complex in Egypt, only the monument's top stone missing. It was in this same year that the last of the pyramid's 144,000 casing blocks were set in place, the lower third covered in off-white inscriptions. This 2815 BC date was the year *1080 Annus Mundi* (same as preflood Hebraic calendar).

But the project was begun in 2905 BC (990 AM), which was precisely *1080 years* to 1825 BC when the patriarch Abraham was in Egypt at Giza translating the pyramid's casing block prophecies and histories, translations concerning judgments, redemption and *resurrection* that became the core material for many of our world's most ancient religious and philosophical works. Most remarkable of all is that this year was 2070 Annus Mundi, 2070 years after Man was banished from Eden in 3895 BC. Abraham was promised to be the father over many nations, and many of these derived through Israelite tribes. Of further synchronicity, exactly 2070 years after the completion of the Great Pyramid (Seal of Israel) was the year 745 BC when the Ten Tribes of Israel (later to be 10 Kingdoms of Europe) were deported by the Assyrians and distributed for assimilation into Medea, Persia, Armenia among the German Scythians.

As this work concerns calendars we must recall that in 713 BC the near collision of the Dark Satellite into Earth altered the number of days it required our world to orbit the sun, adding to its ellipse 5.24 days. This well-remembered disaster (see *Anunnaki Homeworld*) was 2070 years to 1358 AD which was the year the Muslim extraction engineers has completed defacing the Great Pyramid of its polished white limestone casing blocks for rebuilding materials after the quake of 1356 that destroyed Cairo.

Our modern global calendar was designed in 526 AD by Dionysius Exiguus, who calculated that Jesus was born in the 754th year of Rome. He miscalculated by two years (Jesus born in 2 BC) and designed the Year of Our

Lord (Anno Domini) calendar to begin at 1 AD, which was actually the 753rd year of Rome. Rome was founded in 753 BC (3142 AM). As demonstrated in *Chronicon AD* and throughout history, this mistake of Exiguus was *divinely inspired*. The BC-AD continuum is best understood paralleled with the Annus Mundi Chronology:

4 BC 3891		AM
3 BC 3892		AM
2 BC 3893		AM
1 BC 3894		AM
1 AD 3895		AM
2 AD 3896		AM
3 AD 3897		AM

Jesus as Christ (the Chief Cornerstone) was born in 2 BC. He is the *focus* and *meaning* of the Anno Domini Calendar and His birth is attested to in three startling ways:

a. Tertullian wrote that Jesus was born 28 years after Queen Cleopatra died in 30 BC (30-28 is *2 BC*);

b. Irenaeus wrote that Jesus was born in the 41st year of the reign of Augustus Caesar: Octavian, who came to power in 43 BC (43-41 is *2 BC*);

c. Vedic scholars assert that the Kali Yuga (Black Age) countdown to the coming of the *Savior* was exactly 3100 years from the start-date of this Indian system in 3102 BC (3102-3100 is *2 BC*).

Jesus was born near the end of the year and became one year old in 1 BC, and was still one year old well into 1 AD (which is also 2 AD). His appearance into the world was the fulfillment of prophecies concerning the Divine Plan to Redeem Mankind. Christ's Anno Domini timeline begins a *2070-year* countdown to the fulfillment of His principle prophetic message— the Resurrection. Before we delve into his amazing event, we have calendrical validation for our 2070-year event by its alignment with a specific *3000 year* timeline.

In the year 931 BC King Solomon died, the third and final regent over a unified nation of all 13 Israelite tribes. At his passing the Ten Tribes of Israel split into its own kingdom while three tribes formed the kingdom of Judah, and like the Egypt of their origin they became the Two Kingdoms. This rift was the *tearing* of Israel. Our 2070 AD date for the Resurrection is exactly 3000 years after this division, but even more startling is that this three millennia-long hiatus was *prophesied*. The prophet Hosea said:

Come and let us return unto the Lord; for he hath torn, and he will heal us; he hath smitten, and he will bind us up. After *two days* will he revive us: in the *third day* he will *raise us up*, and we shall live in his sight.

—Hoses 6:1-2

In more than one passage do we read in Scripture that a *day* unto the Lord is as a *thousand years*. Thus we see here a definitive three thousand year period when God will *raise us up* to *live*. In 931 BC Israel and Judah were *torn* and 186 years later the Assyrians dismantled the Israelite kingdom and deported them, ultimately leading to their migrations as Germanic nations into the Balkans, Asia Minor, Russia and Europe. A thousand years after 931 BC was 70 AD when the Romans under Titus destroyed Jerusalem and Judea using *German* legions (descendants of Israelites). Over a million Jews died and 97,000 were sold into the Slave Markets concluding this first 1000-year "day." A thousand years later we find that all the European kingdoms that descended from Israel were now in 1070 AD *Christian* nations. As per the prophecy, Israel had been *revived*. In only a few years they would initiate the Holy crusades to get back Jerusalem from her enemies. At this time every nation in Europe had populous Jewish communities, both Israelite and Jewish having no clue they were of the same stock. In the next 1000 years these Christian nations would rule the world and colonize the Americas and isles of the world. 1070 AD concludes the second day (2000 years). At the conclusion of the *third day*, at the end of the total 3000 years, Israel and Judah are *reunited in resurrection* with all who are *adopted by faith* in 2070 AD with the beginning of the *Kingdom of God*.

This year of 2070 AD is 18 years after the arrival of the Seven Kings, which under the post-2046 AD Condensed Calendar of 240 days a year is *4320 days*. By this time God will have removed from life *every righteous human on earth*—the entire planet populated by the wicked. 2070 AD brings judgment upon the Anunnaki as this is *108 years* after the completion of the Anunnaki Chronology in 1962 AD.

World history validates the significance of the 3000-year timeline. Theopompus long ago related that according to the Magi of the east a god reigns over the world for 3000 years before he is cast down by an usurper who likewise assumed the throne for 3000 years. (13) It is to be recalled here that the Anunnaki Chronology began in 5239 BC with their divine appointments and ended 3000 years later with their imprisonment in 2239 BC at the Flood. The Anunnaki Rebellion 600 years into their Chronology, in 4639 BC, was 3000 years to 1639 BC when the dying Jacob (Israel) in

Egypt adopted the sons of Joseph, Manesseh and Ephraim into the family of Israel, whose descendants would become mighty Germanic and ultimately American nations. The restoration of the Earth into a stable orbit beginning the Great Pyramid's Astronomical Chronology in 4039 BC was 3000 years to the 1039 BC birth of King David and start of the Messianic lineage of kingship. The 1039 BC Throne of David timeline was 3000 years to 1962 AD end of the Anunnaki Chronology. Further, the descent of the Anunnaki before the Flood in 3439 BC was 3000 years to the completion of the Parthenon at Athens, which depicts the War of the Titans and Giants (Anunnaki and their Nephilim offspring). The Flood in 2239 BC was 3000 years before the "second Babylon" was founded with the 762 AD start of the Abbasid Dynasty at Baghdad, Iraq. Planet Phoenix darkened the sun and initiated a worldwide catastrophe in 1687 BC felling many of the still preserved stone cities of the world 3000 years before NIBIRU passed close to Earth in 1314 AD when it was seen by many as a "great black darkness" over Europe and China. The Exodus of Israel from Egypt in 1447 BC was 3000 years prior to 1554 AD when a comet illuminated the heavens *552 years* (Phoenix Cycle) before Armageddon in 2106 AD. The year 6000. It was a *comet* that caused the cataclysmic episode during the Exodus when Israel left Goshen, the region of the Great Pyramid. 1554 AD was 5448 Annus Mundi, paralleling the 5448-inch height of the Great Pyramid's flat-topped apex. As this entire thesis is predicated upon the synchroni cities and alignments of calendars, we must take note that 1447 years after the start of the Islamic Hijrah calendar in 622 AD which marked Mohammed the prophet's *departure* (an exodus) from Medina ends amidst the year 2070 AD—*1447 BC* being Israel's *departure from an evil world* (Egypt).

The start of this Year of Our Lord (Anno Domini) 2070 date-event, a virtual chronographical cenotaph of One Who Died Yet Still Lives to share life with those that believe, God visited men *in the flesh* as Yeshua (Jesus) and proclaimed that all men would receive imperishable bodies. He was born through a mortal woman to assume the *likeness of man* that mankind can become the *image of god*. At the end of the 2070 AD event He summons the righteous dead to come out of the earth as they are completely *remade*, joining the Lord who does *not* yet descend to Earth.

This 2070 years is encoded in the Trilithons of Stonehenge and found prominently in the chronometry of the Great Pyramid's internal dimensions, the pyramid a symbol for resurrection as each stone in the monument of Man identifies a human soul in the Body of God. This is a global *exodus* from an evil planet of God's chosen, redeemed and elect, people removed so that God can unleash His fury on a disobedient world in the form of the Seven plagues of the Vials of Wrath. The resurrected are every man, woman and child who had ever lived in every epoch of mankind since 3895 BC who had been *sealed* by God (this mark the divine opposite of the Mark of the Beast) and will come *back to life*. And not just the righteous, but the wicked dead shall be resurrected and will remain to suffer on Earth under the dominion of the Anunnaki, destined to suffer the Plagues of Wrath. The Resurrection event will be a total physiological change in the human body to the genetic level, activating millions of latent genes thereby allowing the human body to realize its true potential when cellular replication and the metabolism will be so amplified that gaping wounds will heal in *seconds* and death can only be achieved by continual and intense burning. Junk DNA is anything but junk. The redeemed of God are given glorified bodies to match their holy spirits, but those left behind on Earth still living and not sealed will be empowered physically, their bodies then becoming eternal repositories of rage, fear, lust and hunger. As the Revelation record claims, "…and Death shall flee from them." The torment of their condition provokes them to pray that the rocks of the mountains should fall on them.

This resurrection and transportation from Earth of the righteous serves to bless them with inheriting the former offices of the Anunnaki who have now all been trapped on Earth so they too can suffer the Vials of Judgment with mankind. As this is the 3000th year of the Divided Kingdom Chronology, which started in 931 BC at Solomon's death, now King Solomon *resurrects* along with the millions of those under the Covenant of the Law to be reunited with their spiritual brothers under the Covenant of Grace. The kingdom of God is now healed, thus the statement in Scripture—Christ brings *healing* in His *wings* (symbol for flight/movement).

The Revelation conveys that in the Last Days 144,000 people will receive the *Seal of the Living God* and be immune from the judgments of the Seven Seals and Seven Trumpets. These are spiritually empowered *prophets*. These are the last humans on earth to die, taken by God in 2070 AD as He had taken Enoch before the Flood and Elijah after it. These spiritual Last Days' giants were prophetically symbolized by the 144,000 white (holy) limestone (once living) casing blocks (most beautiful and last laid parts of pyramid architecture) set onto the Great Pyramids. These holy ones, numbering 12,000 from each of Israel's 12 Tribes were also represented within the spatial dimensions of the Empty Sarcophagus in the Chamber of the Empty Tomb, known popularly as the King's Chamber in the Great Pyramid. This sarcophagus has always been empty and was discovered in 820 AD by Al Mamoun, the Caliph of Baghdad. 820 AD is 1296 years before Armageddon in 2106 AD (6000 AM), or 144 x 9 (number of *judgment*). The sarcophagus has an inside volume of 72,000 cubic Pyramid Inches but the entire stone container has a spatial mass area of 72,000 p" for a combined stone (material body) and inside space (air-spirit) of 144,000 cubic Pyramid Inches once its thin sliding granite lid is restored. This means that the stone itself perfectly matches in area mass the volume of its *contents* (the resurrected spirit receives as an inheritance a body equal to its spiritual integrity and power). Interestingly, 2070 AD is the *only* year in the Last Days from 1902 AD to 2106 AD that has its isometric counterpart *144 years* earlier, in 1926 AD. The epicentral year for the Last Days is 1998 (666 x 3). In 1926 NBC debuted with 24 radio stations, the first radio broadcasting network, broadcasting *Christian* programs concerning the promise of the *resurrection*. Radio waves are merely a different wavelength than *light* waves on the electromagnetic scale, the light being the Gospel. The new radio technology allowed men to spread the Word of God around the globe.

The Resurrection event is terribly misunderstood, and the many passages in Scripture concerning the resurrection have been contorted and twisted by theologians and ministers in their attempt to justify their faith in a totally unscriptural Christian myth known as the *Rapture*, a clever doctrinal tool that keeps the people riveted to their seats when the offering plates are passed around. Essentially, the concept is correct but the timing and teachings about the apocalypse attached to it are not. Believers *will suffer the Apocalypse*, but not the Seven Plagues.

Beginning in 2070 AD, *every* sentient being that has ever lived—Anunnaki, Nephilim hybrids or men—will either be with God receiving inheritances (as Sons of God) or on Earth with the Adversary suffering *punishment* for 36 years and preparing for the Great War... Armageddon.

The Monument of Man complete, the creation awaits 36 years for the Creator to descend at Armageddon as the Chief Cornerstone, the *Keystone* to a portal only the elect can enter. This 36 years is under the post-2046 AD Condensed Calendar of 240 days a year, thus 36 years is *8640 days* (864 being Foundation of Time number). In Greek the word God has the geometrical value of 864. (14) The duration of 36 years (6 x 6) forms the geometry of a keystone with the dimensions of 10 x 10 x 10 x 6 (36). The Chief Cornerstone now has a *foundation* to rest upon, an image that further demonstrates the geometry of His pyramid.

Billions of people on Earth are now under the authority of the Beast, the False Savior now turned Destroyer of the souls of men. He has successfully entombed lost souls in virtually superhuman bodies, allowing for them to bear and live through incredible pain, surviving the most horrendous conditions. This is why the obscure statement

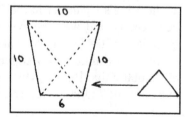

is made in Revelation that the righteous shall from this point remain righteous, and the wicked shall continue wickedly.

The Keystone is figurative for the Stone Uncut by Human Hands, the Stone the Builders Rejected, the Messiah Who will return to Earth once He has sufficient building materials to complete His eternal temple; redeemed humanity who will be pillars (repositories of divine knowledges) throughout the creation within whom God will dwell. The door or gate fit into the stone structure is not finished until the *keystone* is fit within it. This 36 year keystone forms a 52 degree pyramid. Esoterically, the sum 36 is thought to be a symbol for the idea of totality because 36 represents the sum of the first four even numbers (2 + 4 + 6 + 8 = 20) and first four odd numbers (1 + 3 + 5 + 7 = 16): 20 + 16 = 36.

The Seven Plagues are executed upon a totally spiritually vacuous world by the Tetramorph according to the Revelation. In the Gospel of Barnabas we also find that after the ruin of the world God shall anoint four holy angels to keep watch (Watchers). These Plagues and the War of Armageddon are detailed in *Chronicon AD*, so we will conclude this study with some sage advice. The priest-prophet Ezra wrote, "Behold, the Plagues draw nigh, and are not slack! (15) And there is no excuse, for as Baruch wrote, "He hath shown us that which is to be, and hath not concealed from us what will befall in the End." (16)

Archive VIII

Making Sense of It All

A Once-Inhabited Moon

Our Moon is many times larger in proportion to Earth than any other lunar body in the solar system compared to its host planet. This is highly unusual. In fact, compared to the combined moon-planet proportions of the four largest moons orbiting Jupiter (Ganymede), Saturn (Titan), Uranus (Titania) and Neptune (Triton), our Moon is still much larger in comparison. The Earth-Luna system is widely out of proportion in this solar system. (1) This is because it is not a true host-satellite pairing. The earth-Moon relationship is actually a *double-planet system.*

Jim Marrs in 2013 in *Our Occulted History,* wrote, "Mainstream science now accepts the theory that the moon originated *elsewhere* and entered the Earth's gravitational field at some point in ancient times. (2) Isaac Asimov notes that the Moon is too large to have been captured by Earth. (3) Luna was *placed deliberately* in its near-perfect circular orbit and its rotation synchronized with its period of revolution so one side always faces Earth. (4) Spence notes that a captured body should have a pronounced elliptical orbit- our Moon's orbit is too circular and scientists are at a loss to explain why. (5)

In the inner solar system, Earth is the only planet to have a moon. Mercury and Venus have no moons and Mars has two asteroids orbiting it, not moons, and these two asteroids did not appear until 1877 AD, first documented by Asaph Hall. Before that they had never been seen though Mars was the object of much scientific study prior to 1877.

The Moon's distance is so perfect it totally occults the sun at eclipse. It is now known to be far older than previously believed. Odd lights have repeatedly been reported by those studying the lunar surface, yet, scientists have found no evidence of volcanic activity on the Moon. (6) Though this is not the focus of this post, we will soon review evidence that the Moon exhibits much evidence of former habitation. Scientific analysis of moon rocks indicates that it is without a core, or hollow. (7) There are many, even scientists, now holding to the position that our Moon contains hollowed deep-interior bases or installations and that it has for thousands of years been used to watch over our world. Whole crater basins have been seen from Earth to have opened like massive doors with light inside from time to time. On the lunar surface are gigantic artificial constructs called the *Shard* in the Ukert Region and the *Tower* in the Sinus Medii, both upright and totally unexplainable by known natural processes. (8)

That the Moon is a recent addition to the inner solar system and the Earth system was the opinion of naturalists over twenty-three centuries ago. Aristotle wrote that the PreAchaean Pelasgians occupied Arcadia *before* there was a Moon in the sky. (9) Anaxagoras and Democritus taught that there was a time in *human* memory when Earth was a without a *moon. (*10)

Hans Hoerbiger was a Viennese engineer who devoted his life to the study of cosmic origins. He held that Luna is a captured planet. (11) The capture of Luna was actually a *steering* of the Moon to its present position and this occurred on one of those anciently venerated Great Years of 600 years known to the Sumerians as the NER Chronology, the history of the cosmos and world in 600-year intervals. Many fragments of this time-keeping tradition have survived around the world. The Moon was attached to Earth's orbit in the year 4039 BCE, or 1800 years (600 x 3) before the Great Flood cataclysm of 2239 BCE.

In 4039 BCE the Moon is moored to the Earth and our world begins rolling more rapidly, the planet beginning to warm. As the frozen hemispheres thaw, the earth and moon are locked in a geosynchronous *rolling* in orbit around the sun, as the same hemisphere on earth faces the same hemisphere of the moon as if the two bodies were connected by an invisible axis. Like a barbell of unequal weights, they roll around the sun as the ice melting into the seas evaporates on the continual-dayside of the planet. A thick vapor canopy spreads from the solar heated hemisphere that knows no night. This melting of frozen glacial sheets and oceans on one side of the planet continues 144 years. Still, small bands of Neanderthal and Cro-Magnon humans live, the solar-facing hemisphere supporting life. Our planet was a frozen fossil-world with minimal life surviving in the caves and subterranean biosphere. Our lunar body earlier had orbited the sun alone after being ripped away from Tiamat's explosion (Astroid Belt) till Earth came along and trapped it in its gravity. Our Moon was formerly called Kingu before it began orbiting Earth. It orbited the 4th world (present Astroid Belt), called Tiamat, which had 11 moons.

Albert T. Clay, Near East scholar and translator, in 1923, wrote that the Tiamat monster conflict at the Creation symbolically *"represents an unfriendly power,"* and that "the belief existed that there had been a great conflict prior to the Creation of the heavens and the earth, between God and the primeval monster, with whom were associated other beings termed *dragons. (12)* As found abundantly in my prior works on Phoenix and NIBIRU, intruder planets and comets coming very close to Earth throughout history by many cultures were referred to as *dragons*. Tiamat's dead body provided water that fell to the earth- a glaciosphere turned vaporous and torn away from a dead world to rain on ours. In 1902 L.W. King wrote that the Moon was as a "Planet that was laid waste." Sitchin notes that the Moon, or Akkadian *Sin,* derived from SU.EN, or *Lord of Wasteland. (13)*

In Porphry's Letter to Anebo the Egyptian as related by Augustine in *City of God X ch. 11,* he wrote that demons *were of the moon,* and *inside it.* Occult tradition derived from Tibet reads- "Here we touch upon a hidden mystery, of which the solution lies revealed for those who seek, in the fact that human beings and certain groups of devas are no longer *found on the moon.* Man has not ceased to exist upon the Moon because it is dead, and cannot therefore support life, but the Moon is dead because man and these deva groups have been *removed from off its surface.*." (14) "The Moon, as you know, is a *shell, an ancient form... " (15)* There are several theorists offering convincing evidence today that many of the impact scars and craters on the Moon's surface were not from meteorites but are actually *blast craters...*the relics of major weapons impacts.

Earth's new orbit, rotation and axial tilt occurring in 4039 BCE is confirmed indirectly in research of Scott Creighton and Gary Osborn in *The Giza Prophecy,* showing convincing evidence of a geoastronomical timeline encoded in the architectural distribution of the Giza monuments identifying the approximate date of 3980 BC (59 years off from 4039) for an ancient poleshift cataclysm when Earth assumed its 23.5 axial tilt. They confirmed their Sphinx timeline by independent analysis of 39" Queens Chamber shaft that pointed directly at Al-Nitak of Orion's Belt in about 3980 BC. (16)   Also from Egypt comes evidence closer to the mark.   The temple of Dendera in Egypt built by the Ptolemys in accord with an ancient plan was designed to commemorate the Zodiac. Paul A. LaViolette, Ph.D, admitting that he did not know why, wrote that Dendera's zodiac encodes the date *4040 BCE. (17)* An estimate only 1 year off from 4039. A stunning find- truly a band of constellations could have no meaning to a planet *not rotating* on its present axis. The Zodiac was literally born on 4039 BCE because prior to the Moon's presence the terrestrial poles would have been different, thus making the band of stars we see today as the Zodiac to have been a totally different strip of the starry heavens.

In this year of 4039 BC an unusual surface-scarred world appeared in a dead orbit around Earth. The Moon. It was once inhabited. Its installations have been reactivated in the last century. We are far from finished in our study of this remarkable object in our every night sky.

The 432,000 Shars of PreFlood Antiquity

William A. Hinson in *Discovering Ancient Giants* wrote concerning the Sumerian histories, "In text after text, whenever the starting point was recalled, it was always this: 432,000 years before the Deluge, the DIN.GIR (gods) then came down to earth from their own world...NIBIRU." (1) Hinson's statement is mostly true save for the inflated 432,000 "years." For the misinformation that has saturated the genre of books published on Ancient Astronaut Theory, we have Zecharia Sitchin to thank.

Sitchin's belief that NIBIRU's orbit was 3600 years derives from a mistake. That the Deluge occurred in the 120th shar induced Sitchin to multiply 3600 *years* by 120 to produce 432,000 "years" from arrival of Anunnaki to the Great Flood, an error even Vedic chronographers made in determining the duration of the Yugas (World Ages). A preflood year was 360 days, the calendrical systems for ALL ancient 3rd millennium BCE civilizations was 360 days a year. Thus a decade was 3600 days. The shar was a term describing a *day* and a *120-year* period. The historically-recorded ten shars from the descent of the Anunnaki to the Great Flood was simply 120 years times ten for a period lasting *1200 years*. This 1200 years multiplied by 360 days a year is 432,000 *days*. Sitchin's mistake was a simple one but it expanded Anunnaki history from twelve centuries to almost *half a million years,* an untenable duration. Anything that is alive that lived as long as 432,000 actual years would be something totally different by the end of such a long period. It is a span of time that would make even major events within it to be of no significance. Sitchin's other error was assuming that NIBIRU had anything to do with the Great Flood cataclysm in 2239 BCE. It did not. That event was caused by the Phoenix.

Just as the shar was a unit of time measuring 120 of something, ten shars being 1200, so too did the *gar* measure distance and length. A gar was 12 cubits, so ten gar would be 120 cubits. (2) Sitchin knew this but still pushed the 432,000 "years" because it fit with his own belief in the evolutionary model, uniformitarianism and the Ice Age chronologies of Establishment academia.

Sitchin noted that the Sumerians held in high esteem the sum of 3600 shars, or *perfect circles.* (3) This shar term also meant *completed cycle.* He assumed that shars referred to years, but shar had also another connotation, that of a king or *Supreme Ruler.* This introduced the added confusion of the manifold traditions of the Ten Kings before the Flood. Babylonian historians wrote that the Ten Kings of the preflood world ruled 432,000 shars. (4) Berossus wrote that the Ten Kings reigned 120 shars. (5) The Ten Kings are associated by many with the Ten Patriarchs of the Genesis text from Adam to

Noah, survivors of the Flood. The shar concept is preserved in Genesis where we learn that Noah was warned 120 years before the Deluge that it was going to transpire. The biblical Noah meets his parallel in the Phoenician Ouranos, the Greek Uranus, according to the 10th century BCE historian Sanchuniathon, was the son of Autochthon. In Plato's writings this Autochthon was one of the Ten Kings of Atlantis (6), a quasi-mythical realm that was destroyed utterly by a flooding cataclysm. The Ten Kings figure prominently on some versions of the Sumerian King-Lists.

These ten kings (shars being 3600 days) equaled 120 years, or a Great Shar.

A shar was 3600 *days*, or ten antediluvian years of 360 days each. To Sitchin's credit, Berossus as cited by Abydenus made the *same* mistake- "now, a shar is esteemed to be three thousand six hundred years..." (7) Sitchin used this as evidence. But Berossus wrote of things already lost to memory in the 3rd century BC, two thousand years after the shar-day system collapsed.

Puranic texts of ancient Vedic Sanskrit reads that there were Four Earth Ages totalling 432,000 years. (8) The actual composition of the Puranic records were circa 1500 BCE, so the misunderstanding between days-years in the older Sumerian shar system is understandable. It is remarkable that the Sumerian and the Vedic records cite the same number...432,000.

Sitchin further assumed that the 120 shars of Sumerian history to the Deluge was 432,000 years, a ridiculous sum, because Joseph Brady in 1972 wrote that a Jupiter-sized planet with a theoretical orbit of 1800 years (1/2 of 3600) would explain discrepancies in Halley's Comet orbit. Sitchin saw this as proof of his shar-year theory.(9)

My position is that the Anunnaki descended in 3439 BCE, which my books affirmatively demonstrate, which was 600 years after the **Capture of Luna** in 4039 BCE and 600 years before the start of the Anunna Dynasty in 2839 BCE, these 600 year periods being Anunnaki NER epochs so famous in distant antiquity. It is my contention that the 432,000 shars interpreted by Sitchin and mimicked by so many others are merely *days* on a 360-day annual calendar and in my books I offer the proofs that these 432,000 shars concern a *1200-year period marking descent of Anunnaki to Great Flood in 2239 BCE.* Note just these few references:

The Vedic Puranas explain that the Kali Yuga Age was a period of *1200 years (10)* The same records mentioned the 432,000 "years." This is evidence they preserved actual history while remaining confused as to the chronology;

Babylonian records of the Antediluvian world specifically refer to a distinct period of *1200 years* involved the gods (11)

Early Arabians believed that they had an ancestor king before the Flood who lived *1200 years*, King Shedd-Ad-Ben-Ad, the founder of civilization. (12)

In my other works on the Phoenix we have seen numerous chronological proofs that the Great Flood occurred in 2239 BCE, the month of May. Simply adding 1200 years to 2239 gives us the date of 3439 BCE as the appearance of the Anunnaki.

The Gihon Flood 3439 BCE Was 1200 Years Before Noah's Flood

3439 BCE is the *only* year in recorded history when one of the 600-year epochs known in antiquity as Great Years, or Anunnaki NER epochs, coincided with the exact year that NIBIRU either entered or exited the inner Sol system. That numerous traditions assert that it was at this time (1200 years before the Great Deluge: 2239 BCE) that the "gods" arrived to Earth is not without significance. One might argue that Sitchin wrote that NIBIRU caused the Great Flood but he was wrong. Planet Phoenix was responsible for the 2239 BCE destruction and it was Phoenix that was named in antiquity. Phoenix's orbit is different than that of NIBIRU and its chronology is firmly established by many proofs [see my Phoenix Chronology]. Further, Sitchin conveyed that the Great Flood was way back during the last Ice Age, which to me is ridiculous. That a flooding occurred during past Ice Ages is probably true, but the *Great Flood* of human memory and global fame throughout antiquity transpired toward the end of the 3rd millennium BCE (2239 BCE), an event dated easily in multitudes of ways that is scientifically verified by data exhibiting tremendous evidence of the worldwide destruction that ended the Early Bronze Age. This data is already found in my Phoenix Chronology.

In the Hebraic records the Watchers [Anunna] descend to earth in the days of Jared, whose name means *descent*, being in the 10th Jubilee, which was the first descent before the Great Flood. A second group of Anunnaki arrived later, also before the Flood. The descent of the Watchers is the central theme of the Book of Enoch and the name of Jared was a commemoration of the event.

This descent does not mark the first appearance of the Anunna but the arrival of the most important figure in the Old World human histories...ENKI. Even the Genesis chronology shows this to be the time *Enoch* is introduced into the biblical narrative. ENKI of Sumerian records is the same as Enoch of the later Semitic traditions.

The Sumerian text reads that Enki descended to Earth- "When I approached Earth there was much flooding..." (1) The *Book of Jasher* notes that at this precise year of 3439 BC in the chronological narrative that the Gihon flooded and killed a third of humanity. The Gihon is the Nile in Egypt, its identity revealed by the Jewish historian Josephus almost two thousands years ago. Enki himself landed in the Snake Marsh among the Gizi reeds. (2) This was a marshland before the Flood, known today as Giza, where the Great Pyramid stands. This monument is also alluded to in the Sumerian text for it was there that Enki built his house, called E.ABZU (House of the Deep), his sacred precinct in Eridu. This links the Sumerian Enki to the biblical person of Enoch, for which many noncanonical and other documents assert was the builder of the Great Pyramid complex. Additionally, Eridu is the biblical Irad in Genesis that was built by *Enoch.*

The *Book of Jasher* reads that, "In the days of Enosh...the Lord caused the waters of the Gihon to overwhelm them, and He destroyed and consumed them, and He destroyed a third part of the earth... and there was no food for the sons of men and the famine was very great in those days." (3) This disaster in the time of Enosh is confirmed in the Jewish Haggadoth text which relates that this was a terrible flood before the Great Flood of Noah's day. (4) The Yezidas of Asia preserve traditions of a flooding more ancient than Noah's, stating that the world was flooded *twice*, the second flood far worse than the first. (5)

A long tablet series found in the ruins of the Sumerian city of Nippur is the source of the text, which reads, "When I approached the earth, there was much flooding." (6) This is in a text narrated by Enki referred to as *The Eridu Genesis Collection.* We have here an ancient Sumerian narrative of the arrival to earth by ENKI that occurred 1200 years (432,000 shars) before the Great Flood, which would date his descent to earth in 3439 BCE. Coupled with this from independent sources like Jasher we have a terrible flooding (same ENKI witnessed) occurring in Egypt killing a third of humanity. Two separate sources telling the same story.

In the biblical chronology of Stephen Jones' work published in his book, *The Secrets of Time,* the flooding of the Gihon is perfectly dated at 3439 BCE, or 1200 years before the Great Flood in 2239 BCE. A Christian fundamentalist, Jones knows nor publishing anything about NIBIRU or planet Phoenix. That the background of these Enochian/ENKITE traditions was ancient antediluvian Egypt is made more profound when we consider this next piece of chronological evidence, which comes entirely from Egypt.

The 3439 BCE date is found perfectly in the chronometry of the Great Pyramid of Giza. Astronomer Royal for Scotland, Charles Piazzi Smythe, in the 1870s determined on-site at Giza that for reasons **unknown to him**, the monument was designed using the descendant passage as a scope to point directly at the star Alpha Draconis (Eye of the Dragon) in the year 3440 BCE, which he said was the preflood pole star. (7) This 3440 BCE date is virtually a bull's-eye for 3439 BCE. The Great Pyramid was built by Enoch/ENKI which is the subject matter of my book, *Lost Scriptures of Giza*.

Using scripture to interpret scripture, a method of paramount import to the Christian apologist, we read in John 3:13 the very mysterious statement that, "And no man hath ascended up to heaven, but he that *came down* from heaven." We are led to believe this was Jesus, but it would be equally true of Enoch because the biblical records make it an important event that Enoch ascended into heaven and was never seen again. This is none other than a biblical admission that Enoch **arrived to earth in descent** before he again **ascended to heaven.**

Enoch/ENKI is a major player in the early affairs of civilized humanity and many more posts are coming concerning this fascinating individual. What is intriguing is that the apocalyptic *Revelation* prophecies record that in the Last Days a **third of mankind shall die** at the appearance of a celestial object in the sky it called Wormwood, though the 200,000,000 "demons" that scour the earth at the same time are *perfect* images of what the ancient Babylonians perceived the Anunnaki to be [not the Sumerians, who consistently exhibited the Anunnaki as tall, bearded Caucasians].

NIBIRU visited in 3439 BCE initiating an antediluvian apocalypse, the arrival of gods. NIBIRU returns in November 2046 to again kill off a third of the human race. This is the subject matter of my book, *Anunnaki Homeworld*.

Explosion of Civilization at Egypt 3439 BCE

It is noteworthy that in the earliest records of the human race the gods are *physical beings* who created earth, and then *visited it*. No other deities are known, no primordial unseen Creator- the oldest texts leave no room for doubt...the only gods the preflood ancients knew *fell from heaven*. It was *after* the Great Deluge and after the disappearance of the Anunnaki did religionists *invent* the Fall of Man traditions by rewriting particulars that had only pertained to the Fall of the Gods. If there is a heavenly conflict, if there is an ongoing war in heaven, if there is to be a reckoning, a divine judgment executed against one or more groups, these have NOTHING to do with mankind. Humans are DNA-in-harvest, victims of offworld manipulation. An *enemy* manufactured humans with the unintended result of the designer DNA creating *sentience* enough that unconfined spirits outside the holosphere were pulled into physical bodies. Humans are biological spirit-prisons and this unintended consequence initiated a rift between opposing Anunna groups. A sufficiently powerful body of opposition rebelled against enslaving mankind and came to Earth as humanity's *benefactors.* These disobedient Anunnaki became the "sinners," or Those From the Moon [Sin] and it was their "fall" that disrupted Anunna plans to keep humans servile, cowed, ignorant and uncivilized. The Fall is predominantly a western religious theme popularized in Babylonia. It was later heavily borrowed and adapted with Jewish dressings for the biblical records.

Professor G.R.S. Mead in *Fragments of a Forgotten Faith, wrote,* "a persistent tradition in connection with all the great mystery institutions was that their several founders were the introducers of all the arts of civilization: they were either themselves gods or were instructed by gods—in brief; that they were men of far greater knowledge than any who had come after; they were the teachers of infant races...souls belonging to a more highly developed humanity than our own... a prior perfected humanity not necessarily earth-born." (1)

Andrew Collins in *From the Ashes of Angels* wrote, "The myths associated with these supernatural beings appear to be no more than the bastardized memories of the way in which survivors of a previous high civilization passed on their skills and capabilities to our own ancestors. If this is so we are dealing with neither the divine nor the supernatural, but with physical beings of flesh and blood communicating on a one-to-one basis with human kind. (2)

Jim Marrs in *Our Occulted History* adds that the Anunnaki found themselves *marooned* on a primitive world, without their infrastructure to manufacture their tools, but still possessing a superior knowledge. (3)   The Fallen Ones, or Those Who From Heaven to Earth Came, were a small group of hundreds of survivors of a planetary cataclysm *away from earth* who were marooned on earth by other survivors who *did not stay,* still in possession of the vehicles of their technology.   This is how high civilization-engineering, agriculture, writing and arithmetic suddenly appeared in the Neolithic during the Ubaid culture of southern Iraq- the birth of Sumer.

Will Hart in *The Genesis Race* wrote, what we "...find is an explosion of development, a quantum leap compressed into a mere fraction of humanity's existence as a species, a radically changed way of being, and an entirely new survival strategy based on the human engineering of plants and animals undreamed of by those of the Paleolithic Period." (4)   These four popular authors were not the first to theorize these things. Charles Fort wrote about offworld manipulation of humans and history 70-80 years ago. The time when this was supposed to have occured is best summed up by Hart. In *The Genesis Race* he wrote, "...a major developmental thrust between *3500 BCE and 1500 BCE*... a sudden explosion of innovation in these distinct areas of the planet."

(5)   These six regions were Egypt, Sumer, Harappa [Indus Valley], China, Mexico and Bolivia-Peru. Hart asserts that at this time a superhuman race taught mankind how to be human. (6)   Hart continues, "The fact that these ancient cultures do not take credit themselves for their achievements only supports the conclusion that indeed the gods were the source of the amazing explosion of growth and innovation that occurred from 3500 BCE to 3000 BCE...." (7)   Also, "There is no traceable, step-by-step path leading to them from the hunter-gatherer way of life. Science has not explained the Sumerians sudden, unprecedented explosion of development." (8)

Almost a hundreds years ago Lewis Spence wrote, "The histories of all peoples commence with a dynasty of god-kings, only shading later into real history as time proceeds. The Greek and Roman dynasties, the Egyptian, the Babylonian, the Mexican and Central American annals, all began with traditional notions of the lives and deeds of heaven-descended monarchs." (9)

Over 50 years before the Ancient Astronaut Theory began taking root many scholars concluded that at this time in history Egypt's civilization suddenly appeared. "The civilization of Egypt at its first appearance was of a higher order than at any subsequent period of its history, thus testifying that it drew its greatness from a fountain higher than itself." (10)

Ernest Renan wrote, "Egypt at the beginning appears mature, old, and entirely without mythical and heroic ages, as if the country had never known youth. Its civilization has no infancy, and its art no archaic period...it was already mature. (11)

Donnelly- "There is no evidence that the civilization of Egypt was developed in Egypt itself." (12)   Citing *Blackwood's* magazine, Ignatius Donnelly continued, "...as soon as men were planted on the banks of the Nile they were already the cleverest men that ever lived, endowed with more knowledge and more power than their successors for centuries and centuries could attain to. Their system of writing, also, is found to have been complete from the very first...as we have not yet discovered any trace of the rude, savage Egypt...Our deepest researches have hitherto shown her to us as only the mother of a most accomplished race." (13)

Of early Egypt, Renan wrote- "It has no archaic epoch." (14)   Osborn wrote, "It bursts upon us at once in the flower of its highest perfection." (15)   Seiss wrote, "It suddenly takes its place in the world in all its matchless magnificence, without father, without mother...as if it had ***dropped from the unknown heavens.***" (16)   Rawlinson wrote, "All the authorities agree that, however far back we go, we find in Egypt no rude or uncivilized time out of which civilization is developed." (17)

Anthropologists cannot account for the leap and the archeologist cannot help but find that the leap occurred *anciently and everywhere*. We understand this mystery as having its origin with Homo Anunna, passing on their knowledge to their own descendants after they had arrived from somewhere else; not a development but an *inheritance*. The beginning of this explosion of development at 3500 BCE according to Hart is an approximate that matches nicely with the 3439 BCE pass of NIBIRU through the inner Sol system, a date demonstrated in *Anunnaki Homeworld*.

600-Year NER Epochs of Anunnaki Are Holospheric Programming

The deeper we penetrate the architecture of reality the more we come in contact with coincidences that defy rational conclusions. Sentience ensnared in webs of deceit. We traverse through life through a fixed medium of probability molds that take on predictive values the more we recognize their presence. The Old World's time-keeping system involving Great Years is a case in point. A 600-year period.

The birth of the biblical Noah is in the 1056th year of the preflood calendar. Factoring the Phoenix Calendar we find that Year One was 3895 BCE, making Noah's birth year to be 2839 BCE, or year 1056. We can employ biblical chronologist Stephen Jones' chronology published in *The Secrets of Time* and find that in using the Bible, the Book of Jasher, works of Enoch, Jubilees and the Assyrian Eponyms, according to him Noah was born at precisely 2839 BCE. Two different sources, with Stephen Jones knowing nothing about the Phoenix or its orbital chronology. A third method is found in the birth of Abraham. The biblical material reveals that he was born 292 years after the Deluge in 2239 BCE, even Josephus writing that Abram was born in the 292nd year after the Flood. This would be 1947 BCE however, it is also 1948 Annus Mundi, or 1948 years from Year One in 3895 BCE. Thus Abraham's birth seems to be a conjunct between two calendrical systems, one counting forward in time and the other backward. This is possible because the two separate time-keeping systems counted as their first months totally different portions of the year, thus the overlap between 1948 AM and 1947 BCE could mark the exact same date if one system counts March 21st [vernal equinox] as New Year's Day and the other January 1st. At any rate, Abram was born 892 years after Noah in the Genesis/Jasher genealogy, so Noah was born in *2839 BCE.*

Why is this relative to Anunnaki studies? Well, 2839 BCE was exactly 600 years after the Anunnaki/Watchers appeared with ENKI in 3439 BCE and built Erudi (biblical Irad). It was 1200 years (600 + 600) after the appearance of the Moon in 4039 BCE (hollowed for observatory installations). Further,

Noah's birth in 2839 BCE marks the final 600 years until the Great Flood in 2239 BCE, the month of May. Abraham's birth marked the intersect between two calendars just as Noah's birth marked the conjunct between two Great Years of 600 year epochs before the Flood. And we cannot omit this reference from the Genesis text: *"...in the six hundredth year of Noah's life, in the second month, on the seventeenth day..."* the floodwaters were upon the earth.

Here is something you just can't make up. In 1895 the historian J.D. Parsons wrote that Noah's birth was *"...at the meeting point of two of those famous cycles of six hundred years so often referred to by ancient writers."* (1) The import of this statement lies in the fact that Parsons did not have a chronology to back up the claim. His information was from an alternative source other than chronology.

The Anunnaki Chronology began in 5239 BCE, counting 600 years to 4639 BCE, then to 4039 BCE when the Moon appeared, then 600 more years to the arrival of the Anunnaki under ENKI in 3439 BCE. These 600 year epochs are mentioned by Josephus and also revered by the Sumerians as a duration specifically related to the Anunnaki, called a NER. These facts are detailed in my work, *Descent of the Seven Kings*. Robert Temple discovered that the later Babylonians preserved a tradition of the 600-year period, calling it the *neros,* a fact he obtained from *"...an extremily obscure old book from early in the nineteenth century,"* titled *The Celtic Druids* (1827) by Godfrey Higgins concerning Stonehenge and other British stone circles. (2) Interestingly, Zecharia Sitchin notes that the Sumerian cycle of 1800 years [600 x 3] was important to the Anunnaki for astronomical reason. (3) 3439 BCE was exactly the 1800th year of the Anunnaki NER Chronology of 600 year epochs that began 5239 BCE.

Concerning the 600 year calendrical nexus points when historical and traditional records claim great personages were born, died, important events unfolded, Edward Carpenter writing in 1920 seems keen to this phenomenon. He uncovered evidence in his researches prompting him to write- "Have there been in the course of human evolution certain, so to speak, *nodal points,* or periods in which the psychologic currents ran together and condensed themselves for a new start; and has such each node or point of condensation been marked by the appearance of an actual and heroic man who supplied a necessary impetus for the new departure, and gave his name to the resulting movement? *Or,* is it sufficient to suppose the automatic formation of such nodes or starting points without the intervention of any special hero or genius, and to imagine that in each case the mythmaking tendency of mankind CREATED a legendary and inspiring figure and worshipped the same..." (4) This is a profound statement made a century ago- that the collective psyche of humanity responds to the linear projections of a framework of nodal apertures in the fabric of space -time inducing us to either become aware of important persons appearing on those nodal dates, or that we *invented them* later and retrospectively assigned them to those nodal dates. No matter which is true the case set forth by Edward Carpenter is true and demonstrable.

Enoch appears (ENKI) as a great benefactor to humanity in 3439 BCE. 600 years later Noah appears in 2839 BCE who will be the savior of humanity through the global cataclysm. 600 years later this same Noah survives the Deluge in 2239 BCE preserving the seed of humanity. Whether any of this is true does not affect Carpenter's observations, for on those *nodal dates* we have by many different chronological methods ascertained these years to all be 600 years apart whether the stories are true or not. The Chinese maintained a tradition that the Great Flood actually marked a major *division in time.* (5) Additionally, 600 years after the Flood was 1639 BCE, the *exact* date Jacob (Israel) died and the promises of the covenant of Abraham passed to his sons, the patriarchs of many tribes that later become whole nations. We can't stop there because 600 years later we have 1039 BCE when David emerges as the savior hero of Israel in the slaying of Goliath the Philistine oppressor. This phenomenon was addressed by Acharya S. in *The Christ Conspiracy,* when she wrote that it was taught long ago that every 600 years "a great man" arises or is born. (6)

No one can accuse me of inventing this 600-year timeline, it is *ancient* and well-documented. Nor did I date any of these events, which were already dated at 3439, 2239, 1639, 1039 BCE by other published sources as shown in my books *When the Sun Darkens, Anunnaki Homeworld* and *Nostradamus and the Planets of Apocalypse.* As many of my readers know, it is my belief that our reality matrix maintains characteristics of a hologram. It is my theory that this reality construct has dimensional architecture that maintains its structure over long periods of time, *programmed routine.* The 600-year NER, or Great Year, the Phoenix Cycle of 552-year epochs, the 414-year Cursed Earth chronology, the 138 year orbit of the Phoenix, 792 year orbit of NIBIRU, 394.5 year orbit of the Dark Satellite. Each one of these is well demonstrated through history in my research and they all lend proof of a vast invisible infrastructure built around and totally confining, *mankind.*

Orbital Chronology of NIBIRU

Zecharia Sitchin, author of the popular *Earth Chronicles* series, never provided a chronology for the orbit of NIBIRU, but merely speculated that its orbit was 3600 years long. As seen in other posts this 3600 "years" was a glaring mistake on Mr. Sitchin's part involving the interpretation of the length of the Sumerian shar. We will not revisit that embarrassment here. Instead,

I offer you the real and *demonstrable* orbit of the object called NIBIRU by Sitchin—but probably known by other names to the ancients. My published works on the subject contain the source materials, and so will upcoming posts.

3439 BCE... Primitive population of Neolithic humans reduced by a third in massive flooding. The year the Anunnaki/Anunna/Watchers/Enki/Enoch appeared and began building technolithic structures in what later would be called Egypt, 1200 years (432,000 days on 360-day year calendar) before the Great Flood of 2239 BCE. NIBIRU exited the inner solar system orbiting Sol.

2707 BCE... NIBIRU entered the inner system beginning its 60-year perihelion period. The 60-year window of opportunity for the Anunnaki to visit Earth is documented in Near Eastern texts;

2647 BCE... 792-year orbit complete. A Chinese tradition concerning the 60-year period dates its origin to "2637 BCE." Knowing nothing about this NIBIRU orbital chronology, Robert Temple's independent reseaqrch uncovered that ancient Egypts associated the 60-year period with the crocodile, a calendar sysmbol, Temple theorizing that the crocodile represented to them the *amphibian aliens*. 2647 BCE marked the Exodus of the Anunna from Earth, beginning the Abandonment & Shock Period of preflood humanity. Social unrest, wars, racial conflicts, rapid loss of technolithic knowledge initiating the Post-Technolithic Period. 2647 BCE was 408 years to the Great Flood in 2239 BCE, this 408 years remembered precisely by the ancient American cultures who claimed that the Fourth Age was the *Water Sun* epoch lasting 408 years, which began their calendar. To recall the exact amount of years, 408, is beyond coincidence. In ancient South America the people practiced ritual magic in the designing of the gigantic geoglyphs of Nazca in an effort to induce the sky gods to return. All around the world cultures began erecting pyramids believing that by emulating the work of the gods (Anunnaki visitors), these gods would return.

[732 years pass with NIBIRU outside the Sol system on its orbit around Nemesis, the Dark Star, Sol's collapsed binary companion star being a dark brown dwarf. 60 + 732 years gives NIBIRU a total orbital period of 792 Earth years]

1915 BCE... NIBIRU entered the inner system beginning its 60-year perihelion period. Ancient Near East texts describe a terrible sky dragon and celestial war that shook the earth. Writings from India describe a great darkness during the daytime and a rain of stones with flames from the sky.

1855 BCE... No records. NIBIRU exits Sol system. 792 year orbit complete.

[732 years pass with NIBIRU outside the Sol system on its orbit around Nemesis, the Dark Star, Sol's collapsed binary companion star being a dark brown dwarf. 60 + 732 years gives NIBIRU a total orbital period of 792 Earth years]

1123 BCE... NIBIRU entered the inner system beginning its 60-year perihelion period. A sky dragon appeared and changed the Mandate of Heaven in China; Shang Dynasty collapses

1063 BCE... No records.   NIBIRU exits Sol system. 792-year orbit complete.

[732 years pass with NIBIRU outside the Sol system on its orbit around Nemesis, the Dark Star, Sol's collapsed binary companion star being a dark brown dwarf. 60 + 732 years gives NIBIRU a total orbital period of 792 Earth years]

331 BCE... NIBIRU entered the inner system beginning its 60-year perihelion period. The Macedonians under Alexander and the Persians under Darius III witnessed a partial eclipse. The Moon dimmed and the sky turned blood red. Modern eclipse computation programs calculate no eclipses for this period seen over the Near East. Weeks later Alexander's forces were terrified to see flames coming out of the sky.

271 BCE... Something totally eclipsed planet Venus . For this to occur, with Venus so close to Earth, an object of great size had to have transited between them. 792-year orbit complete.

[732 years pass with NIBIRU outside the Sol system on its orbit around Nemesis, the Dark Star, Sol's collapsed binary companion star being a dark brown dwarf. 60 + 732 years gives NIBIRU a total orbital period of 792 Earth years]

462 CE... NIBIRU entered the inner system beginning its 60-year perihelion period. No records.

522 CE... 792-year orbit complete.   Earthquakes devastated Olympia in Greece. Sky dragons were seen over Britain, a celestial war of monsters, raining great droops of blood followed by a dearth. This could be Phoenix, as 522 CE in the *only* year in all recorded world history that NIBIRU and Phoenix were passing through inner solar system at same time. A strange star appeared over Britain, attached to a ray that ended in a dragon. 522 CE was the beginning of the Dark Age when written records became scarce.

[732 years pass with NIBIRU outside the Sol system on its orbit around Nemesis, the Dark Star, Sol's collapsed binary companion star being a dark brown dwarf. 60 + 732 years gives NIBIRU a total orbital period of 792 Earth years]

1254 CE... NIBIRU entered the inner system beginning its 60-year perihelion period. No records.

1314 CE... 792-year orbit complete. Plague fogs, quakes and disasters in China but over Europe is seen a great Black Darkness that blots out the stars. This ends the period known as the Seven Comets Over Europe. The Great Famine of Europe from 1314-1317 CE began a 40-year period of disasters, plagues and famines worldwide that killed *a third of the global population.*
[732 years pass with NIBIRU outside the Sol system on its orbit around Nemesis, the Dark Star, Sol's collapsed binary companion star being a dark brown dwarf. 60 + 732 years gives NIBIRU a total orbital period of 792 Earth years]
2046 CE... NIBIRU entered the inner system beginning its 60-year perihelion period. Called Wormwood in the Apocalypse text, a third of humanity again killed just as in 3439 BCE. Anunnaki invasion of Earth (described bodily in Revelation prophecies). David Davidson's 80-year old research on geometry of Great Pyramid reveals that he was convinced that the monument conveyed an *orbital chronology* that ENDS in 2045 CE. It is the 2046 CE proximity of NIBIRU to Earth that reduces the *day, night, sun, moon, and stars by a third* because our planet will be MOVED and begin spinning faster causing destruction that will kill off *a third of mankind.*
2106 CE... 792-year orbit complete. NIBIRU exits the Sol system after the Anunnaki on planet for 60 years. 2106 CE is the 6000th year from 3895 BCE that serves as the Ancient World's *Year One,* marking the year of a major poleshift that *reset* civilization back to a 0 point. This 3895 BCE global lithospheric displacement rearranging the coasts and continents, slipping entire landmasses beneath the seas, is the reason why in 3439 BCE when the Anunnaki arrived they found a human race living no different than animals (according to the Sumerian records and the archeological evidence). When the Anunnaki arrived it had been 456 years since the 3895 BCE poleshift had ended every civilization on the planet.
This orbital chronology is the subject matter of my book *Anunnaki Homeworld* and its data-packed sequel, *Nostradamus and the Planets of Apocalypse.* I have here provided the orbital history of NIBIRU but we have much ground to cover before we conclude that all the evidence has been amassed. My own books are packed with extensive bibliographies because I believe that all source materials need be honored, and that all who read my conclusions see for themselves that I invent no dates to support a theory, that the dates were already published in works preceding my own.

Gamma Radiation Burst Records Document NIBIRU's Proximity

The accounts of Anunna origin seem confusing- out of the sea or out of the sky. But the most popularized account is not original, but an anachronistic misunderstanding of older records. Originally, the oldest writings, Sumerian, depicted the Anunnaki as having *dropped from heaven.* They were not amphibian. Nephilim is Hebrew for *the fallen ones*, or *those who dropped down .(1)*   That this refers to fallen angels is purely religious invention.

After the Great Deluge the Sumerians texts were translated into Akkadian and Babylonian. These translators found multitudes of references to Anunnaki having appeared on earth from "...out of the Deep." This Deep [ABZU] was originally an *astronomical* designation for the largely unknown abyss of southern hemispheric space...the region of space below our solar system that cannot be viewed from the northern hemisphere. In Babylon artists showed gods emerging from the *sea*, a terrestrial abyss and soon after reliefs gave such marine deities *amphibious characteristics.* Later scribes compounded the association until the gods almost a thousand years after the Great Flood in 2239 BCE were represented as part fish. Even later in time they would be represented with wings to symbolize their origin from the sky and ability to fly. And the concept of angels was born.

Excavated tablets from the Sumerian city of Nippur tell of the arrival of the Anunna to a mountainous region. They set up a camp in a fertile valley and called their settlement EDIN. (2)   These are the Kharsag Tablets, and EDIN is a name implying a *walled enclosure.* (3)   An Anunna female called the Serpent Lady was among them, known as NINKHARSAG. In Egyptian, the hieroglyph and word for *goddess* also means *serpent. (4)*   The explanation we get in Genesis that Eve means The Mother of All Living is a borrowing from the older goddess religion of antediluvian antiquity. The Mother Goddess was *the* center of all preflood religious observances.

From this anciently popular Sumerian account the Jews borrowing heavily from the Babylonian libraries invented the Adam, Eve, Garden of Eden and serpent themes that found their way into the composition of Genesis. From EDIN groups of Anunna spread out to become the ruling elite over the indigenous humans who were living as beasts without culture, written language or an infrastructure. These Anunnaki founded the dragon and serpent dynasties so popular in traditions about the preflood world.

That the ancients provide no clear data on NIBIRU suggests that the knowledge of this object was already obscure by the advent of writing systems. The oldest known writings in the world do not antedate 2200 BCE. We have traditions claiming things were written down prior to this time and there are references in the oldest texts that they were copies of yet more ancient documents, but we simply have no examples. Even the most sophisticated technolithic architecture found in ancient Egypt is absolutely bereft of any hieroglyphs, pictographic texts or writing of any kind.

3439 BCE begins the 792 years of Anunnaki residence among humans on earth before the Flood, to the year 2647 BCE when NIBIRU passed through the inner solar system one last time prior to the Great Flood. Robert Temple had no date for this time but we'll borrow his terminology, this being the Anunnaki *Contact Period.* William Brambley called them the *Custodial Society* in his monumental work *The Gods of Eden.* NIBIRU is the Planet of the Crossing according to Zecharia Sitchin. NIBIRU is one of the 50 divine names in the *Enuma Elish;* the 49th name. (5) The Babylonian *Enuma Elish* reads- "Nibiru shall hold the crossing of heaven and earth...let 'crossing' be his name." (6) Robert Temple remarks that in the *Enuma Elish* text NIBIRU is described not as a planet but as a *star.* (7)   Sitchin wrote that NIBIRU orbited its own star, not Sol, located in the Deep. It appeared in the Sol system seeking a new *destiny [orbit].* When it appeared in the Sol system it had the longest circuit [orbit] of all of Sol's planets. (8)   NIBIRU approached planet Tiamat and destroyed her, capturing some of her eleven moons, KINGU (Luna) among them. NIBIRU continued on, finding a destiny and returned to the Deep. (9) NIBIRU returned later to plunge through the debris of Tiamat and over time her remnants filled her former orbit as the Asteroid Belt. Sitchin noticed that the Sumerian records refer to NIBIRU as the Planet of the Crossing, that the other known planets were told not to cross *above nor below (10)* , referring to the ecliptic plane on which all the other known planets orbit.

According to the author of *Ancient Alien Question,* NIBIRU's existence as a planet is questionable- no Sumerian texts call NIBIRU a planet. (11) But NIBIRU is mentioned in post-Sumerian cuneiform texts but not as a mysterious planet, but as a description of *known* planets like Jupiter and Saturn as published in 1900 in *The Reports of the Magicians and Astrologers of Nineveh and Babylon in the British Museum* by Reginald Campbell. NIBIRU of the Anunnaki is more probably a dark red dwarf binary companion to Sol with an Anunna-populated world, moon or superconstruction that uses it as a ferry. It must also be noted that even a supergiant planet the size of Jupiter if near Pluto would be *invisible to earth.* Too far away. Neptune is huge and Uranus much closer to Earth and both gigantic worlds are invisible without telescopes. NIBIRU will not be visible from earth until 2043 to 2045 before its arrival in November 2046. But by this time it won't matter. The Phoenix will have already transited and totally changed the contours of our world, coastlines, mountain ranges, drying ocean beds replacing many regions that were thickly populated just hours prior to its May 16th, 2040 passage. See *Phoenix Calendar.*

Evidence for the existence of the NIBIRU brown dwarf dark star derives from an unexpected source. Scientist Paul A. LaViolette, Ph.D. shows that the historic spacing of cosmic ray peaks in the geologic record shows that it occurred 14 times in the last 6000 years, gamma ray bursts bathed earth. The first saturation is approximately dated 3300 BCE. (12)   The radio telescope findings are close to NIBIRU's 3439 BCE passage date. As an approximate they are exact. As the small brown dwarf star is within its perihelion period to Sol it would occasionally release energy in the form of flares spewing cosmic radioactive particles. Though LaViolette does not mention NIBIRU, the dating of the gamma ray bursts are too coincidental to ignore. These findings show that something saturates earth with a cloud of ionized gas. I venture that this object bursts with gamma ray activity upon close approach to perihelion, LaViolette documenting a period coinciding with the NIBIRU visitation from 1123-1063 BCE, again in 522 CE and 1314 CE. Because the perihelion period is 60 earth-years long before NIBIRU exits the inner system till its return 732 years later, *seven* of the cosmic ray peaks can be attributed to NIBIRU (50%), this including the first [3439 BCE] and the *last* time it was in the inner system in 1314 CE. About 40% of the gamma ray bursts occurred within 500 years of one another, 650-1050 CE (six bursts) and five of the six occurred as NIBIRU was returning *toward* the inner Sol system. These were not proximity saturations but immense wave fronts from *detonations*, or x-flare activity from NIBIRU or our own sun. LaViolettes research accounts for 13 of the 14 radiation pulses.

In late 1960s Dr. Anthony Hewish, 1974 Nobel Prize recipient in Physics, working at Mulard Radio Astronomy Observatory discovered in the *southern* sky radio emissions from an extinct star that had blown up or collapsed circa 4000 BC. Totally independently, at the same time, George Michanowsky, deciphered an ancient Sumerian star catalogue text concerning the *same* southern region of the heavens that told of a star explosion. (13)   In my published works and other posts it is my position that this nova or binary companion collapse is what so heavily damaged the planets and moons of our solar system, the origin of Phoenix, the Dark Satellite and NIBIRU, the Astroid Belt and comets. The existence of a dark brown dwarf binary companion still near to the Sol system is the subject of Andy Lloyd's interesting work published as *The Dark Star.*

NER Chronology Full of Deceit and Coincidence

Charles Fort had a theory almost a century ago that Earth was being watched, observed by intelligent overseers, that mankind was considered as *property.* My research as published in several books seems to bear this out, none more than *Descent of the Seven Kings* where I detail and analyze the 600-year epochs of world history from 5239 BCE to 1962 CE that make up the Anunnaki NER Great Year Chronology.

We have examined the 3439 BCE descent of the Watchers/Anunnaki and the person of ENKI/Enoch that occurred 600 years after the appearance of the Moon to orbit the Earth, or Capture of Luna. 3439 BCE appearance of the Anunna was also 600 years before the birth of Noah and the 1st regnal year of a dynasty of Nephilim Kings over Egypt. Noah's own birth was in the biblical narrative 600 years before the Great Flood of 2239 BCE, a Phoenix-caused cataclysm. This disaster that largely depopulated the planet was 600 years before the death of Jacob in 1639 BCE and introduction of the Egyptian-Josephite peoples into the family of Israel (Hyksos Amorites). Jacob (Israel) died 600 years before the 1039 BCE birth of David, the Nephilim-slayer, killer of Goliath and other Anakim-Philistine giants who became King of Israel.

That some of these events NEVER happened does not matter, that David was borrowed from a Canaanite epic about a giant-slayer does not make a difference. That Noah was born at the beginning of a 600-year period and was still alive 600 years later when the Great Flood occurred, whether true or not, does not matter. The veracity of these accounts has little to do with what is occurring. The individual stories come from source materials from widely separated texts. When studied and put into their chronologies they all fit perfectly within the 600-year framework. How? The dates were derived from different authors and chronological studies, the biblical narratives, Book of Jasher, Enochian texts... how can real and fictive events *thousands of years* after they are said to have occurred, be put together in a perfectly sequential timeline of 600-year intervals?

Everything we perceive in our reality is the echo of something actually thought of or implemented at a higher dimension. Charles Fort was not wrong—we are *owned.* Deceived. Even our histories are manufactured because these designs are control mechanisms and that allow offworld manipulators to guide the flow of modern events. The 600-year Anunnaki epochs are nodal points where religious programming is patterned, where actual governments are toppled and set back progress and development and where humanity experiences tragic exterminations, whole populations decimated that are at peace and show signs of impending progress. Remember, our own modern technological, information-based civilization is less than *150 years old.* If our owners only have a 600-year window of opportunity to base their projections on our progress to keep us at Ground Zero Development then they must have a continuous stream of data from observation posts (many lunar craters are such devices) as well as Earth-based agents.

The manipulation is ancient and quite revealing, demonstrating that (A) something wants to keep humans *mis*educated, ignorant and primitive, often introducing accusations against Group B; (B) something seeks to be mankind's benefactor but has been severely demonized throughout history. The Great Deluge story became the most prolific piece of propaganda *ever.* All variations of the idea attribute the blame for the Great Flood on earth to MAN for his rebellions against God and because of the wicked children of the angels who taught humans forbidden secrets- all lies being the ***opposite of the truth.*** The friendly Anunna who taught humans how to live were demonized by those Anunna seeking to keep mankind enslaved. After the Deluge in 2239 BCE the slavery continued in the form of *religious programming.* The priesthoods took the reins of public education and soon had all people believing they were born in sin. History repeated itself when the spiritually free movements of Gnosticism were stamped out by the official Roman Church that continued to perpetuate a religious institution inducing men to blame themselves for their physical and spiritual plight.

The 600-year intervals are curious because of the events that transpired and how those events shaped the histories that followed. Remember, our reality construct maintains the architecture of a hologram, events are not random but serve as reflections of prior events just as new events that unfold are actually ghosted reflections from a future already set in stone in the collective though we as individuals have great freedom to decide what, where we want to be. This is better covered in my work, *Nostradamus and the Planets of Apocalypse.* The underlying theme of the 600-year Anunnaki NER date-events is that of *religious programming,* not any particular religion—for they all have their use in population control. The second theme evident is *change of government.* The third is widespread *depopulations.*

Continuing into more relative history, 600 years after the 1039 BCE birth of David was 439 BCE when the Parthenon Temple atop the Acropolis at Athens completed, exactly 3000 years after the Anunnaki/Watchers descended in 3439 BCE. 1800 years after the Deluge in 2239 BCE and 1200 years after the death of Jacob in 1639 BCE, 600 years after the birth of David. The Parthenon was adorned in fantastic reliefs of the War of the Titans and Giants with a depiction of Nereus, the ancient Achaean *Noah* who survived the Flood and whose Greek name preserved the Sumerian NER (=600) in NER-eus. This temple was the center of the Greek world and was built to commemorate a *goddess*, Athena, who epitomized the Virgin [parthenonos is Virgin Chamber]. This concept was born in the Near East when virgins were placed in opulent temple bedrooms to entice gods to descend.

Moving another 600 years we arrive at 162 CE when a pandemic disease afflicted China for eleven years and spread throughout the east to the west infecting the Roman Empire for 16 years. Entire provinces belonging to Rome were depopulated. Amidst the massive loss of life the Han Dynasty fell initiating an Asian Dark Age that lasted over four centuries until the emergence of the Tang Dynasty. (1)

Readers of my published works will know that 1902 was the end of the Cursed Earth system known in antiquity, a Phoenix calendar. 1902 CE began the Giza Course Countdown of pyramid levels to the final year when the Chief Cornerstone descends to finalize the monument, whatever or whomever this chief cornerstone is. In 1902 a farmer plowing a field near La Majorra in the mountains of Veracruz State discovered the Tuxtla Statuette, later acquired by the Smithsonian Institute. It was a squat, bullet-shaped headed human with a duckbill and wings covered in 75 Epi-Olmec glyphs. Its own inscribed Long-Calendar date is March 162 CE which in 1902 made it the oldest Long-Count calendar found. (2) Curious how this date of 162 CE marks a further end to an old culture that met a cataclysmic end toppling their civilization in 31 BCE at transit of Phoenix, now found in 1902 CE when Phoenix again transited bathing the planet in hundreds of millions of tons of red dust. This is exactly what you would expect in a holofield. Separate calendrical systems often intersect at key nodal points.

We move forward through history another 600 years. The Observers find humanity rising in population levels but most of the world suffers in a widespread Dark Age. Literacy is virtually nonexistent save for the quills of the priesthoods. The year is 762 CE. The Jewish Exilarch Solomon died, leader over foreign Jewish activities in Persia and throughout the Islamic world. His hereditary successor, his nephew Anan ben David Hassini, was rejected by the elders who opted instead to install his younger brother Chanaya as Exilarch. Anan fled to Palestine founding his own synagogue, calling upon Jews everywhere to abandon the corrupt Talmud and obey only the inspired Word of God in the Pentateuch (Genesis to Deuteronomy). His sect became influential, known as the Karaites, or Followers of the Text, and Anan's view and teachings about Jesus was much more positive than the Talmudic one. He urged Jews to resist the Rabbinate, for he thoroughly believed that the rabbis were modern Pharisees bents on propagating the traditions of men rather than the will of heaven. (3) This Kairite movement still exists today. This event of 762 CE caused a major rift in Judaism still extant today. The value of such division between groups of the same faith is that it perpetuates the belief system by both groups supporting it but differing only in minor issues. A control mechanism.

This year of 762 CE marked the first year of the Abbasid Dynasty in Baghdad. The region of ancient Babylon, Baghdad is thoroughly planned out and would remain a Muslim center even today.

On the other side of the planet 762 CE marked an important event. The Mayan conclave met at Copan to *correct the calendar*. The skywatchers served as the culture's *chronologists*. Altar Q at Copan depicts these 16 skywatchers. The following year in 763 CE the decision of the Copan skywatchers was published on monuments throughout the realm of the Maya.(4) Interestingly, 762 CE is the 6000th year of the Anunnaki NER chronology of 600 year epochs from its start in 5239 BCE.

Continuing along the 600-year periods we get to 1362 CE. England, long under French influence, in this year began opening Parliament in English rather than in French and English began in the language of the law courts as well. (5) This marks a major awakening among the English and French peoples as other nations in Europe begin to stir. Global depopulations occurred from 1314 CE passage of NIBIRU on through 1348 CE when the Great Black Death plague run its course. 1362 CE marks the beginning of exploration and awareness, the foundation of Western Civilization of post-Dark Age antiquity. In fact, in 1362 the Norse-Goth expedition of King Magnus of Norway surveyed North America and left behind the Kensington Stone inscription discovered in 1898 as proof of their presence across the interior. (6) This region later to become Canada and the United States of America.

The final 600 year epoch ends in 1962 CE but the events of that year require an entire section by itself.

End of the Anunnaki NER Great Year Chronology

The 600 year Anunnaki NER Chronology throughout history has consistently visited upon us at those key nodal dates the themes of the Moon, of visitors from the Deep of space, of calendar systems and of religious programming. What exactly occurred in 5239 and 4639 BCE is purely conjectural, but the dates from 4039 BCE to 1962 CE, or 6000 years evenly, are not unknown. 1962 CE marks the end of the 600-year NER calendar of the Anunnaki so we should find that many events that transpired in this year directly reflect these same themes carried on through these epochs of human history.

1962 CE was the final year the astonishing underground cities of Turkey remained unknown and hidden. In 1963 the entrance to a vast subterranean metropolis called Derinkuyu was accidentally discovered, covering an estimated 2.5 square miles. It has between 18-20 underground levels though only 8 of them are open to the public. Advanced drainage, ventilation shafts have evidence of drilling- thousands of chambers to support a population between 100,000 and 200,000. Amazingly, underground tunnel systems connect Derinkuyu to other subterranean cities and a total of 36 such underworld cities have already been found by 2004. Derinkuyu is pre-Hittite, probably antediluvian or even PreAdamite (pre-4039 BCE). Great planning was required and Andrew Collins theory is most plausible- these cities were designed by a population seeking protection from a coming force of nature, to avoid dying out in some foreseen cataclysmic episode. (1) In 1962 CE Arizona Cavalcade was published, written by Joseph Miller, which cites a 1909 Phoenix Gazette news article about the amazing discovery of a mysterious underground city complex in the Grand Canyon. (2) Underground facilities were built extensively at Giza in Egypt below the Great Pyramid but are closed off from pulic inspection today.

Such underground projects are not only on Earth. In 1962 CE meticulous observations of an anomalous bulge at the Martian equator by nine respected astronomers resulted with astrophysicist, Dr. E. J. Opik, concluding that such a bulge may be hollow, an artificial construction, like a shelter. (3) Vladimir Terziski, a Bulgarian-born engineer and physicist, claims there to be a joint U.S.-Russian base on Mars since 1962. Dr. Richard Boylan holds that we have had military bases on the Moon and Mars since 1962. (4) In 1962 CEs scientific examination of the Moon found that its interior was less dense than its interior; NASA scientist Gordon MacDonald concluded that "...it would seem that the Moon is more like a hollow than a homogenous sphere." (5) Jim Marrs quotes MIT's Sean C. Solomon concerning new findings by the lunar orbiter, "...indicating the frightening possibility that the Moon might be hollow." (Our Occult History p. 19) The hollow moon position was supported by Russian scientists Vasin and Shcherbakov, who claim that the Moon is not an artificial satillite but a hollowed-out planetoid, fashioned by some advanced civilization. (6) In 1962 CE the U.S. landed Ranger 3 on the moon and John Glenn became first American to orbit the earth, doing it three times in a Mercury capsule called Friendship 7.

Radio telescopes in 1962 began detecting strong xrays coming from the Cygnus region of space, the Cygnus Rift, a great black tear in space. Scientists first detected solar wind in 1962 and on July 8th scientists detonated a megaton atomic weapon 248 miles above the earth. In 1962 the ultra secret Cheyenne Mountain Complex is completed near Colorado Springs, a massive underground facility with tunnel systems leading to other underground bases and underworld cities. Here, underneath the United States, the most intelligent people on the planet manufacture technologies unknown to the private sector. This is also the NORAD Command Center, the Air Force Space Command, the Space Defense Operations Center and the Air Defense Command. This complex provides a day-to-day picture of precisely what is in space and where it is located. (7) Many researchers are convinced that the Cheyenne Mountain underworld contains a whole joint human-extraterrestrial joint operations center. 1962 CE was first year of operations for Wright-Patterson Air Force Base's Foreign Technology Division. (8) Since 1947 as the T-2 Intelligence of Air Material Command, it was at Wright-Patterson Field that U.S. scientists attempted to reverse-engineer the debris from the Roswell UFO crash. The Naval Ordnance Lab manufactured Nitinol from the "memory metal" in 1962, a titanium-nickel alloy. Titanium was not a human discovery, but developed from the 1947 Roswell debris. Researchers note that prior to 1947 CE there exist no government references to titanium. (9)

1962 CE began the Close Encounters of the Fourth Kind—abductions of unwilling humans for genetic experimentations, fetal extractions and implantation of tracking devices. In 1962 scientists discovered that Venus is hot and rotates in a retrogade motion, both facts predicted by Immanuel Velikovsky. (10) In 1962 Dr. Carl Sagan urged the scientific community at the American Rocket Society in November to reexamine ancient myths and traditions for evidence and clues that Earth has been visited by extraterrestrial species in antiquity. (11) In 1962 CE Dr. James D. Watson and Francis Crick awarded the Nobel Prize for Physiology or Medicine for their discovery of the double-helix DNA construction. Crick holds that DNA is too complex and so perfect that it is not the result of evolution, that its origin lies elsewhere. DNA is alien. (12)

Many believe 1962 began a spiritual darkening over America, a curse on the nation. All those material blessings that made America supreme in the past began to wane—crude oil production, coal mining, steel manufacturing, pig iron production, nickel mining, aluminum and zinc, rubber, copper, lead, tin, bauxite, chromite, gold, electricity production. Merchant fleet tonnage diminished, as did automobile production, as other nations began out-producing the United States. By 1966 the statistics were alarming, showing a rapid decline in all of these national resources productions. (13) In 1962 CE U.S. Supreme court on a 6-1 decision ruled it unconstitutional to pray in public schools. (14) The Southern Baptists went the opposite extreme, overwhelmingly passing a resolution concerning absolute faith in the biblical records as the infallible Word of God. (15) Few biblical scholars are Southern Baptists. That much of the biblical material is of proven Babylonian, Elamite, Egyptian, Ionian and Gnostic origin is ignored. Even the Vatican was feeling it in 1962. Rome held a council of 3000 men under Pope John XXIII to consider ways it can relate to the 20th century world. (16) By 1962 the Vatican was losing the battle against Protestantism concerning the making available of the

Holy Writ to the public which Rome refused to do for centuries. In 1962 the Christian Gideon's Association celebrated its 50,000,000th freely distributed King James Bible in hotels and other public places. (17)

The year 1962 CE is the 6000th year since the Capture of Luna, or Moon, once an inhabited world, which was 144 years before 3895 BCE when the lithospheric displacement virtually created a new heavens and new earth as ocean beds dried becoming new landmasses after populated continents became oceans beds. The year 1962 CE is also 144 years before 2106 CE, which is the 6000th year from the poleshift of 3895 BCE whic h began Year One of the 1656 years before the Great Flood in 2239 BCE. The Revelation prophecy of the coming of a new heavens and new earth is precise, but NOT as the religionists believe. It will occur in 2106 CE...a population-eradicating poleshift.

In Closing

Prophetic knowledge is not a sacerdotal ethos to be perceived by some privileged elect, but is essentially time-released and brought to light in the generation right before fulfillment. Often the case, especially with the biblical prophets, the seers that divulge future secrets to their contemporaries were ignored thereafter. This is the inveterate condition of human psychology. Equally dangerous is the total acceptance of prophetic messages too antecedent to the unfolding of the divined events, for as Neitzsche once put it, "...when a matter becomes clear it ceases to concern us." Blind certitude assuming a prescience unprovable or undemonstrable is illogical, immature, and delusional. It is for these reasons that this author meticulously elucidates on the mechanics of arcane mathematical geometry, comparative timelines, cross-calendrical parallels and calendrical isometrics because these systems verify the *when* of events already prophesied. In the mirror of reality an historian gazes at the reflection of a prophet.

Only by understanding what was hidden in the Zodiac does the Sphinx in Egypt, the largest statue in the world, become comprehensible, the peculiar geometry of the Great Pyramid with its chronometrical enigmas no longer remain unfathomable, and the prophetic texts of a hundred olden cultures synthesize into a tapestry of a future fragmented in antiquity *after it was already known.* Stonehenge, Newgrange, Carnac, the Aztec Stone of the Fifth Sun, the Greek Parthenon, avenues of Angkor Wat in Cambodia, Toltec pyramids, Mayan Long-Count date monuments, the Temple of the Inscriptions and thousands of other ancient mysteries lose their mysteriousness once these are seen to convey a precise knowledge of the Anunnaki, the Seven Kings, NIBIRU, Phoenix and the *calendars* attached to them. Even the Doors of Valhalla and the Great War of the Ragnarok are broken memories of the future.

All enigmas from antiquity lead to Giza in Egypt, this silent geometrical apocalypse time capsule. However, the Great Pyramid and Sphinx conjoined are merely the earth side half of a galactic calendar among the stars. Though the Zodiac knowledges antedate the composition of the Book of Revelation by millennia, the source material is the same. The Revelation record finds its origin in seemingly dateless Sumerian texts that preserve acute descriptions and mathematics of NIBIRU and Phoenix, obscure texts that make Revelation to be a Sumerian scientific treatise on the Last Days. Though written in the Greek language the Revelation is distinctly Sumerian, conveyed by a literary deluge of symbols and imagery that were alien to the most erudite Greek minds, already lost in Hebraic antiquity—but would have been perfectly understandable to the average literate Sumerian scribe versed in the theological iconography of his people. This is not at all to say that Revelation is a forgery. On the contrary, the fact that Sumerian was *extinct* by the time of the composition of the text discredits such a supposition. Prophetic texts are intended best for those who are about to suffer the situations of their content. The Revelation is a perfect record of the history of Earth in the final years before and after the appearance of Phoenix and NIBIRU into the inner system…as well as the Anunnaki.

As our learned father of critical thinking, Aristotle, once wrote, "…all learning proceeds entirely or partially by means of things that are previously known." And for this reason we must look backwards, for our predecessors knew great secrets about our solar system that have not yet been admitted by the learned of our own civilization. Our inability to fully understand our ancestors has critically warped our perceptions of the present. This is entirely relevant because today's academics merely assume to know former sciences and histories, making them to be the worst of students, their presumption of knowledge and pretended wisdom hindering them from suspending their ego and learning something new. It is these contemporary sages, ignorant of the truly archaic and incredible convergences terminating between 2040-2052 AD that make Niccolo Machiavelli to be a prophet, who wrote, "…we see that men are frequently in the greatest danger when they *think themselves most secure.*"

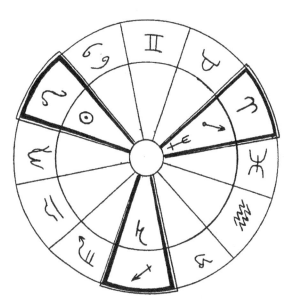

Fire Trigon △

In the Beginning was a virtual Golden Age, a reign of peace when humanity enjoyed the produce and results of their labor. The act of procreation was pleasurable, but many chose to abuse the doctrine of "one flesh" and committed sexual abominations that led to spiritual adultery that alienated them from God. The ground was cursed and husbandry was necessary, but those who believed on the promises of their forefathers knew a Savior was coming [typified by Orion]. These were the spiritual virgins having the knowledge and wisdom of God to be living stones in the Building of God. Their iniquity will not be remembered, but attributed to the Wicked One who tried to seduce them. When he and his kingdom is cast into the Abyss will the faithful receive eternal gifts and the fruits of the Earth, for their works among men will be rewarded.

It was known in the beginning that Man would fall prey to the Adversary but provision was made to cover his sin by slaying of the Lamb. Fire has been prepared for purification of the holy and destruction of the evil. God will strike the kingdoms of men with a sword [comet with tail] and a third of Earth will be consumed in flames as a burnt offering [Great Pyramid is altar] as well as a third of the rebel Anunnaki that departed heaven to pollute humanity. It was they who brought the Flood, ending the Draconian Epoch with a pole shift that will be reversed in the Apocalypse. The kingdoms of this world, the Adversary assuming a temporary kingship over them, will end when the True King returns, strips him of his garments [goatskin of Aries] and gives them to His true subjects: the Redeemed.

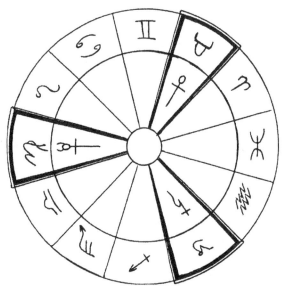

Earth Trigon ▽

In the beginning the two Great Pyramids were built to convey the knowledge of both good and evil, of creation and destruction, eternal life and the Second Death—its divine messages disseminated throughout the kingdom of men around the world in thousands of fragmented texts and beliefs. For those who take heed to the Stone shall escape the Great Judgment at the end of the Age. One of the pillars was lost at the Great Flood as a result of the poleshift but the surviving pillar at Giza remained as an eternal testimony [book] that God destroyed ancient Earth by water, and that they who possess the knowledge of good shall *pass through* His judgment and into a New World as did Noah on the Ark through the Flood , the true Water Bearer.

Air Trigon △

In the beginning was prepared under the Earth a place of imprisonment for those that rebel against the Creator, and that Earth itself is the foundation by which heaven shall be supported. In the End the rebellious prisoners shall be released upon Earth's surface [transition from Crab in Water to Scorpio on Earth] to waste away mankind in afflictions, violence, pestilence and Great War that first arose in the primordial past. The Anunnaki will revisit Earth, giving rise to the fiery judgment of the consumption in the Second Death. But the redeemed of God, the last of His creation, shall become *first* over the angels and the breach between heaven and earth healed *through mankind.*

Water Trigon ▽

Signs in Opposition

Two signs of the Zodiac directly across from one another are Signs in Opposition. The motifs attached to these signs in opposition confirm each other's veracity. A sign's opposite is exactly six signs away and in all six pairs of opposites the signs compliment each other.

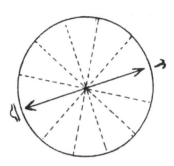

ARIES-LIBRA

Atonement and judgment for sin providing balance in the Creation and made known in His monumental Book.

TAURUS-SCORPIO

Two kingdoms at variance among Men: Messianic Golden Age civilization and Draconian dominion of Hell and Death.

GEMINI-SAGITTARIUS

The ancient world and our own generation have been warned of global judgments by the pillars of stone that guarded the Word of God.

CANCER-CAPRICORN

The inescapability of Hell to rebellious men is the final end to the Adversary as well, just as the faithful shall receive their reward.

LEO-AQUARIUS

As God destroyed the Old World by water so too will Earth in the Last Days be bathed in flames, and by the same mechanism: comet impact and poleshift.

VIRGO-PISCES

The righteous are the number of stones required to make the Building of God that [as a pillar] will *support* the Chief Cornerstone.

Note: There are many other latent messages to be discovered within the Zodiac by the application of *squares* instead of trigons, hexagons and even tangents. Geometrical message-hunting is by the assimilation of all known motifs, ideas and concept attached to the particular Zodiacal sign, the relative esoteric, all the stars in the signs domain, ruling planet characteristics.

Complete Bibliography

Three Books of Occult Philosophy, Henry Cornelius Agrippa, annotated by Donald Tyson (Llewellyn) 16 century AD

Hidden Mysteries: ETs, Ancient Mystery Schools and Ascension: Joshua D. Stone (Light Technology Publishing)

Sight Unseen: Science, UFO Invisibility and Transgenic Beings: Budd Hopkins and Carol Rainey (Atria) 2003

God's Laughter: Man and His Cosmos: Gerhard Staghun, trans. from German by Steve Lake and Caroline Mahl (Aaron Asher Books: HarperCollins (1990)

Great Disasters: (Readers Digest Assoc.) edited by Kaari Ward, 1969

The Secret Language of the Stars and Planets: A visual Key to the Heavens: Geoffrey Cornelius & Paul Devereaux (Chronicle Books)

The Black Death: Johannes Nohl (London, George Allen & Unwin LTD. 1926)

The Black Plague: George Deaux (1347) (New York, Weybright & Talley, INC. 1969)

Simple Kabbalah: Kim Zetter (Conari Press)

The Art of War: Niccolo Machiavelli

Encyclopedia of Wicca and Witchcraft: Raven Grimassi (Llewellyn Pub.)

Northern Tales: Howard Norman (Pantheon)

Book of the Hopi: Frank Waters (Penguin)

The Natural Genesis (1883): Gerald Massey Vol. I & II (Black Classic Press)

Ancient Egypt Light of the World (1907): Gerald Massey Vol. I & II (Black Classic Press)

The Meaning of the Glorious Quran: trans. Arafat K. El-Ashi (Amana)

Epic of Gilgamesh: trans. Maureen Gallery Kovacs (Standford Univ. CA)

Dictionary of Deities and Demons of the Bible: edited Karel Van der Toorn, Bob Becking & Peter Vander Horst (Brill: William B. Eerdman's Pub.)

An Introduction to the Complete Dead Sea Scrolls: Geza Vermes (Fortress)

Greek Myths: Robert Graves (Penguin)

Mythology of Mexico and Central America: John Beirhorst (William Morrow & Co. INC. NY)

Ancient Man: Handbook of Puzzling Artifacts: William Corliss (Sourcebook Project)

Ancient Structures: William Corliss (Sourcebook Project)

Epic of Gilgamesh: trans. N.K. Sandars (Penguin)

The Science of God: Gerald Schroeder (Free Press)

Secrets of Time: Stephen Jones (God's Kingdom Ministries)

Apocalypse of Baruch (Destiny)

The Odyssey: trans. Robert Fagles (Penguin)

Strong's Exhaustive Concordance: (Word Pub.)

Missing Links Discovered in Assyrian Tablets: E. Raymond Capt (Artisan)

Cruder's Concordance (Barbour)

God is Red: Vine Deloria (Delta Books)

The True Bible Code: 2000 (The Lord's Witnesses)

Lost Books of the Bible and Forgotten Books of Eden: (World Bible Publishers)

The Book of Jubilees: trans. Rev. George H. Schodde (Artisan)

Mars Mystery: Graham Hancock (Crown)

Archeology and the Land of the Bible: Vol. II Ephraim Stern (Doubleday)

Out of the Flame: Cherokee Beliefs and Practices of the Ancients: *James Adair (1775) (Cherokee Language and Culture)*

Mythology: Edith Hamilton (Little, Brown and Co., Boston)

The Glory of the Stars: E. Raymond Capt (Artisan)

Antiquities of the Jews: Flavius Josephus, trans. William Whiston 1736 (Hendrickson Pub. 1987)

Encyclopedia Americana (Grolier)

New Evidence of Christ in Ancient America: Blaine M. Yorgason, Bruce W. Warren and Harold Brown (Stratford Books)

The Odyssey: Homer, trans. Robert Fitzgerald (Doubleday Anchor)

The Age of God-Kings: Timeframe 3000-1500 BC (Time-Life, Alex. VA)

Bulfinch's Mythology: Edmund Fuller (Dell)

Dictionary of First Names: Patrick Hanks & Flavia Hodges (Oxford Univ.)

Daniel the Prophet: Noah Hutchings (Hearthstone)

The Book of Enoch: trans. Richard Lawrence, Ll.D. (Artisan)

The Book of Jasher (Artisan)

Dake Annotated Reference Bible: Finnis Jennings Dake (Dake Publishing)

Gladiator: Witchcraft, Propaganda, and the Rise of the World Hero: John D. Christian (Rivercrest Publishing)

Philosophy of Aristotle: Renford Bambrough, 1963 (Mentor)

Nile Valley Contributions to Civilization: Anthony T. Browder (Institute for Karmic Guidance)

Book of the Dead: trans. E.A. Wallis Budge (Grammercy Books)

Necronomicon: 1977 (Avon 1980)

Pole Shift: John White (ARE Press)

Gospel of Barnabas: trans. Lonsdale & Laura Ragg (M.B.I.)

The Earliest Civilizations: Margaret Oliphant (Facts-On-File)

The Student Bible Dictionary: Karen Dockrey, Johnnie Godwin, Phyllis Godwin (Barbour)

Early Man and the Cosmos: Evan Hadingham (Walker & Co.)

Herodotus: The Histories: *trans. Aubrey de Silincourt & revised John Marincola (Penguin)*

Dialogues of Plato: Jowett translation; edited J.D. Kaplan (Pocket Library 1955)

Beyond Good and Evil: Frederick Nietzsche 1886 (Walter Kaufmann trans. Vintage)
Astronomy: Kristen Lippincott (Dorling Kindersley)
The Mystery of Numbers: Annmarie Schimmel (Oxford Univ. Press)
The Wycliffe Bible Dictionary
Temple of Wotan: Ron McVan (14 Word Press)

The remaining publications availabl through Book Tree (1-800-700-TREE)

Galactic Alignment: John Major Jenkins (Bear & Co.)
Myths and Legends of the Ancient Near East: Fred Gladstone Bratton (Barnes and Noble Books)
Origin and Significance of the Great Pyramid: C. Staniland Wake (1882, Reeves & Turner, Book Tree)
Atlantis: Mother of Empires: (1939) Robert B. Stacey-Judd (Adventures Unlimited)
Beginnings: The Sacred Design: Bonnie Gaunt (Adventurers Unlimited Press)
The Shadow of Atlantis: Alexander Braghine (1940) (reprint Adventures Unlimited)
Ancient Pagan and Modern Christian Symbolism: Thomas Inman (1869) Peter Eckler (Book Tree)
Stellar Theology and Masonic Astronomy: 1882, Robert Hewitt Brown (D. Appleton & Co., Book Tree)
Symbols and Legends of Freemasonry: J. Finlay Finlayson (1910, Book Tree)
The Land of Osiris: Stephen S. Mehler (Adventures Unlimited)
Darwin's Mistake: Hans Zillmer (Adventures Unlimited)
History of Baalbek: Michael ALouf (1890 First Ed.) (Book Tree)
Kybalion: Three Initiates (1912, Book Tree)
Sepher Yetzirah: trans. Dr. Isidor Kalisch 1877 (Book Tree)
Dimension of Paradise: John Michell (Adventurers Unlimited)
Origin and Evolution of Freemasonry: Albert Churchward 1920 (Book Tree)
The Fountainhead of Religion: Ganga Prasad 1927 (Book Tree)
The Great Secret: Life's Meaning as Revealed Through Ancient, Hidden Traditions: 1922 Maurice Maeterlinck (Book Tree)
Herder Dictionary of Symbols: trans. to English by Boris Matthews (Chiron Press)
America's Secret Destiny: Spiritual Vision of the Founding of a Nation: Robert Hieronimus, Ph.D. (Destiny)
Symbols, Sex and the Stars: Earnest Busenbark (Book Tree)
The Magus: A Complete System of Occult Philosophy: Vol. I & II: Francis Barrett 1801 (Book Tree)
Book of Enoch: trans. R.H. Charles 1912 (Book Tree)

Enuma Elish: Seven Tablets of Creation: 1902, Vol. I & II: L.W. King (Book Tree)

Ancient Symbol Worship: (1875) Hodder M. Westropp & C. Staniland Wake (Book Tree)

Babylonian Influence on the Bible and Popular Beliefs: (1897) A. Smyth Palmer (Book Tree)

Nature Worship: (1929) Ted. St. Rain (Book Tree)

Lost Language of Symbolism: (1912) Harold Baylay (Book Tree)

The Popul Vuh: (1908) Lewis Spence (Book Tree)

Atrahasis: trans. Albert T. Clay (1922, Book Tree)

The Vedas: (1892) trans. Ralph T.B. Griffith (Book Tree)

Pistis Sophia: Agnostic Gospel: trans. 1921 G.R.S. Mead (Book Tree)

The Wisdom of the Knowing Ones: Manly P. Hall (Philosophical Research Society)

Sun Lore of All Ages: (Book Tree)

The Chronology of Genesis: A Complete History of the Nephilim: Neil Zimmerer (Adventures Unlimited)

From the Ashes of Angels: Forbidden Legacy of a Fallen Race: Andrew Collins (Bear & Co.)

The Story of Astrology: Manly P. Hall (Philosophical Research Society)

Our Cosmic Ancestors: Maurice Chatelain (Temple of Golden Publications)

Gods of Eden: Egypt's Lost Legacy and the Genesis of Civilization: Andrew Collins (Bear & Co.)

The Light of Egypt: The Science of the Soul and Stars: Vol. I & II 1889, Thomas Burgoyne (Book Tree)

Evolution Cruncher: Vance Ferrell (Evolution Facts, INC)

The Doctrine of Sin in the Babylonian Religion: Julian Morganstern (Book Tree)

Lost Cities of China, Central Asia and India: David Hatcher Childress (Adventures Unlimited)

Lost Cities of Ancient Lemuria, and the Pacific: David Hatcher Childress (Book Tree)

Lost Cities of North and Central America: David Hatcher Childress (Adventures Unlimited)

The Stones and the Scarlet Thread: Bonnis Gaunt (Gaunt)

The Pagan Book of Days: Nigel Pennick (Destiny Books)

The Orion Prophecy: Patrick Geryl & Gino Ratinckx (Adventures Unlimited)

When Men are Gods: G. Cope Schellhorn (Horus House Press)

The Great Pyramid: Its Divine Message: (1927) D. Davidson & H. Aldersmith, (12th edition republished by Book Tree)

The Book of Jasher: trans. Albinus Alcuin 800 AD (M.M. Noah & A.S. Gould, NY, 1840, republished 2000 by Book Tree)

The Divine Pymander: trans. John D. Chambers (Book Tree)

Origin of Biblical Tradtions: Hebrew Legends in Babylonia and Israel: Albert T. Clay 1923, orig. pub. Oxford Univ. Press, New Haven (Book Tree)

The Secret Books of the Egyptian Gnostics: Jean Doresse (MJF Books)

The Gods of Eden: William Bramley (Avon)

The Wars of Gods and Men: Zecharia Sitchin (Avon)

When Time Began: Zecharia Sitchin (Avon)

Divine Encounters: Zecharia Sitchin (Avon)

The 12th Planet: Zecharia Sitchin (Avon)

The Secret in the Bible: Tony Bushby (Joshua Books)

The Destruction of Atlantis: Frank Joseph (Bear & Co.)

Maps of the Ancient Sea Kings: Charles Hapsgood (Adeventures Unlimited)

Antigravity and the World Grid: David H. Childress (Adventures Unlimited)

Atlantis: The Antediluvian World: Ignatius Donnelly & Edgerton Sykes (Kessinger)

Atlantis in America: Navigators of the Ancient World: Ivar Zapp & George Erikson (Adventures Unlimted)

The Archko Volume: trans. by Drs. McIntosh and Twyman (Book Tree)

Gods and Men: The Attainment of Immortality: W.J. Perry, 1929 (Book Tree)

Secret Cities of Old South America: Harold T. Wilkins, 1952 (Adventures Unlimited)

The Origin and Evolution of Religion: Albert Churchward, 1924 (Book Tree)

Behold a Pale Horse: William Cooper (Light Technology Publishing)

Crop Circles: Signs of Contact: Colin Andrews with Stephen Spignesi (New Page Books)

Crop Circles, Gods and Their Secrets: Robert Boerman (Frontier Publishing)

The End of Days: Armageddon and Prophecies of the Return: Zecharia Sitchin (William Morrow) 2006

The Book of the Damned: Charles Fort, 1919 (Book Tree) 2006

Our Haunted Planet: John Keel (Glade Press) 2002, orig. pub. 1971

Phenomenal World: Joan d.Arc 2000 (Book Tree)

Tertium Organum: P.D Ouspensky 1919 (Book Tree)

Mankind: Child of the Stars: Max Flindt & Otto O. Binder, 1974 (Ozark Mountain Pub.)

Invisible Residents: Ivan T. Sanderson (Adventures Unlimited Press) 1970

Aryan Sun Myths: The Origins of Religions: Sarah Elizabeth Titcomb, 1899 (Book Tree)

Atlantis in America: Lewis Spence, 1925 (Book Tree)

Far Out Adventures: edited by David Childress (Adventures Unlimited)

Time and the Bible's Number Code: Bonnie Gaunt (Gaunt)

Genesis Revisited: Zecharia Sitchin (Avon)

Our Occulted History: Do the Global Elite Conceal Ancient Aliens? (William Morrow) Jim Marrs

Space Travelers and the Genesis of the Human Form: Joan d'Arc (Book Tree

Worlds in Collision: Velikovsky (A Laurel Edition)

Ponder On This: Alice A. Bailey & Djwhal Khul (Lucis Pub. Co. NY)

The Giza Prophecy: The Orion Code and the Secret Teachings of the Pyramids: Scott Creighton and Gary Osborn (Bear & Co.)

Earth Under Fire: Humanity's Survival of the Ice Age: Paul LaViolette (Bear & Co.

Discovering Ancient Giants: William A. Hinson (Seaburn)

Elder Gods in Antiquity: M. Don Schorn (Ozark Mountain Publishing)

Underworld: The Mysterious Origins of Civilization: Graham Hancock (Three Rivers Press)

Flying Serpents and Dragons: R.A. Boulay (Book Tree)

The Lost Book of Enki: Zecharia Sitchin (Bear & Co.)

The Genesis Race: Will Hart (Bear & Co.)

The History of Atlantis: Lewis Spence (Adventures Unlimited reprint)

Our Sun-God: Christianity Before Christ: John Denham Parsons (Book Tree reprint)

The Sirius Mystery: New Scientific Evidence of Alien Contact 5000 Years Ago: Robert Temple (Destiny)

Pagan and Christian Creeds: Edward Carpenter (Harcourt Brace & Howe, reprinted by Book Tree)

The Christ Conspiracy: The Greatest Story Ever Sold: Acharya S. (Adventures Unlimited)

The Ancient Alien Question: Phillip Coppens (New Page Books)

The New World Order: A Ralph Epperson (Publius Press)

The Mystery of the Olmecs: David Hatcher Childress (Adverntures Unlimited)

A New Look at God's True Calendar: Dankenbring (Triumph Prophetic Ministries)

The Lost Realms: Zecharia Sitchin (Harper)

History in Quotations: Reflecting 5000 Years in World History: M.J. Cohen and John Major (Cassel)

Secret History of Extraterrestrials: Len Kasten (Bear & Co,)

Alice in Wonderland and the World Trade Center Disaster: David Icke (Bridge of Love)

Inside the Real Area 51: The Secret History of Wright-Patterson: Thomas J. Carey & Donald R. Schmitt (New Page Books)

The United States and Britain in Prophecy: Herbert Armstrong

Encyclopedia of World Dates and Facts: Gordon Carruth (Harper Collins Publishers)

The Great Pyramid: Its Secrets and Mysteries Revealed: Charles Piazzi (Bell Pub. , orig. pub. 1880)Smythe:

A Short History of the World: H.G. Wells (Book Tree reprint)

Ancient Mysteries: Peter James & Nick Thorpe (Ballantine)

Chapter-By-Chapter Bibliography

Archive One
Anunnaki Origin of World's Oldest Calendars

1. Missing Links Discovered in Assyrian Tablets 15
2. The True Bible Code 614
3. The Pagan Book of Days 7
4. Jubilees 23:14
5. Our Cosmic Ancestors 107
6. Our Cosmic Ancestors 32
7. The True Bible Code 22
8. The Great Secret 26
9. Voices of Our Ancestors 188
10. The Great Pyramid: Its Divine Message 106
11. Origin of Biblical Traditions 125-126
12. The Great Secret 122-123
13. The Great Secret 123
14. The Great Secret 123
15. The True Bible Code 22
16. The 12th Planet 248
17. The Natural Genesis VOl. II 184; Antediluvian World 4, 7
18. Atlantis: Mother of Empires 212; Antediluvian World 4, 7
19. John D. Morris, Back to Genesis, Institute for Creation Research: Secret Cities of Old South America 262
20. The Doctrine of Sin in the Babylonian Religion 13
21. The Doctrine of Sin in the Babylonian Religion 90-91
22. The Natural Genesis VOl. I 322
23. The Natural Genesis Vol. II 104
24. Ancient Egypt Light of the World Vol. I 322
25. The Doctrine of Sin in the Babylonian Religion 91
26. The Doctrine of Sin in the Babylonian Religion 79
27. The Natural Genesis VOl. II 84-85 & Ancient Egypt Light of the World Vol. I 323
28. The Natural Genesis Vol. II 84-85
29. The Great Pyramid: Its Divine Message 105, 76-77
30. The Great Pyramid: Its Divine Message 555
31. The Origin and Significance of the Great Pyramid 112-114
32. The Origin and Significance of the Great Pyramid 112-114
33. The Origin and Significance of the Great Pyramid 112-114
34. The Histories, Herodotus Book II 4 pg. 87
35. The Land of Osiris 109
36. Symbols, Sex and the Stars 293
37. Early Man and the Cosmos 217

38. Early Man and the Cosmos 219
39. Atlantis: Mother of Empires 71
40. Herder Dictionary of Symbols 179
41. Book of the Hopi 17
42. Sun Lore of All Ages 23-24
43. The Great Pyramid: Its Divine Message 173
44. Mythology 255
45. Antiquities of the Jews Book I 3.9
46. Symbols, Sex and the Stars 302
47. The Story of Astrology 82
48. The Story of Astrology 81
49. Symbols, Sex and the Stars 302
50. Symbols, Sex and the Stars 302
51. Galactic Alignment 104
52. The Doctrine of Sin in the Babylonian Religion 92
53. Sex, Symbols, and the Stars 293, 245
54. The Doctrine of Sin in the Babylonian Religion 92
55. The Natural Genesis VOl. II 321
56. Mythology 38
57. Romans 16:15
58. The Natural Genesis VOl. II 147
59. Babylonian Influence on the Bible and Popular Beliefs 58
60. The Doctrine of Sin in the Babylonian Religion 92-93
61. Secrets of Enoch 20:1
62. Ancient Pagan and Modern Christian Symbolism 7 & The Mysteries
     of Numbers 150
63. Jubilees 4:22-23
64. The Doctrine of Sin in the Babylonian Religion 10-11
65. Wars of Gods and Men 104
66. Lost Language of Symbolism 12
67. Lost Language of Symbolism 13-14
68. Wycliffe Bible Dictionary 64
69. Lost Language of Symbolism 13
70. The Doctirne of Sin in the Babylonian Religion 87
71. The Vedas 116
72. The Doctrine of Sin in the Babylonian Religion 88
73. Babylonian Influence on the Bible and Popular Beliefs 59
74. Babylonian Influence on the Bible and Popular Beliefs 59
75. The Natural Genesis Vol. II 149
76. Book of the dead 509
77. Book of Enoch, trans. Charles 18:6 notes
78. Enoch 18:11-14, 21:1-3
79. Revelation 17:3-11
80. Ancient Egypt Light of the World VOl. II 567
81. Genesis Rabbah 10, 7
82. Apocalypse of Baruch LVI:12
83. Enoch 7:7
84. Jasher 4:18

85. Enoch 68:17-18
86. Jasher 2:20
87. Epistle of Barnabas 14:11
88. Nile Valley Contributions to Civilization 125
89. Atrahasis 16-17
90. The Natural Genesis VOl. I 484, Records of the Past, Sayce Vol. II 109
91. Jubilees 4:15
92. Cruder's Concordance
93. Cruder's Concordance
94. The Natural Genesis Vol. II 22
95. The Natural Genesis Vol. I 201
96. The Shadow of Atlantis 97
97. The Dialogues of Plato 18-19
98. The Land of Osiris 109
99. Cruder's Concordance
100. Herder Dictionary of Symbols 148
101. The Origin of Biblical Traditions 139
102. Evolution Cruncher 639-640
103. Leviticus 10:1-2
104. Judges 8:29-9:57
105. 1 Samuel 14:50-2 Samuel 3:30 & 2 Samuel 1:23
106. 1 Samuel 14:50-51
107. Strong's Concordance Hebrew/Aramaic/Chaldee lexicon no. 5369, 5216, 5214, 5135
108. 2 Samuel 13, 18:5-17, 31-33
109. Missing Links Discovered in Assyrian Tablets 187
110. The Origin and Significance of the Great Pyramid 105
111. Deuteronomy 2:9-10, 20
112. Joshua 15:13
113. Symbols, sex and the Stars 143
114. Enoch 92:3-6
115. Antiquities of the Jews Book I
116. Enoch 10:18
117. Symbols, Sex, and the Stars 293
118. The Natural Genesis Vol. II 186
119. The Great Secret 59
120. Galactic Alignment 127
121. The Mysteries of Numbers 97
122. The Mysteries of Numbers 97
123. The Pagan Book of Days 110-111
124. The Great Pyramid: Its Divine Message 49
125. Babylonian Influence on the Bible and Popular Beliefs 59
126. Herder Dictionary of Symbols 19
127. Galactic Alignment 13, 16-17
128. Mythology 269
129. Wisdom of the Knowing Ones 139
130. Book of the Dead 386-387

131. Lost Language of Symbolism 84
132. Poleshift 124
133. The Origin and Significance of the Great Pyramid 104-106
134. Sepher Yetzirah 55-56 note 40
135. The Secret Books of the Egyptian Gnostics 292-293

Archive Two
End of the PreAdamic and PreFlood Worlds

1.   The Shadow of Atlantis 112
2.   Enuma Elish: Seven Tablets of Creation VOl. II 209
3.   Chronology of Genesis: A Complete History of the Nephilim 1
4.   The Natural Genesis VOl. II 241
5.   Enoch 64:1-3; Destruction of Atlantis 120; Secret Cities of Old South
                                               America 48, 403
6.   Greek Myths 407
7.   Mythology 133
8.   Darwin's Mistake 95
9.   God's of Eden: Collins 21
10.   Darwin's Mistake 96
11.   Philosophy of Aristotle 116
12.   Darwin's Mistake 95
13.   Sun Lore of All Ages 6
14.   Sun Lore of All Ages 131; Antediluvian World 209
15.   The Natural Genesis Vol. II 220
16.   God is Red 155-156
17.   The Shadow of Atlantis 39
18.   Myths and Legends of the Ancient Near East 13
19.   Beginnings: The Sacred Design 172
20.   Prophecy Flash! 2012 AD and End of Days pg. 12 (Triumph
                                               Prophetic Mini.)
21.   Gospel of Barnabas 17 (pg. 18 chapt. 35)
22.   Beginnings: The Sacred Design 173
23.   Enuma Elish: Seven Tablets of Creation Tablet 1 lines 23-24
24.   Babylonian Influence on the Bible and Popular Beliefs 5
25.   Babylonian Influence on the Bible and Popular Beliefs 80
26.   Philosophy of Aristotle 46
27.   Plato's Symposium, Dialogues of Plato 174; Theogany 27
28.   Symbols, Sex and the Stars 312
29.   The Vedas 105
30.   The Natural Genesis Vol. II 98
31.   Mythology 87
32.   Greek Myths 34
33.   Epistle of Barnabas 5:14
34.   God is Red 155
35.   Book of the Hopi 16

36.   God is Red 155
37.   Book of the Hopi 16
136.   Sun Lore of All Ages 48; Secret Cities of Old South America 114;
        Antediluvian World 96; Gods and Men 10-15
137.   Sun Lore of All Ages 218-219
138.   Genesis 1:16
139.   Fountainhead of Religion 226
140.   Secret Books of the Egyptian Gnostics 358
141.   Epistle of Barnabas 1:8
142.   Philosophy of Aristotle 322, Ethics Book III
143.   Wycliffe Bible Dictionary 1028
144.   Babylonian Influence on the Bible and Popular Belief 63
145.   Origin and Significance of the Great Pyramid
146.   The Great Pyramid: Its Divine Message 25
147.   Book of the Dead 391, 425, 430
148.   Mars Mystery 159
149.   The Natural Genesis Vol. II 68
150.   The Natural Genesis Vol. II 68
151.   Quran surah 56:62
152.   Lost Cities of North and Central America 524
153.   The Natural Genesis Vol. II 5
154.   The Natural Genesis Vol. II 147
155.   Secret Books of the Egyptian Gnostics 165
156.   Secret Books of the Egyptian Gnostics 285
157.   Secrets of Enoch 29:2-4
158.   Book of Adam and Eve I 56:13-14
159.   Secret Books of the Egyptian Gnostics 60
160.   Quran surah 15:26-27, 55:14-15
161.   Quran surah 51:56, 7:38
162.   Quran surah 7:11-12, 18:50
163.   Quran surah 6:128, 34:40-41
164.   Book of the Dead 391
165.   Book of the Dead 391
166.   Book of the Dead 430
167.   Wars of Gods of Men 96, 97
168.   Wars of Gods and Men 97
169.   Origin of Biblical Traditions 79
170.   Atrahasis 43
171.   Enoch 8:6
172.   Wars of Gods and Men 98
173.   Myths and Legends of the Ancient Near East 43
174.   Jubilees 16:2-3
175.   The Natural Genesis Vol. II p. 111
176.   The Natural Genesis Vol. II 98
177.   The Natural Genesis Vol. II 98
178.   Jubilees 19:19
179.   An Introduction to the Dead Sea Scrolls 152
180.   Book of Adam and Eve I 57:9-10

181. Book of Adam and Eve I 47:7-8
182. Pistis Sophia, First Book 19
183. The Natural Genesis Vol. II 111
184. Light of Egypt: Science of the Soul and Stars Vol. II 64
185. Student Bible Dictionary 157
186. Evolution Cruncher 103-105
187. Astronomy 39
188. Astronomy 41
189. Wars of Gods and Men 35
190. Divine Encounters 111
191. When Time Began 86
192. New Evidence of Christ in Ancient America 13
193. Herodotus, The Histories Book II p. 86
194. Evolution Cruncher 49
195. The Magus: A Complete System of Occult Philosophy Vol. II 169
196. Symbols, Sex and the Stars 161
197. Enoch 92:14
198. The Great Pyramid: Its Divine Message 323-326, annote. A Tables XVII-XIX
199. The Mysteries of Numbers 275
200. Beyond Good and Evil 17
201. Kybalion 17, Intro
202. Symbols, Sex and the Stars 310
203. Dictionary of First Names 390
204. Our Cosmic Ancestors 157
205. Dimenions of Paradise 181
206. Symbols, Sex and the Stars 168
207. Symbols, Sex and the Stars 99
208. The Mysteries of Numbers 150
209. Herder Dictionary of Symbols 78
210. Symbols, Sex and the Stars 355
211. Student Bible Dictionary 39, see map
212. Student Bible Dictionary 98
213. Babylonian Influence on the Bible and Popular Belief 2
214. Dictionary of Deities and Demons of the Bible 3
215. The Bible as History 83
216. Symbols, Sex and the Stars 161
217. Symbols, Sex and the Stars 161
218. Symbols, Sex and the Stars 161
219. Herder Dictionary of Symbols 153
220. The Mysteries of Numbers 272
221. Our Cosmic Ancestors 56
222. Dimensions of Paradise 181
223. Symbols, Sex and the Stars 95
224. The Great Pyramid: Its Divine Message 106
225. Dimensions of Paradise 180
226. Ancient Structures 269
227. The Stones and the Sacred Thread 36d

228. Herodotus, The Histories Book II 123 p. 131
229. Symbols, Sex and the Stars 159

Archive Three
Gizean Secrets of the Zodiac

1.   Enuma Elish: Seven Tablets of Creation vol. II 141-155
2.   Wycliffe Bible Dictionary 1527
3.   Age of the God-Kings 35
4.   Encyclopedia Americana 4, Wars of Gods and Men 272
5.   From the Ashes of Angels 252
6.   Babylonian Influence on the Bible and Popular Beliefs 99
7.   Jasher 11:6
8.   History of Baalbek 54
9.   Dictionary of Deities and Demons of the Bible 25
10.   Dictionary of Deities and Demons of the Bible 32-33
11.   Dictionary of Deities and Demons of the Bible 25
12.   Symbols, Sex and the Stars 10
13.   The 12th Planet 110
14.   The Doctrine of Sin on the Babylonian Religion 115
15.   Babylonian Influence on the Bible and Popular Beliefs 100-101
16.   Secret Language of the Stars and Planets 68-69
17.   Encyclopedia of Wicca and Witchcraft 189
18.   Enuma Elish: Seven Tablets of Creation Vol. II lines 60-90
19.   Enuma Elish: Seven Tablets of Creation Vol. II Tablet 7 line 100
20.   Enuma Elish: Seven Tablets of Creation Vol. II Tablet 6 line 25-55
21.   Symbols, Sex and the Stars 61, 149
22.   Dictionary of Deities and Demons of the Bible 403
23.   Epic of Gilgamesh: trans. Kovacs lines 17-20 p. 3
24.   Atrahasis 42-43
25.   Secret Language of the Stars and Planets 70
26.   Dictionary of Deities and Demons of the Bible 403
27.   The Greek Myths 180
28.   Bulfinch's Mythology 15
29.   The Greek Myths 37
30.   The Greek Myths 120
31.   The Greek Myths 39
32.   Mythology 83
33.   The Greek Myths 131
34.   Mythology 234
35.   Greek Myths 362
36.   The Greek Myths 463
37.   Secret Language of the Stars and Planets 94
38.   The Greek Myths 451
39.   The Odyssey: trans. Fagles 507
40.   Secret Language of the Stars and Planets 63

41. The Greek Myths 182
42. The Origin and Significance of the Great Pyramid 115-116
43. Herodotus, The Histories Book II 43 P. 102
44. The Vedas 33
45. Dimensions of Paradise 172
46. Herodotus, The Histories Book II 7 p. 88
47. The Light of Egypt Vol. I p. 65
48. Simple Kabbalah 106
49. Psalm 19:1-2
50. Enoch 80:102
51. Enoch 105:23
52. The Divine Pymander 134
53. Enoch 3:2
54. Symbols, Sex and the Stars 280
55. Stellar Theology and Masonic Astronomy 7
56. Beyond Good and Evil 44
57. Our Cosmic Ancestors 121, 123
58. Symbols, Sex and the Stars 275
59. Symbols, Sex and the Stars 279
60. Nature Worship 11
61. Symbols, Sex and the Stars 102
62. Dictionary of Deities and Demons of the Bible 649
63. Glory of the Stars 105
64. Stellar Theology and Masonic Astronomy 43
65. Herodotus, The Histories Book VII 193 p. 435
66. Glory of the Stars 101
67. Secret Language of the Stars and Planets 107
68. Book of the Hopi 149
69. Secret Language of the Stars and Planets 107
70. Dictionary of Deities and Demons of the Bible 628
71. Secret Language of the Stars and Planets 90
72. Secret Language of the Stars and Planets 90
73. Glory of the Stars 51
74. Mythology of Mexico and Central America
75. The Natural Genesis Vol. I 298
76. Symbols, Sex and the Stars 298
77. The Greek Myths 152
78. Secret Language of the Stars and Planets 96
79. Doctirne of Sin in the Babylonian Religion 99
80. Herder Dictionary of Symbols 34
81. Herder Dictionary of Symbols 101
82. Herder Dictionary of Symbols 101
83. Symbols, Sex and the Stars 60
84. The Greek Myths 451
85. Glory of the Stars 65
86. Glory of the Stars 65
87. Symbols, Sex and the Stars 20
88. Doctrine of Sin in the Babylonian Religion 72-73

89.   Mythology 118-119
90.   Mythology 126, Herder Dictionary of Symbols 88
91.   Glory of the Stars 93
92.   Glory of the Stars 91; Aryan Sun Myths 30, 108-109
93.   Glory of the Stars 91
94.   The Light of Egypt Vol. II 13
95.   Philosophy of Aristotle 56, Metaphysics Book II:1
96.   Philosophy of Aristotle 137, Logic
97.   Galactic Alignment 91
98.   The Great Pyramid: Its Divine Message 254
99.   Galactic Alignment 152
100. Galactic Alignment 152
101. The Greek Myths 154
102. The Great Pyramid: Its Divine Message 25
103. Lost Language of Symbolism 84
104. Astonomy 61
105. Symbols, Sex and the Stars 126
106. The Light of Egypt Vol. II, 15
107. Symbols, Sex and the Stars 167
108. The Natural Geneis Vol. II 343
109. Cruder's Concordance
110. Symbols, Sex and the Stars 312
111. Evolution Cruncher 640
112. Galactic Alignment 169
113. Myths and Legends of the Ancient Near East 11
114. Symbols, Sex and the Stars 152
115. Symbols, Sex and the Stars 151
116. Symbols, Sex and the Stars 152
117. Acts 28:11
118. Galactic Alignment 166, Myths & Legends of the Anc. Near East 45
119. Gladiator 89
120. Beyond Good and Evil 90
121. Fountainhead of Religion 82
122. Herder Dictionary of Symbols 206
123. The Light of Egypt Vol. II 139
124. Symbols, Sex and the Stars 51
125. Glory of the Stars 113
126. The 12th Planet 189
127. Origin and Evolution of Freemasonry 127
128. Dimensions of Paradise 170
129. Herder Dictionaryof Symbols 47-48
130. Glory of the Stars 127
131. Glory of the Stars 131
132. Herder Dictionary of Symbols 50
133. Fountainhead of Religion 142
134. Lost Language of Symbolism 282
135. Glory of the Stars 123
136. Glory of the Stars 121

137. Glory of the Stars 39
138. Glory of the Stars 123
139. Herodotus, The Histories Book IV 5 p. 218
140. Glory of the Stars 22
141. Glory of the Stars 133
142. Herder Dictionary of Symbols 61-62
143. The Natural Genesis Vol. II p. 2
144. Herder Dictionary of Symbols 189
145. Herder Dictionary of Symbols 210
146. Symbols, Sex and the Stars 278
147. Fountainhead 68
148. Enoch 39:1, 41:1
149. The Orion Prophecy 75
150. Job 21:6
151. Proverbs 16:2
152. Psalm 62:9
153. Stellar Theology and Masonic Astronomy 204
154. Symbols, Sex and the Stars 122-123
155. The Great Secret 143
156. Fountainhead of Relligion 4
157. Astonomy 6
158. Glory of the Stars 14
159. Glory of the Stars 51
160. Glory of the Stars 51
161. Glory of the Stars 51
162. Herder Dictionary of Symbols 63
163. The Great Pyramid: Its Divine Message 250
164. Symbols, Sex and the Stars 278
165. Herder Dictionary of Symbols 135
166. Herodotus, The Histories Book IV 94 p. 245
167. The Greek Myths 477
168. Out of the Flame 68
169. The Natural Genesis Vol. I p. 331
170. Herodotus, The Histories Book I 172 p. 68
171. Glory of the Stars 63
172. Glory of the Stars 62
173. Herder Dictionary of Symbols 117
174. Herder Dictionary of Symbols 178
175. Ancient Structures 307 illustration
176. Herder Dictionary of Symbols 211
177. Symbols, Sex and the Stars 71
178. The Earliest Civilizations 23
179. The Great Pyramid: Its Divine Message 250
180. The Stones and the Sacred Thread 49
181. Symbols, Sex and the Stars 259
182. Astronomy 63
183. Glory of the Stars 87
184. The Great Secret 130

185. The Light of Egypt VOl. II 26
186. Symbols, Sex and the Stars 152
187. The Light of Egypt Vol. II 26
188. Symbols, Sex and the Stars 150
189. Herder Dictionary of Symbols 189
190. Herder Dictonary of Symbols 204
191. Symbols, Sex and the Stars 153, 223
192. Enoch 22:9
193. Psalm 19:1-4

Archive 5

Charting the History of the Iron Empire

1. Three Books of Occult Philosophy 673
2. Archko Volume p. 18
3. Antiquities XI.5.2
4. 2 Esdras 13:40-46
5. Phenomenal World 180, citing Cisco Wheeler

Archive 6

2052 AD Return of the Fallen Ones

1. Crop Circles, Gods and Their Secrets 139
2. The End of Days 311
3. Tertium Organum 43
4. Antigravity and the World Grid 128
5. The Mysteries of Numbers 106
6. The Herder Dictionary of Symbols 58
7. Atlantis in America 156
8. Antigravity and the World Grid 15
9. The Lost Realms: Skywatchers in the Jungles: Sitchin
10. A New Look at God's True Calendar 55-56, Dankenbring, (Triumph
    Prophetic Ministries)
11. Beyond Good and Evil 35
12. Psychic and Occult Views and Reviews: Mag. Psychic Review Co.
    140 St. Clair St. Toledo, OH pgs. 74-75, Martha J. Keller, Secretary
13. Invisible Residents 28
14. 2 Esdras 5:20
15. Book of the Damned 195
16. Book of the Damned 217

17. Book of the Damned 196
18. Book of the Damned 143
19. Hidden Mysteries 4
20. Crop Circles: Signs of Contact 124
21. Lost Cities of North America 510
22. Mankind: Child of the Stars 26
23. Hidden Mysteries 4-5
24. Kenny Young, MUFON
25. Behold a Pale Horse 200
26. Behold a Pale Horse 196
27. Behold a Pale Horse 202
28. Behold a Pale Horse 202-204
29. Sight Unseen 357
30. Crop Circles, Gods and Their Secrets 136-140
31. Behold a Pale Horse 215
32. God's Laughter 213
33. God's Laughter 213
34. Our Haunted Planet 174
35. Invisible Residents XIX/Cosmic Pulse of Life 271
36. Mankind: Child of the Stars 25
37. Epistle of Barnabas 14:11
38. Mankind: Child of the Stars 25
39. Mankind: Child of the Stars 32-33
40. Mankind: Child of the Stars 219
41. Far Out Adventures 459
42. The Wars of Gods and Men/Mankind Emerges
43. Great Disasters 15
44. Great Disasters 15
45. Stones and the Scarlet Thread 202
46. Stones and the Scarlet Thread 202
47. Hidden Mysteries 714
48. Sight Unseen 181

Archive 7

What Shall Come to Pass

1. Luke 21:25-26
2. Revelation 4:6-8
3. Revelation 5:6
4. Dimensions of Paradise 80
5. Dimensions of Paradise 78
6. Nature Worship 83
7. Revelation 7:1-4
8. Enoch 53:5-6

9.   Enoch 40:1-3, 9
10.   Enoch 18:13-16
11.   Enoch 54:12
12.   Quran surah 18:94-100

Archive 8

Making Sense of It All

A Once-Inhabited Moon
(1) Genesis Revisited p. 114-115; (2) Our Occulted History p. 19; (3) ibid p. 19; (4) ibid p. 19; (5) Atlantis in America: Spence p. 232; (6) Our Occulted History p. 16-17; (7) ibid p. 18; (8) ibid p. 23; (9) Space Travelers and the Genesis of the Human Form, citing Velivoksky, Ovid); (10) Worlds in Collision: Velikovsky); (11) Atlantis: The Antediluvian World p. 38; (12) The Origin of Biblical Traditions p. 69; (13) The 12th Planet p. 233; (14) Ponder on This p. 272; (15) ibid p. 273; (16) The Giza Prophecy p. 127-1238, 235; (17) Earth Under Fire p. 81;

The 432,000 Shars of PreFlood Antiquity
(1) Discovering Ancient Giants p. 200-201; (2) Atlantis: The Antediluvian World p. 62; (3) The 12th Planet p. 247; (4) Secret Cities of Old South America p. 116; (5) The 12th Planet p. 248; (6) Atlantis: The Antediluvian World p. 168; (7) The 12th Planet p. 248); (8) Elder Gods in Antiquity p. 321; (9) The 12th Planet p. 247; (10) Underworld p. 239; (11) The Gods of Eden p. 44; (12) Atlantis: The Antediluvian World p. 174

The Gihon Flood 3439 BCE Was 1200 Years Before Noah's Flood
(1) The 12th Planet p. 291; (2) ibid p. 291; (3) Book of Jasher 2:3-7; (4) Flying Serpents and Dragons p. 132; (5) Ancient Egypt Light of the World Vol. II p. 567; (6) The Lost Book of Enki p. 8; (7) The Great Pyramid: Smythe p. 370

Explosion of Civilization at Egypt 3439 BCE
(1) Fragments of a Forgotten Faith p. 26-27; (2) From the Ashes of Angels p. 360; (3) Our Occulted History p. 171; (4) The Genesis Race p. 168; (5) ibid p. 3; (6) ibid p. 4; (7) ibid p. 56; (8) ibid p. 75; (9) The History of Atlantis: Spence p. 104; (10) Atlantis: The Antediluvian World p. 108; (11) ibid p. 109; (12) ibid p. 184; (13) ibid p. 185; (14) ibid p. 189; (15) ibid p. 189; (16) ibid p. 189; (17) ibid p. 189

600 Year NER Epochs of Anunnaki Are Holospheric Programming
(1) Our Sun-God: Christianity Before Christ p. 33; (2) The Sirius Mystery p. 377; (3) Flying Serpents and Dragons p. 57; (4) Pagan and Christian Creeds p. 218; (5) The Great Pyramid: Its Divine Message p. 173; (6) The Christ Conspiracy p. 338

Gamma Radiation Burst Records Document NIBIRU's Proximity
(1) Flying Serpents and Dragons p. 86; (2) From the Ashes of Angels p. 205; (3) ibid p. 204; (4) The Sirius Mystery p. 267; (5) The Sirius Mystery p. 156; (6) ibid p. 157; (7) ibid p. 157; (8) The Lost Book of Enki p. 48-49; (9) ibid p. 52; (10) ibid p. 55; (11) The Ancient Alien Question p. 53; (12) Earth Under Fire p. 356-357; (13) The New World Order p. 94

NER Chronology Full of Deceit and Coincidence
(1) A Short History of the World p. 128-129; (2) The Mystery of the Olmecs p. 199-200; (3) A New Look at God's True Calendar p. 55-56, Dankenbring (Triumph Prophetic Ministries); (4) The Lost Realms p. 79; (5) History in Quotations p. 211; (6) Ancient Mysteries p. 391

End of the Anunnaki NER Great Year Chronology
(1) From the Ashes of Angels p. 283; (2) Lost Cities of North and Central America p. 316; (3) Elder Gods in Antiquity p. 67; (4) Secret History of Extraterrestrials p. 60; (5) Our Occulted History p. 19; (6) Space Travellers and the Genesis of the Human Form p. 28; (7) Alice in Wonderland and the World Trade Center Disaster p. 212-213; (8) Inside the Real Area 51 p. 63; (9) ibid p. 70-71; (10) Our Haunted Planet p. 71-72; (11) ibid p. 39; (12) The Ancient Alien Question p. 227; (13) The United States and Britain in Prophecy p. 156-158; (14) Encyclopedia of World Dates and Facts p. 818-819; (15) ibid p. 818; (16) ibid p. 819; (17) ibid p. 819

In Closing

13. Origin and Evolution of Religion 130
14. Time and the Bible's Number Code 124
15. 2 Esdras 16:37
16. Apocalypse of Baruch LXXXV:8

Other Important Works by Jason M. Breshears

The Lost Scriptures of Giza (Paperback & Kindle)

Centuries after a cataclysmic depopulation of the world, mankind sought to replicate the one great monument that survived from the previous age. Pyramids were erected everywhere as colonies of survivors thrived, but none have matched the Great Pyramid of Giza in size and meaning. Its secrets are now uncovered and explored in this important groundbreaking book. This book also reveals:
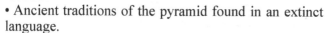
• Ancient traditions of the pyramid found in an extinct language.
• An ancient body of teachings holding that Enoch was the architect of the Giza monuments before the Great Flood.
• New discoveries of the amazing teachings and ministry of Abraham at the Great Pyramid in Egypt.
• A secret body of obscure scriptures in the Bible that refer to the Great Pyramid.
• Ancient knowledge that the Great Pyramid complex was long ago beneath the Mediterranean Sea.
• Ancient Egyptian accounts of the discovery of the Great Pyramid, with Egyptian based memories of Abraham visiting the Giza site.
• Secret traditions regarding the Sphinx and why it appears older than the pyramids – but is not.
• Historical records showing that the Great Pyramid was built to preserve knowledge and survive through a planetary cataclysm.

When the Sun Darkens (2009) paperback & ebook

Numerous times throughout Earth's history there have been major cataclysmic events. These events have resulted in large-scale climactic changes, mythological stories of floods and visitations from the skies, and sometimes the complete extinction of life. The major planetary body that has caused much of this carnage has been referred to by many names. Jason Breshears has termed it Phoenix, based on his research into the distant past and what it was usually called by witnesses. By piecing together ancient documents from the most reputable sources available, we have, in this book, the

most extensive and accurate rendering of the cycle of the Phoenix, including when it will come again. Some of us, according to the author, will live to

see its return. Beyond the foundational scientific evidence, the author ties in various Bible prophecies that relate directly to it. Many books exist on this subject, but few have broken new ground like this one, due to the extensive research involved. After years of researching into chronological and calendrical systems from around the world I made a single profound discovery not found in ANY published books EVER. Over thirty ancient destructions and eyewitness accounts specifically dated and confirmed by multiple recorders from widely separated civilizations left us writings today that DATE the appearance of a vast red object approaching earth and passes leaving earthquakes, volcanic ruin, floods and a red, mud, rain or reddish dust blanketing our atmosphere. These findings, coupled with what ancient writers mentioned of the very old legends of the Phoenix, led me to write *When the Sun Darkens*, published by Book Tree of San Diego in 2009. My discoveries did not end with the publication of this work, but so much new materials came into my possession that I had to write *Nostradamus and the Planets of Apocalypse*.

Nostradamus and the Planets of Apocalypse (Paperback & Kindle)

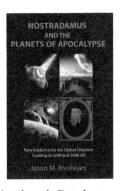

This book maps out the entire historical chronology of planetary cataclysms starting in 4309 BC, covering the cyclical return of Nibiru, the planet Phoenix, and more. It also reveals the code for understanding the prophecies of Nostradamus, showing when they have occurred in the past, or when they will occur in the future. It takes the work of Mario Reading, who first broke the code, and shows how it perfectly applies to all of Breshears' previously made cataclysmic predictions for the years 2040 and 2046. Mr. Reading made mistakes in interpreting some quatrains for the years 2001-2012 that did not involve his code, so his work has been largely dismissed. Breshears brings Reading's work back to life with stunning clarity, and takes it one step further in our understanding of prophetic events. Also covers the predictions of Mother Shipton, who was not only a contemporary to Nostradamus, but made the exact predictions Breshears and Nostradamus made concerning two large scale global catastrophes that will occur six years apart. Despite the many predictions of others, the year 2012 passed with no worldwide cataclysmic events because, according to the author, they were never interpreted or explained correctly, until now. The author remains unmatched in his in-depth research regarding historical and geological cycles, which in turn allows him to accurately map major planetary events, past and future, many of which are outlined in this book.

Anunnaki Homeworld (2011) paperback

The Anunnaki is a legendary race that appears in the oldest documents preserved by mankind. They are said to inhabit an outermost planet that orbits our sun in an extremely elliptical orbit. Each time this planet gets near to the earth it creates planetary cataclysms. Many researchers claim it will be returning soon. The work of Zecharia Sitchin, author of the Earth Chronicles series of books, focuses on the Anunnaki and their previous visits. Many have asked Sitchin, "When will this planet return?" He never gave an exact date, but said it was more than halfway back. Jason Breshears gives an
exact year, and does so confidently, due to his extensive research. He delves not only into historical records, as Sitchin had done, but also uses scientific cycles and mathematical formulas that relate to our concepts of planetary time and orbits. The historical records, chronologically presented by Breshears, help in identifying cyclical patterns. He also employs advanced geometry, interprets complex crop circle patterns, and uses biblical prophecy in support of some of the astronomical events he has predicted. He does not cover much on the mythical aspects of the Anunnaki gods themselves, but focuses more on the actual sciences that can predict their return. Ancient stories and carefully documented proof are two different things. For these reasons, this book is highly recommended.

This work restored what our scholars have lost. The *truth* about our planet's past and future. This author's prior work, *When the Sun Darkens*, concerned the history and 2040 AD return of planet Phoenix, a fragmenting and uninhabited world having little bearing on then present thesis. The fact is herein demonstrated that there is indeed a *second* wandering planet that occasionally visits our inner solar system, a gigantic broken and present *populated* world that is now fast approaching Earth and will arrive at 2046 AD. This planet is NIBIRU, and its orbital history completely forged the unfolding of human events.

This is the Anunnaki Homeworld and its return was a constant fear of the ancients. The most magnificent architectural wonders from the Old World, the Great Pyramid and Stonehenge, as well as the earth's most archaic dating systems all remain as mute witnesses of the presence and orbital chronology of this alien planet. Even the modern misinterpreted Mayan Long-Count system, when *accurately interpreted, as will be shown herein, was a sophisticated countdown to the exact date of the return of NIBIRU* and its Anunnaki occupants in 2046 AD. The popularized year of 2012 AD was never the end of the Mayan system, and this will be conclusively proven in this book.

The pyramid was not a tomb. Stonehenge was not a temple. It is not mathematically possible for 2012 AD to be the end of the Mayan Long-Count calendar (Editor- Breshears' book published 2011, written 2009, **three years before** 2012). These are the assumptions of men trained to think one-dimensionally, those blind to the silent atavistic patterns appearing mysteriously in our grain fields that beckon us to search deeper into the messages of universal geometry. We are being warned. These warnings concern 2046 AD.

Whatever preternatural forces are at work behind these amazing crop formations, it is abundantly clear that the exact same formula exployed in interpreting the three-dimensionasl calendrical geometry of Stonehenge I and II and also the method for understanding the *calendrical messages of crop patterns*. READER BEWARE... what the masses believe and what this thesis demonstrates cannnot both be true.

Secret to Changing Your Life (2017) (Paperback & Kindle)

There's a ton of self-help books at every trash dump in every major city. You've seen them, read them and they didn't work. There's a reason for this. A single fact about how we view the world around us that remains unmentioned by these authors.

This explosive book shows exactly what mental practice was employed by the author that fundamentally CHANGED EVERYTHING in his life. From inside a prison cell with no resources, no money, very limited access to anything he needed, he changed a single thing about how he perceived the world around him and suddenly received help from the most unusual places, secured four publishing contracts as a convicted felon still in prison, received not one, but THREE paroles after 26 years and was released at 43 years old. He has only been out of prison 59 days and has already released four more books on Amazon with a California publisher about to release another of his nonfiction works. This man herein shares with you a secret that OPENED EVERY POSSIBILITY in his life, forever altering the dynamics of his existence for his benefit. He claims that he is not special in any way, that ANYONE can do what he did and declares that what he reveals in this book will PROVE IT.
—Jason M. Breshears

All my life I thought myself independent from the masses, a rogue, tough guy making my own way. How deceived I was. After decades of living the wrong way, in a passive state of reactive impulses I was shocked into being STILL. For the first time in my life I observed what was occurrring around me, what had been transpiring all around each one of us our entire life. I

WOKE UP and this simple act CHANGED MY FREQUENCY. No longer in resonance with the negative, and requiring NO EFFORT ON MY PART, I broke through the condition of bondage and entered a realm where EVERY DAY things go my way. Now no one nor any thing stands as a barrier between me and the things I seek to do and experience. So profound is this change that I often infect those I'm closest contact to and they too enjoy the benefits, profiting by my contact. Do not deny yourself that which is rightfully yours. Start LIVING. What I will show you can be found nowhere else.

Accept this singular tenet and your world will change. You will become a concentration of vast creative potential, an auric field saturated with all of the knowledge and power acquired in life ready to be drawn upon at will, a vortex that pulls people and favored circumstances to you through the illusionary barriers of time-space. Nothing can be beyond the reach of your will. No boundaries exist because all is connected. Your power will be magnified in patience and trust, knowing that events, circumstances and things are instantly moved by your thoughts, aligning toward you by repetitive thinking in the positive...drawn more and more into your life through daily streams of thought and expectation. As your daily behavior reflects these thoughts, what you want begins manifesting in your life. The holospheric Oversoul will both obey the master or afflict the slave; the master has all he wants andbuilds his own life, the slave remains adrift in a chaotic sea of thought-constructs belonging to others.

About Jason M. Breshears
Breshears has authored 17 books and several articles, 10 works available on Amazon. His research bibliography is currently at 1157 nonfiction books read and data mined during a 19-year period, approximately 250,000 pages from many rare works as old as four hundred years, including translations of texts dating as far back as four thousand years. His core conclusions, discoveries and observations are being released on nephilimarchives.com in 2017. As a pen & ink illustrator and graphic artist, most of his book covers and interior artwork are done by himself.

Breshears is one of the only researchers in the world who specializes in ancient chronological systems, focusing on global antiquities from 4309 BCE to 522 CE, many of his historical discoveries can not be found in any other works. For this reason he was awarded with multiple publishing contracts with Book Tree in San Diego.

Also in 2017 Breshears will start his new company, Ophis, a consultation service that will employ PREPS, or Pattern-Recognition Event Prediction Software for personal and business applications. Ophis development emerged naturally out of his extensive studies on time-space anomalies and complex calendar systems of ancient technolithic civilizations.

Personal Note from Jason: I'm witty with a dark sense of humor, my pendulum swings between gladiator and goofball. I value smartasses. A free spirit, humor my ally, I embrace my deviance, finding solace among the shadows. I recognize that I see the world around me through a lens different than my peers. A pirate philosopher playing both sinister and sacred, I honor no God- my spirituality is measured in my actions toward others. Implacable in my beliefs until overwhelmed with new information, love meatballs but dislike spagetti, scrape the good stuff out of tacos and subway sandwiches and the toppings off of pizza. Life's too short for shells and crusts. I sing in the shower, drink my coffee black, love short-haired dogs and I'm hoping heaven has grilled-cheese sandwiches. I'm all-American, a patriot who has studied and admired the history of this great nation and I'm upset with the morons who are ruining it. My friends are few, but genuine. In a world that thrives on artificiality I take care to identify friends from fictions. In summary, I've never been accused of being normal.

My Philosophy: Though all men are created equal, they do not remain that way. In this age males are many but men are few. But there are some of us that rise above the rest and have the right to represent our gender as a whole... men of peace with capacity for war, we who speak what others are afraid to say, the apex of both the sacred and the profane. I am one of these men, just as evil as I am holy, separated by sin but bound to God, a student and teacher from the occult to Christianity. Poets and philosophers, visionaries and Vikings, we few have a divine right to claim that we are men...all others are merely males. The following are my beliefs, the architecture of my personality:

* "The man of principle never forgets what he is, because of what others are." —Baltasar Gracian

* "The real voyage of discovery consists not in seeking new lands, but in seeing with new eyes." —Marcel Proust

* "I am something more than I suppose myself to be, and perhaps all those perfections which I attribute to God are in some way potentially in me." —Rene Descartes

* "A man's worth is not measured by his accomplishments, but in what he strives to accomplish." —Cicero, 1st cent. BCE

* LIVING is the purpose of life.

* "A person who sees what he wants to see, regardless of what appears, will some day experience in the outer what he so faithfully sees within." -Ernest Holmes, 1919

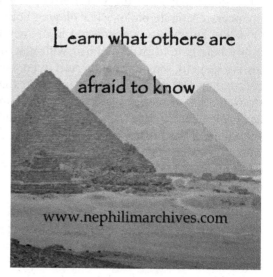

Printed in June 2023
by Rotomail Italia S.p.A., Vignate (MI) - Italy